The Stock Trader

How I Make a Living Trading Stocks

◇◆◇◆◇◆◇◆◇◆◇◆◇◆◇◆◇◆◇

Tony Oz

GOLDMAN BROWN
Laguna Hills, California

Published by Goldman Brown
P.O. Box 3043, Laguna Hills CA 92654

ISBN 9780967943534

Printed in the United States of America.

To My Wife Jodi and My Kids Jordan & Jennifer

You have made my life complete!

I love you.

Disclaimer

TABLE OF CONTENTS

Chapter 25

Chapter 26

Epilogue

Acknowledgements

Many thanks to my wife Jodi, my son Jordan, and my daughter Jennifer for making me smile every day. I want to thank my dear friend Rick LaPoint who worked with me every day from the initial setup for the challenge through writing the last page of this book. I couldn't have done it without you.

Thanks to Townsend Analytics, Janice Kaylor, Danilo Torres, Mary Heim, and Margaret Hafner.

Special thanks to Steve, Ross, Keith, Mark, Brian, Beth, Meg, Gail, Henry, Courtney, David, Phil, Jeramie, Shawn, John W, John G, Mat, Brenton, Kenny, Forest, Michael, and the rest of the crew at MB Trading. You have provided me with state-of-the-art customer support throughout the challenge.

Thanks to all the members of the Market Technicians Association, and special thanks to all my students. You have inspired me to write this book for you.

Foreword

I sat down at one of four monitors, still only half-awake while sipping my third cup of coffee since 3:30 am. The trading day starts early in California, and it took almost an hour to get here. But whenever a great trader invites me to watch them trade, I feel compelled to take full advantage of such a golden opportunity. Little did I know how extraordinary this experience would turn out to be.

For his second Book, a follow-up to his instant classic, Stock Trading Wizard, Tony Oz wanted to show the world how he trades stocks for a living. And as I watched for the next four weeks, all of his trading activities were documented in a detailed trading diary. The idea was simple, and the formula classic. He would invite everyone to take an intimate look into his activities as he explains the strategies and processes behind his actions. It's a recipe that has worked for centuries, as Master entrusts to Apprentice a lifetime of knowledge and experience.

After having received an exciting challenge from the founders of the International Online Trading Expo, Tim Bourquin and Jim Sugarman, Tony planned to hold nothing back, providing all the decisive details of each trade, including the thoughts, strategies, surprises, and problems, and how he dealt with the moment-by-moment challenges the Market presented him.

Such a book had never been attempted before. No trader has ever put their reputation on the line with this kind of honesty. It's easy to search through past trades and present the best ones. But no trader has come forth in advance with the candor to say, "For the next four weeks, I will reveal my every move, for better or worse, entries and exits, winners and losers, with all my profits and losses."

Presented in these pages, 116 Round Trips are documented, including the charts, illustrations, and formulas. Tony explains the research and preparation; the joys and frustrations; the exhilarating victories and disappointing defeats. And of course, the blow-by-blow descriptions of each battle between Emotions, Decisions, Market Makers, and Technology.

In this fascinating account, readers will quickly find themselves immersed in the action as Tony weaves his narrative. The chess game never lets up, as The Stock Trader matches his wits with the best the Market can throw at him.

And by an astonishing coincidence of timing, trading for this book was in full swing during the Great Crash of April, 2000. When the devastation was complete and the carnage had exhausted itself, The Stock Trader rose from beneath the rubble triumphantly wielding his profits, unbowed and unscathed, from a Market where over Two Trillion dollars had been obliterated within a mere fourteen days.

Most traders would agree that studying the actions, strategies, and emotions of a great trader is an opportunity anyone, regardless of experience or viewpoint, can benefit from. This book is a treasure in that regard, and is sure to become a classic, as Tony demonstrates with his simple methods, that you too, can make a living trading stocks.

Rick LaPoint

CHAPTER 1

The Challenge

As I watch TSLA on my Level II screen trading at $1780 per share, I am drawing support and resistance lines on my charts and placing limit buy and sell orders just as I did twenty years ago. It is amazing that while the ticker symbols of the stocks I trade today may have changed, my trading system has remained the same.

This fact has prompted me to update the book, *The Stock Trader*, and release this new edition. I believe you can learn a lot from the challenge and the trading that took place over four weeks, and I believe those of you who are restricted to trading exclusively on the long side will greatly appreciate the trading strategies featured in this book.

With zero commissions for equity trades now prevalent across the online trading industry, there is a newfound edge for stock traders. I recommend investing your time to learn as much as you can about stock trading, so you can leverage the zero commissions edge. For those of you looking to learn my trading system, buckle up and enjoy the ride.

* * * * * * * * *

Following the success of the stock trading manual I published in 1999, I was challenged by industry leaders to show that the strategies featured in the book work in real life. To do so, I would start from scratch as if I was a beginner. I would research and select the right broker. I would open an account with $50,000 and follow all the money management and risk management rules outlined in this book. I would trade for a period of four weeks, starting on a date selected in advance. I would feature all trades - winners and losers - from concept to completion.

The goal is quite simple. I would invite the readers to spend four weeks with me to learn how I trade stocks for a living. I really liked the idea and challenge. I felt it would be beneficial for anyone who considers trading stocks for a living to see how I do it. I accepted the challenge, and it was decided that I would have the account ready to start the trading challenge no later than the end of March.

Choosing a Broker

This is a very important element of the setup procedure. I knew from past experience how important it is to have my account with a broker I can trust. I want to make sure that I take the time here and stress the importance of selecting the right broker and the right trading software in order to increase the chances of success. This is the most important part in the business of stock trading, because the broker both holds the funds and provides the tools for trading the funds. If anything does not work as well as it should, the consequences can be disastrous. Keep that in mind when you are selecting your online trading broker.

I took the following steps in the process of selecting an online broker for the four-week trading challenge

First, I eliminated all browser-based brokers since real time trade execution and reporting is a must. While this may seem like a big problem that was only true twenty years ago, I have had instances in the year 2020 with reputable online brokers who offer award winning trading software that had serious problems with timely reporting of trade executions. Some customers reported as long as 45-minute delays to get their trade confirmations. Always do your research in that regards before you select a broker.

Next, I eliminated brokers who did not offer full access to the market and all available market makers and ECNs. This was a lot more relevant twenty years ago than it is today. However, having an understanding on how your orders are routed is important as it may represent a strength or weakness to your overall trading system.

Then, I focused on the functionality and stability of the trading software the broker offered. This is as important today as it was twenty years ago, and it spills over from desktop to mobile version of the trading software as well.

Finally, I selected a broker who had all the above requirements, offered the best customer service, offered low commissions, and had a reputable clearing firm behind it. In this case, the clearing firm was Southwest Securities. This is also truly relevant today. Before you select a broker, research their customer service availability and response time by calling. Ask yourself if you can trust the broker in times of chaos. The clearing is also important as it represents additional hurdles especially if a firm is self-clearing or not.

Once I chose a brokerage firm, I filled out a new account application and sent it in with a check for $300.00 for the data feed. My account was issued within a couple of days, and I wired $50,000 into the account on 3/17/00. I was ready to make the first trade on Monday 3/20/00. The time frame for the challenge would be for the four weeks starting on Monday, 3/20/00 and ending on Friday, 4/14/00.

I feel it is extremely important that I disclose that I have never had an account with this brokerage firm prior to the above date. Consequently, it made the challenge very real. I was going to trade a new account with a new broker just as a beginner trader would.

CHAPTER 2

Setting the Rules

The first rule has to do with risk management. When you manage risk, you always have to think of what would happen should something go wrong. Although this may seem like a pessimistic point of view, it is an essential element of proper risk management. We have set the following guidelines for money management and risk exposure for all trades that will take place in the following four weeks.

Risk capital is set at $50,000. Margin may be used for a total buying power of $100,000. Maximum amount of money to be allocated to one stock position may not exceed $30,000 on the most aggressive position and should be around $25,000 for most stocks. This will ensure I will not put all the eggs in one basket. The exception to the rule will be index-tracking stocks such as SPY, QQQ and DIA. Since these stocks track a basket of 30 to 500 stocks, a single position in one of these stocks is already diversified. Consequently, the entire buying power of $100,000 may be allocated to such a position.

I must take into account the volatility of certain stocks, and manage risk properly. I may use the entire buying power to hold positions overnight and be fully extended if I so choose, but I must have a very good reason for doing so.

At the end of each week, all realized profits will be swept out of the account. If I have $800 in profits for the week, I will order a check for that amount and start the next week fresh with $50,000 in risk capital. If I have a losing week, I do not add money back into the account. I will work with the remaining capital until I get back over $50,000, in which case I will draw checks again. This will prevent me from losing a lot if I hit a slump.

To keep things more challenging, I may not short sell stocks. This seemed a little odd to me at first, but the argument made was that many traders don't have access to an extensive short list or are trading accounts that are restricted from short selling. In order to not distort any of the performance, I will have to trade only one side of the market – the long side. I had no idea how much more challenging this rule was going to make things during the next four weeks.

Preparing for Day One

Sunday, March 19, 2000.

     My day begins when the market is closed. At some point between the close of the market and the open on the following day, I will do my research. I normally like to do it at night. When I am finished with my research, I should have an idea as to what positions I want to be in during the next trading day. I will take notes, write out trading plans, and go to sleep.

     I use technical analysis to help me find potential stock trades for the next day. Technical analysis is used to determine supply and demand for a stock based on price behavior over a certain period of time. There are many patterns in which a stock has traded in the past that will help me forecast the potential future price movement for that stock. I try to keep things very simple and I only trade patterns that I understand.

     I will use two types of charts to illustrate the setups that I will be trading over the next four weeks, bar charts and candlestick charts.

Bar Charts

     Each bar shows four different price fields for any given day. These price fields include the **opening** price of the day, the **high** price of the day, the **low** price of the day, and the **closing** price of the day.

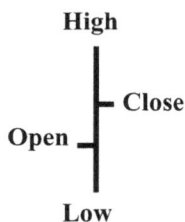

Opening Price – This is the execution price of the first trade of the day.

High – This is the highest price point that the stock traded at that day.

Low – This is the lowest price the stock traded at that day.

Closing Price – This is the price of the last trade of the day.

6

Candlestick Charts

Candlestick charts record the same data; however, it is somewhat easier to see the range between the opening price and the closing price for the time period the candle stick covers. Here are the differences between a white candle and a black candle.

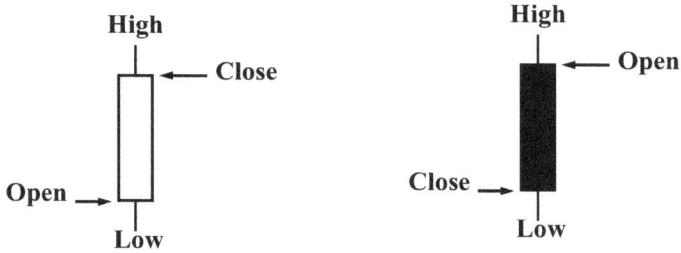

High
← Close

Open →
Low

High
← Open

Close →
Low

A white candle means that the closing price was higher than the opening price. A black candle means that closing price was lower than the opening price.

There are a few patterns, that I base most of my trading decisions on, which I found easy to understand and implement. Those patterns consist of the trend or overall price direction a stock is trading in, and support and re-sistance. I strongly believe that most complex patterns and indicators which will derive from certain mathematical calculations of price behaviors will try to confirm the obvious pattern. I learned that focusing on the simple pattern has been very profitable for me over the years.

Support and Resistance

I will try and use a very simple example of how I look at support and resistance levels or how I implement the laws of supply and demand in my trading. I will use a hypothetical example to illustrate the idea of support and resistance. Let's say that at 9:30 AM, XYZ stock opened for trading at 43.50. The stock started trading down, and at 10:30 AM the stock was at 41.50. The stock then started to trade higher and at 1:30 PM it was trading at 44.50. The stock then traded in a tight trading range between 44 to 44.50, and the last trade at 4:00 PM was at 44.12. Let's chart the data of the trading day for XYZ Stock.

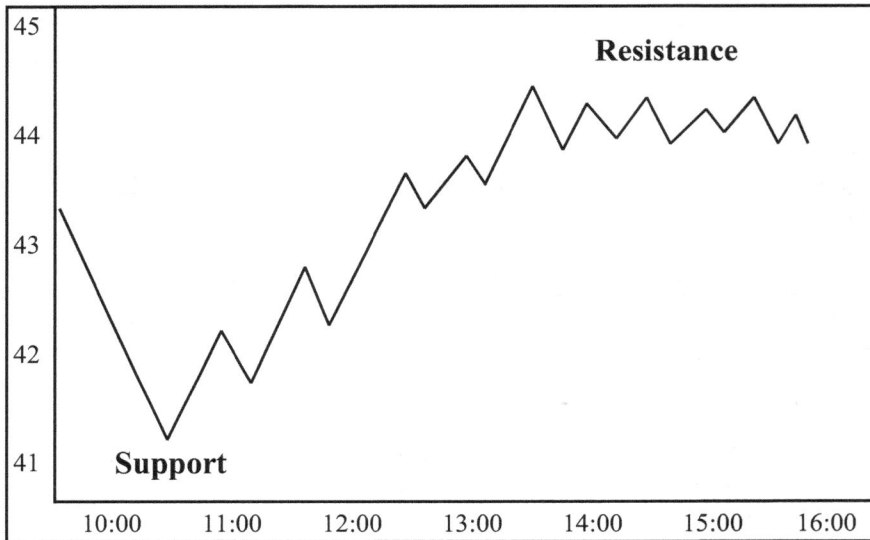

As you can see, XYZ traded down from 43.50 to 41.50 where it found a bottom (support), then traded back up to 44.50 where it topped out (resistance). The question is, why? Why didn't XYZ go lower than 41.50. Why didn't it go higher than 44.50? The answer, of course, is found in the laws of supply and demand.

The laws of supply and demand for any product or service are very simple.

1. If quantity demanded is greater than quantity in supply, prices will go up.
2. If quantity in supply is greater than quantity in demand, prices will go down.

The reason XYZ share price did not go any lower than 41.50 is simply because the quantity in demand was greater than the quantity in supply. The reason XYZ share price did not go higher than 44.50 is simply because the quantity in supply was greater than the quantity in demand.

The next question is, why was the quantity demanded higher than the

8

quantity supplied at 41.50, and why was the quantity in supply greater than then the quantity in demand at 44.50? In other words, what determines supply and demand in the stock market?

The reason there was more quantity in demand at 41.50 is simply because investors' expectations were for the stock to go up in price. The reason there was more quantity in supply at 44.50 was because investors' expectations were for the stock to go down in price. In other words, supply and demand in the stock market is determined by investors' expectations.

If we study the price behavior for XYZ stock in more depth, I can expect a few things to happen in the future based on what took place in the past. The first thing will be that if XYZ traded back down to 41.50, buyers should step in and buy the stock. Next, if XYZ trades back up to 44.50, it will face some selling pressure. This easy to understand concept is the foundation of my trading system, and almost every setup I trade is based on this simple idea, that is to say, on changes in supply and demand.

Changes in Supply and Demand

If XYZ would be able to trade at a higher price than 44.50, then it would suggest that investors' expectations have changed. If XYZ is able to trade at a lower price than 41.50, then it would suggest that investors' expectations have changed, as well. These changes in investors' expectations, or changes in supply and demand, for a stock are very common, and I would try to capitalize and profit from these changes over the next four weeks.

Searching for Potential Trades

I have three main sources for potential trades. The first one is a watch list of 35 stocks that I follow on a daily basis. This list is my Constant watch list (although I do make changes to it once in a while). The second source is a scan I run after the market closes. This scan looks for different criteria and presents me with stocks that require further analysis. The third source is a scan I run during the trading day, which also looks for specific criteria to be met. Over the next four weeks, I will disclose how I found each and every trade prior to executing it. I will be covering methods of producing a Constant watch list, and I will also be covering different scanning criteria, which you may use in your own trading, later in this book.

Running the Overnight Scan

The first scan I ran was for stocks that have pulled back in price over the last three days. I am looking for stocks that are pulling back in price from their 52-week high and are at or near support levels. The formula for the scan is:

Oz Pullback Swing Trade (Bottom Fisher)

VolAvg20 > 350,000
Last > P Low
P1Close < P2Close
P2Close < P3Close
P3Close < P4Close

Explanation:
VolAvg20: Average volume the stock has traded over the last 20 days.
P Low: Previous Day's low.
P1Close: Previous day's close
P2Close: The close the day before
P3Close: The close the day before P2
P4Close: The close the day before P3

Tips and Guidelines

What you are about to read in this book is very educational. Therefore, there will be many illustrations that will require both time and a high concentration level on your part. This book was not intended to be a novel, but a text book of many lessons of how I trade stocks for a living. In order for you to get the most out of this book, I am including the following tips and guidelines, which I suggest you follow.

Every case study which features an executed trade will include a chart that shows the pattern I was trading. **It is extremely important that you take the time to analyze each and every chart and understand exactly what took place.** I understand that there is lot of technical information that slows down the flow of the action; however, it is that technical information that is so important to learn.

Every stock I will be trading over the next four weeks will be referred to by its ticker symbol. I will say I bought 200 shares of INTC at 33.18. INTC is the ticker symbol for Intel. Since I am including charts for every executed trade, you will be able to know the company name, if you simply read it off the chart.

I will also be referring to Market Makers by their four letter code. To avoid confusion, I will put this code in italics to differentiate it from the ticker symbol. I will say something like *SBSH* was a serious seller. If you want to know who the Market Maker is, you can go to *www.nasdaqtrader.com.* Click on the symbol directory link. In the search box, check the following fields:

10

Symbol, *Start With*, and *Market Participant*. Enter the four letter code into the *Search For* window and click *Execute Search*.

Here are some tips on how to get the information out of the charts that I will feature in the book.

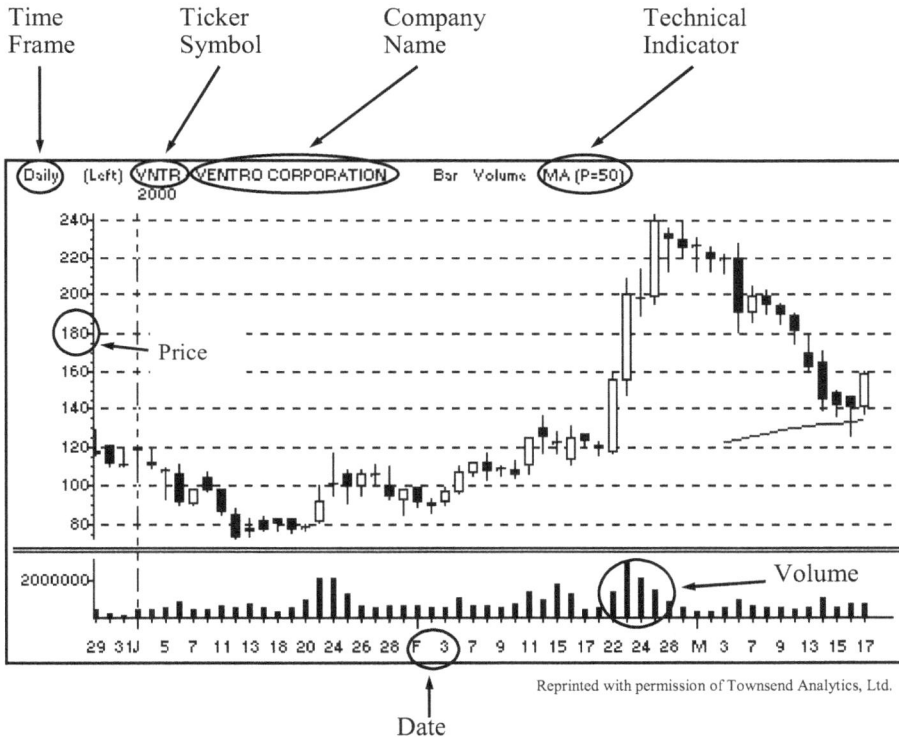

Reprinted with permission of Townsend Analytics, Ltd.

The technical indicator shown in this chart is MA, which stands for Moving Average. (P=50) means that the average covers 50 Period = 50 Bars. In this case it is a 50-Day Moving Average (since it's a "daily" chart in which every candle charts the price action for one day).

Intraday Chart (Single Day)

Intraday Chart   Time Frame for each Bar

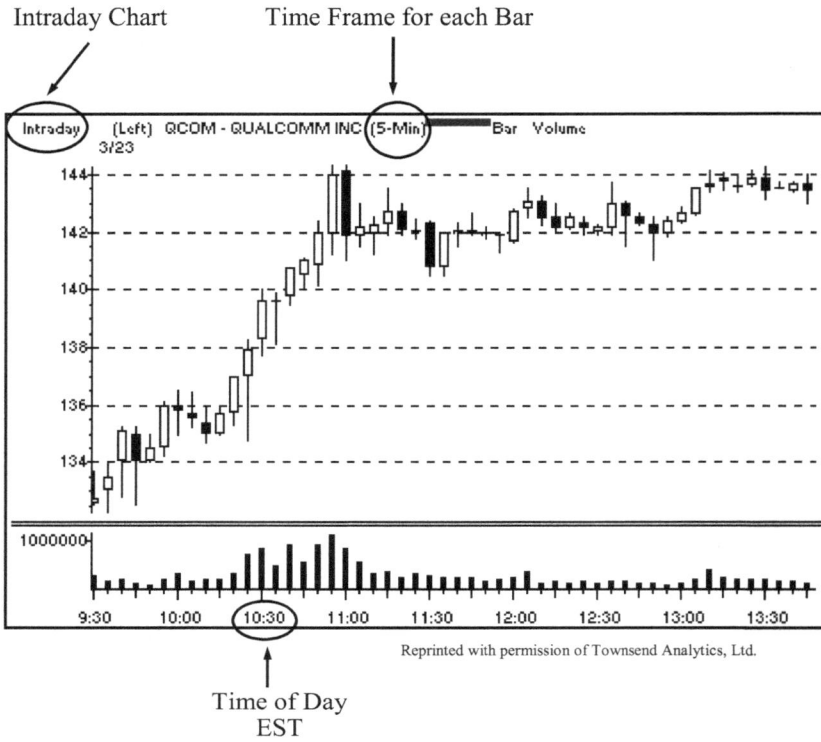

Reprinted with permission of Townsend Analytics, Ltd.

Time of Day
EST

Multi-Day Intraday Chart

Date

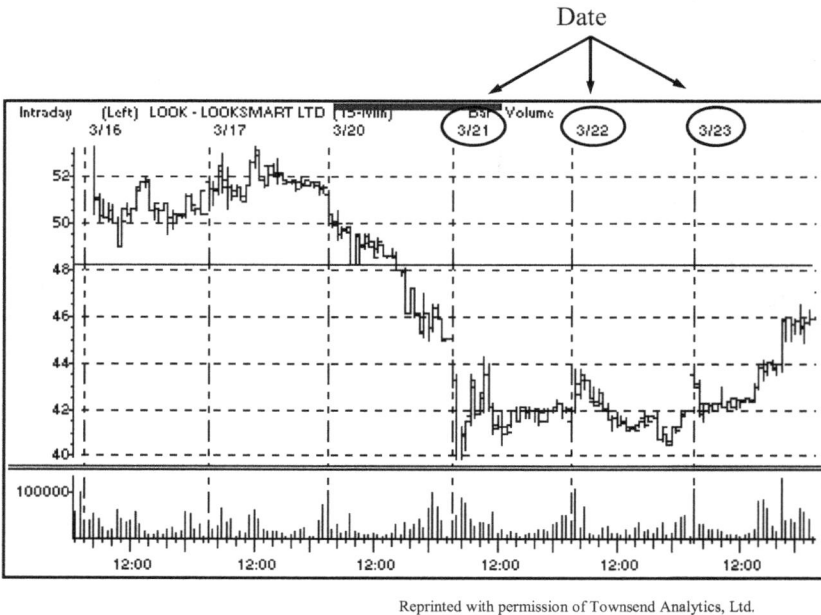

Reprinted with permission of Townsend Analytics, Ltd.

12

One of my goals in writing this book was to give the readers the sense that they are sitting right next to me while I execute the trades. I wanted readers to know the battles that take place inside my head. In my attempt to do so, I have included some of the extra important things that takes place while I trade. I wanted the reader to be a fly-on-the-wall observing all the action.

I think it is also important that you understand that I use RealTick^{TM} III order execution software in my trading. This software is not the traditional order routing software which you might be used to. This software allows me to control the routing of my trades by cutting the middle man out. Consequently, I have more order routing options to choose from, which may at times make things a little complicated to understand. The five order routing options I will be using in my trading over the next four weeks will be SOES, SelectNet, ARCA, ISLAND and ISI. All listed stocks are automatically routed to ISI. As to Nasdaq stocks, I will be using one of the other four order execution routs listed above depending on the situation I am presented with.

Over the next four weeks, there will be trades that I will enter one day and exit sometime in the future. In order to keep some mystery as to what takes place next, I won't tell you where or when I exit the trade until it actually takes place; consequently, I will go on to feature the next trade I get into. This might be somewhat confusing to you. In an attempt to keep things organized, at the end of each trading day, I will list my open positions that I am holding overnight, along with a daily profit and loss statement.

Every trade that I execute will include a trade record in a table format. This table will show the capital allocated to the trade and the profit or loss realized on that trade.

With these tips and guidelines in mind, fasten your seat-belt and enjoy the ride.

CHAPTER 3

Evaluating Risk/Reward Ratio

A trader should never risk more than he can make on a trade. I try not to risk more than 1/3 of what I am looking to make on a trade. In other words, my reward is normally three times greater than the risk I will take. If I am looking to make three points on a trade, I can only risk one point, so if I enter a stock at 50, and my price target is 53, I will have to cut the trade if the stock falls below 49. If the setup I look at does not present me with this ratio or better, I will not enter it. This will be one of the rules I will try to follow religiously over the next four weeks.

Stop Loss

One of the keys to successful trading is an effective stop loss system. Over the next four weeks, I will utilize the following strategies to limit my downside risk. I will first take into account the risk/reward ratio presented by the setup I am going to trade. Next, I will take into account the maximum allowable drawdown on my position. Then, I will define where technical support is found.

I will use one of the following strategies for the placement of a stop loss:

Below today's low

Below yesterday's low

Below secondary intraday support levels

Below multi-day intraday support levels

Below 50% retracement of last rally

Below an index day's low or intraday support levels

Once I am in a trade in which the initial stop loss was never activated, I will use trailing stops to protect profit. I will be monitoring the overall market, the individual stock, and the Market Makers to determine such exit points.

Stop Loss Strategies

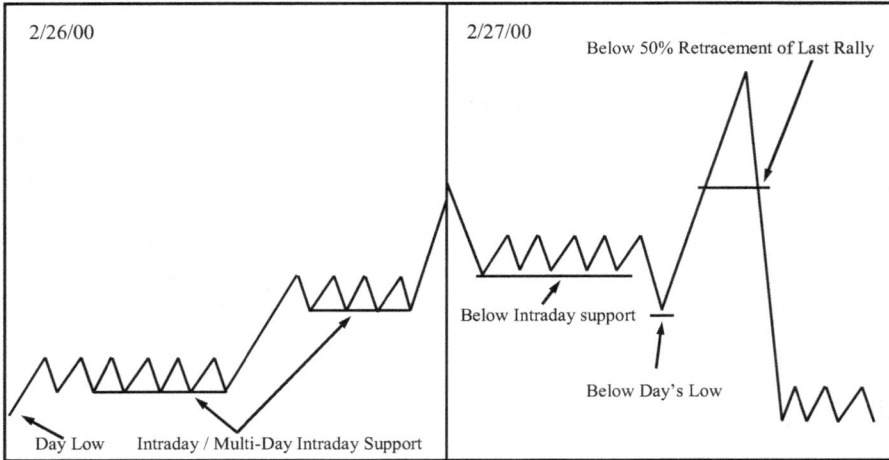

The above 2-day intraday chart shows the different strategies for the placements of stop loss and trailing stop orders that I will be using over the next four weeks.

The final candidates for potential trades on Monday, March 20, 2000

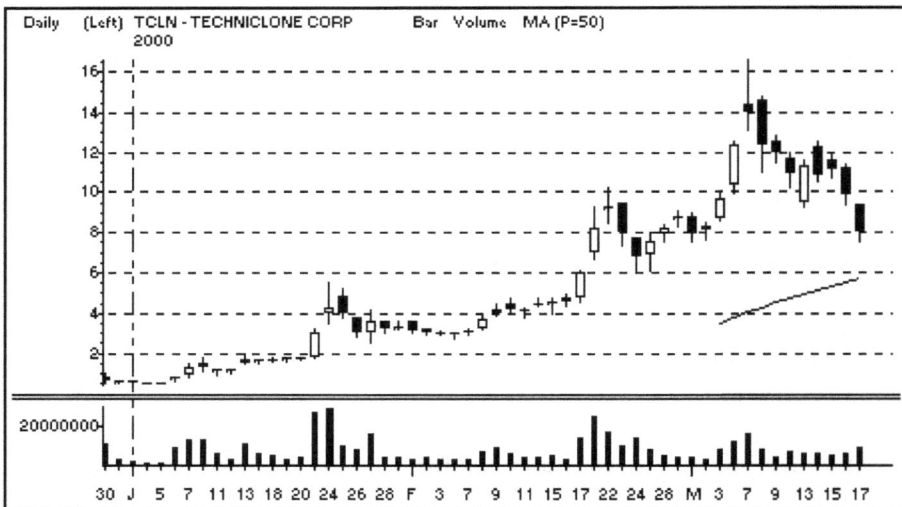

TCLN has come down in price from 16.62 to 7.50. I was going to watch the stock to see if it could bounce back up in price if it reached the following support levels:

$6.00 – This was the low the stock hit on 2/24/00, and was able to trade up from there.

16

$5.72 – This is the price level where the 50-day closing price moving average lies.

$5.50 – This is the price level set by the stock on 1/24/00 on the high of the day. This is the same high that was taken out on the breakout on 2/17/00.

If TCLN goes down to these price levels and is able to trade back up, my price targets will be between 10 - 12 a share. The 10 level was the high set on 2/22/00, and the 12 level was the high set on 3/14/00.

The next thing was to determine the stop loss. I left that field open, and I made a little note to myself saying that depending on where I enter the stock, set a stop loss at 0.18 below the low of that trading day.

Reprinted with permission of Townsend Analytics, Ltd.

IFMX has made a 52-week high at 21 and pulled back to 17.25. My trading plan for this stock is to buy it at 16.50, which was the high the stock made on 2/7/00. My stop loss is at 15.87, and my price target is 19 - 23. My plan is to buy 300 shares at 16.50. I will add 300 shares at 16.87 should the stock show strength. I will sell 300 shares at 18.87, and trail a stop behind the remaining 300 shares. I will give it a chance to move to new high ground.

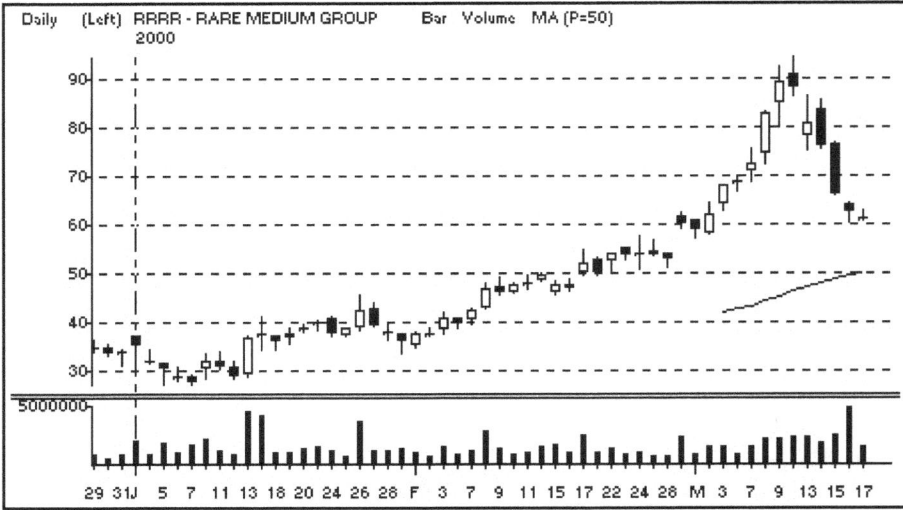

RRRR has pulled back from 94.75 to 60.50. The last trading day, the stock closed below the previous day's close, but it did not trade at a lower price than the previous day's low. My plan is to buy the stock if it trades higher than 63. My stop loss is to be placed at 60.37. My price target is 75 which was the low the stock made on 3/13/00.

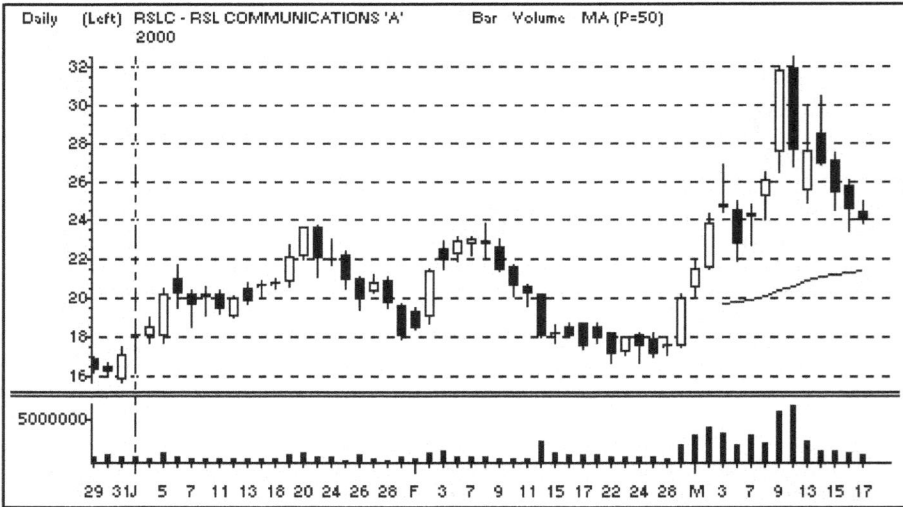

RSLC has pulled back from a 52-week high at 32.50 and was at support levels around 24. The stock did trade lower the previous day and hit 23.37. The close yesterday was the lowest closing price in nine trading days. The 50-day moving average is at 21.50, and I will be looking for a possible bounce at that price level. My price target will be 24, and my stop loss will be placed 0.12 below the low of the day.

18

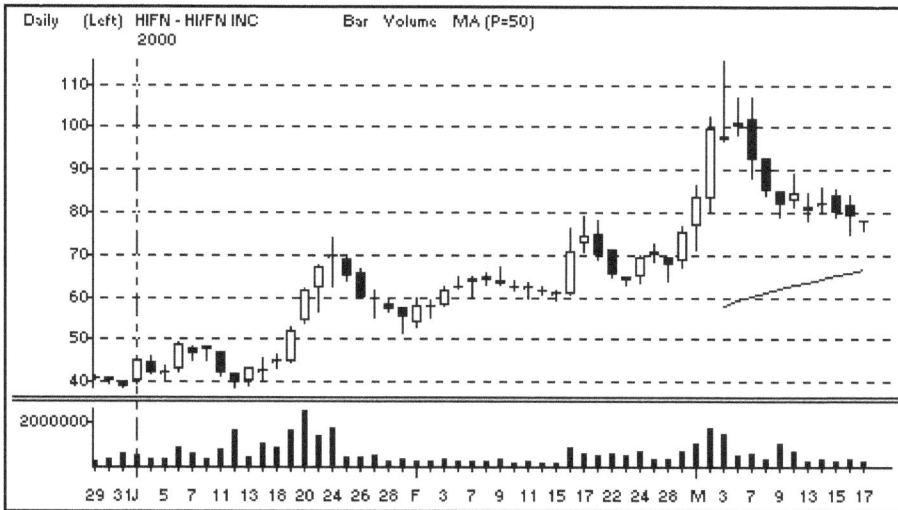

HIFN pulled back from a high of 116 to 76. It closed near the high of the day at 78.06. My plan is to buy HIFN if it trades higher than 78.38. My stop loss is at 75.87, which is 0.12 below the low of the day. My target is 89, which was the high on 3/10/00.

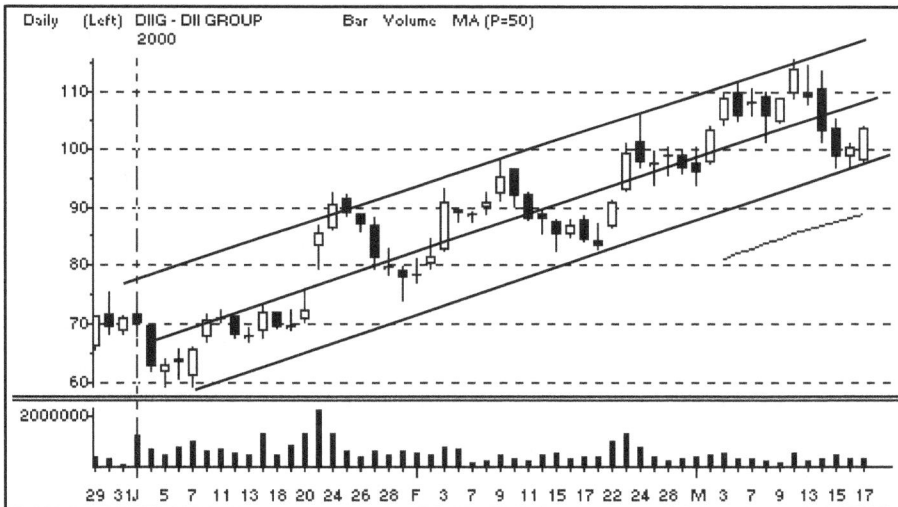

DIIG is trading in a rising channel. It held the trendline and is now looking to turn up. My plan is to buy the stock should it trade higher than 103.75, my stop loss will be at 99.75. My price target is 115 − 125. I found this potential trade on my Constant watch list, which I analyze everyday.

CHAPTER 4

The Early Warning

DAY ONE

Monday, March 20, 2000.

The time has come, and I was now to capture all my trades, executed over the next four weeks, for all the world to see. I have to admit I was extremely nervous, yet anxious to get the show on the road. I had my potential trades in my market-minder window ready to be followed. The trading plans were well outlined, and now it was a matter of simply executing the trading plan.

The trading day starts very early in Southern California. I like to get up at least 90 minutes before the open to check on market conditions and be alert early in the trading day. More often than not, there is a big news story, which sets the tone for the trading day. Today was no different, and the story of the day had to do with a company that might have been cooking the books (the company said it was revising its 1999 and 1998 revenue and operating results, "due to its evolving business model" and were later hit with a lawsuit by angry shareholders as a result). I was very familiar with this company and knew of individuals who were long the stock.

Gap Open

In case you didn't know, stocks which trade today at a certain price and close at a certain price can open the next morning at *any* price. In other words, if a stock closed its trading today at 100, there is no saying where it will open for trading tomorrow. In fact, it can open for trading at 697, or it can open for trading at 20. It might not even open for trading at all the next day. This is some of the risk that is taken when you hold a position overnight. Here are some examples: On Friday, May 1, 1998, ENMD traded last at 11.75. There was a very positive story about the company in one of the major news publications over the weekend. The first trade on Monday morning, May 4, 1998 took place at 82. This is not a mistake! The stock gapped up at the open almost 600%. In March of 1995, IDC was halted intraday. They lost a lawsuit in which they were trying to get compensation from MOT for patent infringement. The stock did not trade the following day at all! It never opened for trading. The last trade before the halt was at 12.87. When the stock finally opened for trading, it was at 5 dollars a share. This was a 61% haircut for the stock.

Today was one of those days and the unlucky ones were the share holders of MSTR.

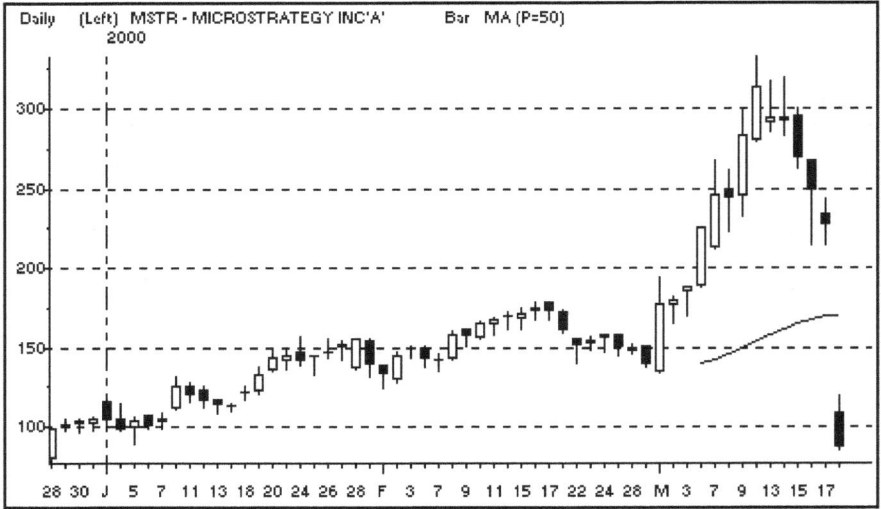

Reprinted with permission of Townsend Analytics, Ltd.

MSTR made an all time high at 333 and pulled back to 226.75 where it closed on Friday. Following the bad news, the stock gapped down to 109.25 and closed at 86.75. It lost 140 points over the weekend from its close on Friday. This was a warning sign for me, a reminder that a big part of risk management is to plan for the worst. I have traded MSTR in the past, so I was familiar with the stock. In fact, I remembered at least one incident when I held the stock overnight in the past, and when something like this happens to a stock you carried in the past, you realize the danger you were in and the risk you were taking. I took this incident as a warning sign as I was looking to make my first trade.

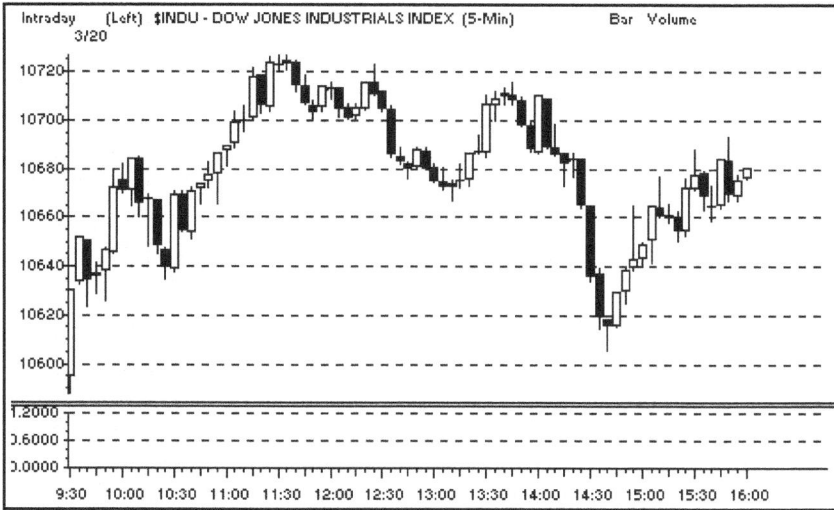

I was monitoring my six candidates and none of them triggered the setup I was looking for. Some gapped up and traded down, while some gapped down below the support levels which I wanted to buy them at. It was becoming a very frustrating day. The indexes were trading in opposite directions. While the Dow was up 85 points, the NASDAQ was down 179 points.

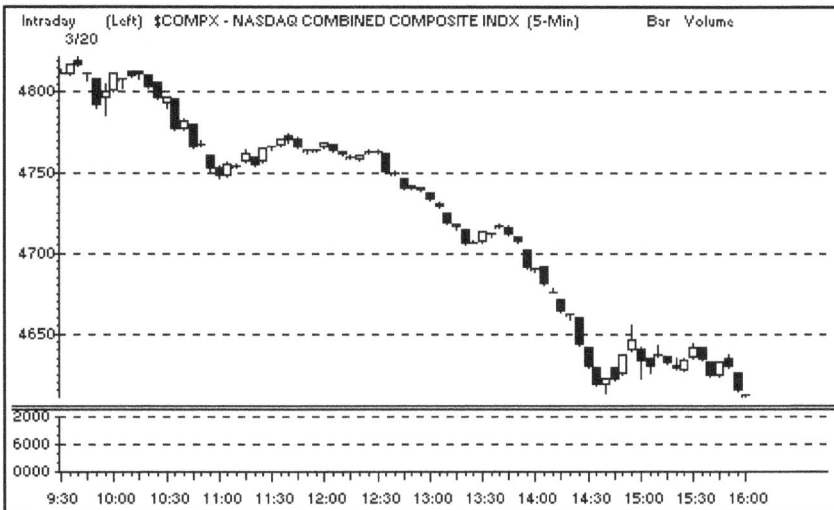

I was very disappointed that I didn't pull the trigger on any of the trades I had planned for today. I felt as if I was a bride who spent the last twelve months planning a wedding, but then didn't have the nerve to show up. And you, my friends, are the guests who have been invited to the wedding only to find out that there will be no ceremony. I am sure you are just as disappointed as I am; however, disappointments are delivered by Wall Street on a daily basis. It is a part of the job. Although I did not execute any trades today, I realized, how important were the lessons learned on the first day of the challenge.

Day One Lessons

Overnight positions are subject to the additional risk of breaking news prior to the market Open. You can sustain serious losses when a stock gaps contrary to your position.

Patience is a key element to successful trading. You don't have to place a trade everyday.

CHAPTER 5

DAY TWO

Tuesday, March 21, 2000

The story of the day is the FOMC meeting in which a possible change in monetary policy might take place. Recent economic numbers suggested that the Fed might raise interest rates at this meeting in an attempt to battle the inflationary threat. While the market often seems to disregard these threats, Alan Greenspan has made ominous warnings about the current economic situation. Most of us are expecting the Fed to raise interest rates today, and the only question is, by how much? Since there was added risk to trading today, I didn't make any trading plans for stocks I studied overnight. My strategy today is to sit tight and watch. I call it the *sniper* strategy, where I sit patiently, observing the movement of the market and specific stocks, and then when I have a clear shot, I will take it.

I got up at 4:45 AM Pacific Standard Time, and I rebooted my machine. I try to reboot my machine every morning before the market opens in order to "clean it out." Since I didn't have any trading plans from my overnight research, I was going to use my intraday scanning software and my Constant watch list to generate potential trades. The news from the Fed that we are all waiting for will not be released until 2:15 PM EST, so there is plenty of time to trade until then.

I was waiting for a high percentage setup. I wanted the first trade to be a winner in order to build some confidence and set a positive tone for the weeks ahead. I was up for four hours already, and I finally saw a setup that I liked.

25

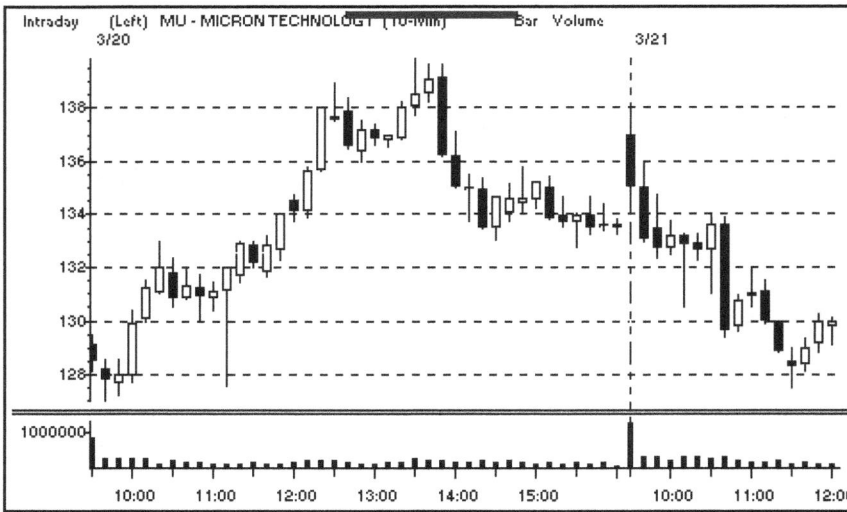

Reprinted with permission of Townsend Analytics, Ltd.

I had MU on my watch list because it made a 52-week high around 1:30 the previous day. I was watching the action on the stock very carefully. Yesterday, 3/20/00, MU traded in a range between 139.75 and 127.50. The stock opened for trading at 129.12 and traded down to 127.50. At this price level, the stock found support, and it turned back up and traded all the way to 139.75, which was the all time high for the stock. MU then traded down and closed at 133.50.

Today, it gapped up and opened at 137. It traded as high as 138 before selling off. The stock traded down and hit 127.50 at 11:30. The same price level that held the previous day, held again today and the stock started moving up in price. I followed it up very closely and was ready to enter an order.

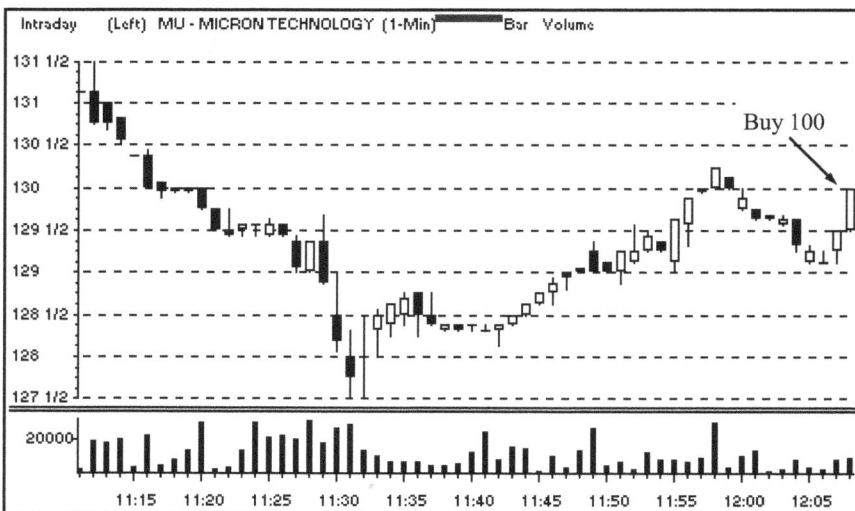

Reprinted with permission of Townsend Analytics, Ltd.

26

As you can see in the chart, MU ran up from 127.50 back up to 130.25, then pulled back to 129.12 around 12:05. The stock was gaining momentum and volume increased. I bought 100 shares at 130. My price target was 133.50- 135. I placed my stop loss at 128.87, which is the price level below the 129.12 lows set at 12:05 PM.

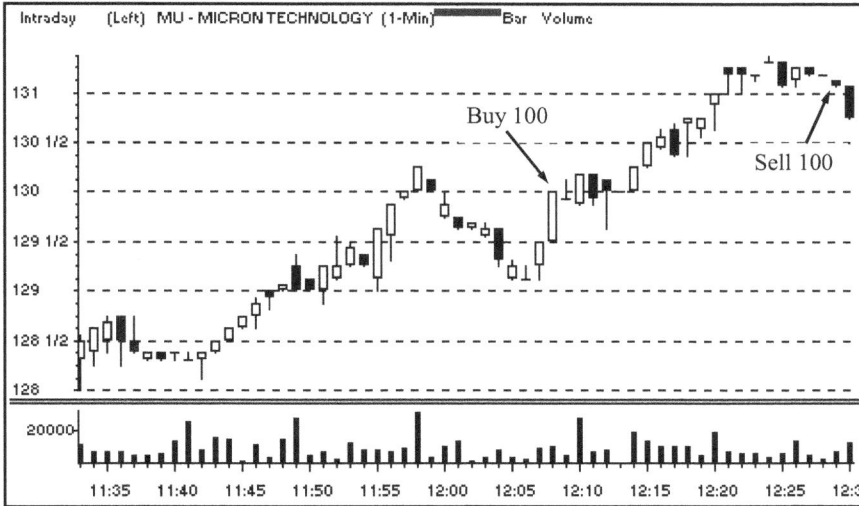

Reprinted with permission of Townsend Analytics, Ltd.

MU traded up to 131.50. I was very nervous the entire time I was in the trade because the Dow broke through the low of the day around 12:18, and it lost 68 points from that point on. The Dow then rallied 68 points, but MU was flat. The Dow turned back down again, and MU looked weak. I sold 100 shares at 131.12 and locked in my profit.

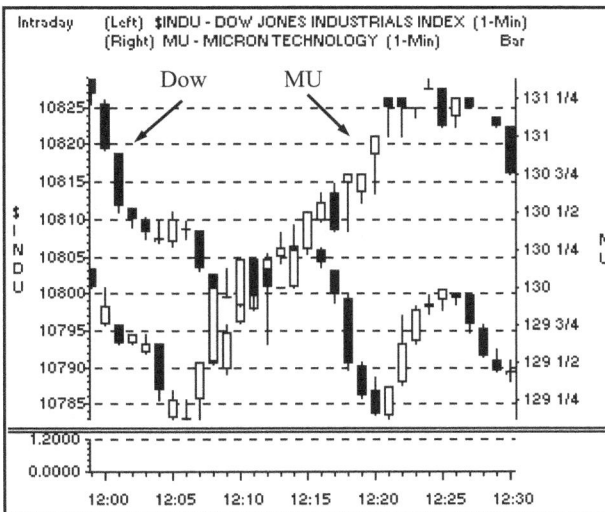

Reprinted with permission of Townsend Analytics, Ltd.

The chart, on the previous page, shows the overlay of the Dow vs. MU. Notice the divergence from 12:13 to 12:22. MU was going up while the Dow was going down. Notice the rally on the Dow from 12:22 to 12:25 while MU was flat. Then the Dow broke down again at 12:27 which is just about the time I pulled the trigger on the sell order. MU followed the Dow this time. It is important to follow the indexes when sitting in a trade.

I will use the following trade record table throughout the book, so we can keep track of the performance. The six fields in the table are:

Source – How did I find the trade.
Investment – The total dollar amount I put into the trade.
Proceeds – The total dollar amount received when I closed the position.
COM – The total commission cost charged by my broker for the trade.
P&L – The net dollar amount I made or lost on the trade after commissions and fees.
Return – The percentage return on the money I had at risk.

Trade Record

Source	Investment	Proceeds	COM	P&L	Return
Watch List 1	13,000.00	13,112.50	10.42	102.06	0.78%

I was happy to get the first trade out of the way. It was no home run, but the 100 bucks or so I made on this trade helped my confidence. I truly felt as if I had *never* traded before this MU trade took place, and I was so excited as if these were the first profits I ever took out of the market.

I was watching my intraday scan, looking for an opportunity. This is when I found CLRN. The stock showed up on my Power Trader Scan . You can find out more information about the scans at www.tonyoz.com

Reprinted with permission of Townsend Analytics, Ltd.

CLRN pulled back from 178.75 to 111. It was in the process of a Reversal Day, and it was taking out the previous day's high. A Reversal Day takes place when a stock opens for trading at a certain price, then trades significantly lower. Buyers step in to buy the stock, and the stock trades up to its opening price and starts breaking out to new intraday highs. The following chart illustrates a Reversal Day. You would normally see higher than average volume on Reversal Days as traders like the strength the stock is showing.

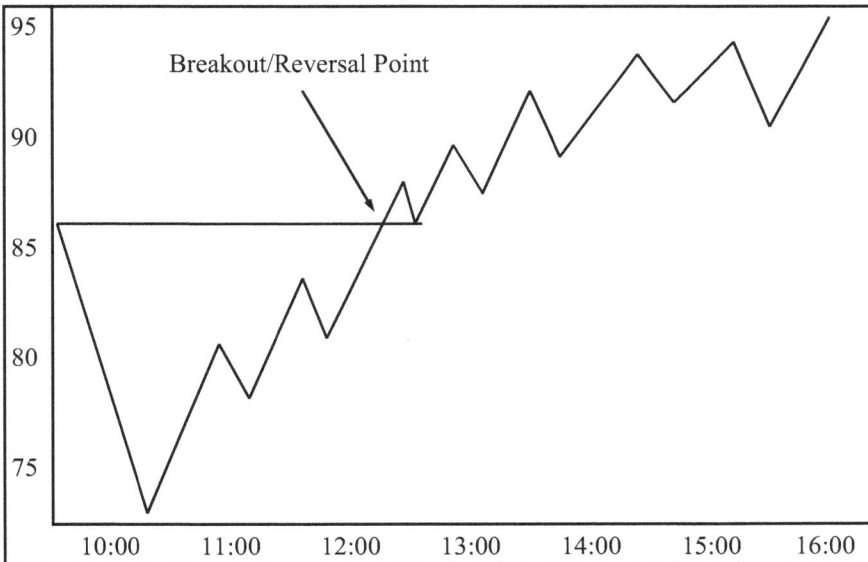

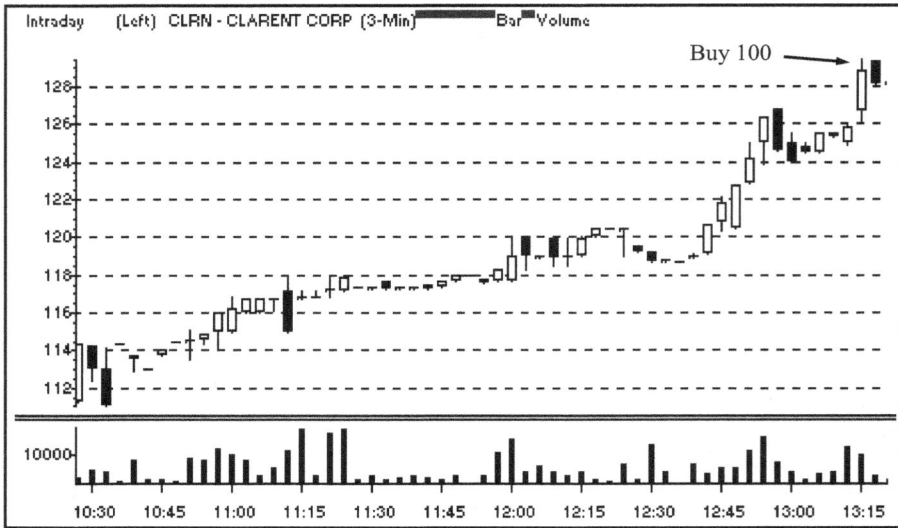

Reprinted with permission of Townsend Analytics, Ltd.

CLRN was showing strength. It took out the high of the previous day and broke out to an intraday high. I bought 100 shares at 129 at 1:15 or so. The price target I had in mind was 140, which was the top three days ago. I placed a stop loss at 126.37, which was just below the tops made at 126.75 around 12:55.

CLRN was very strong, and it took the 130 level out. It was now trading at 135. I moved my stop loss up to 133. I was looking for five more points on the upside, but I wasn't willing to risk more than two points. I was also worried about a couple of things:

1. The stock has run up from 111 to 135. There is always a possibility of a sharp pullback after a move like that.
2. The Fed will announce their decision within the next 45 minutes.

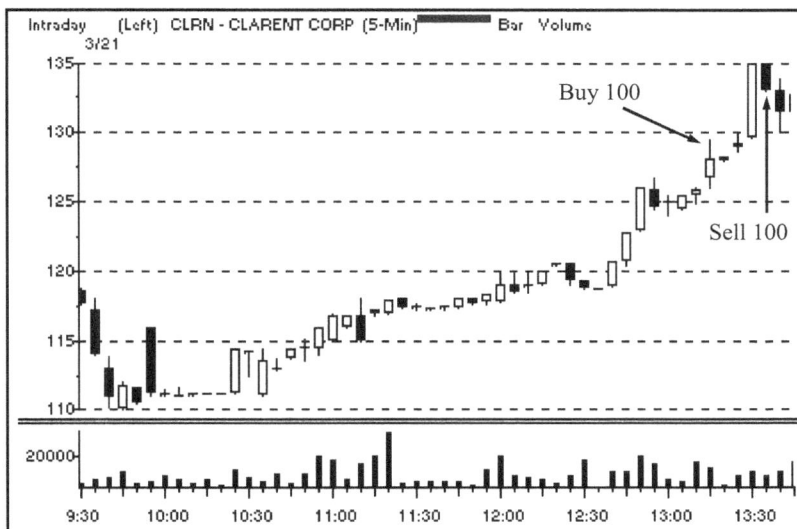

Intraday (Left) CLRN - CLARENT CORP (5-Min) Bar Volume
3/21

Buy 100

Sell 100

CLRN pulled back from 135 and was now trading at 133. I executed my trailing stop and sold 100 shares at 133. The stock would go as low as 130 and then run back up to 140, after the Fed made the announcement; however, I followed my strategy and sold once the stock hit 133. These are the rules of discipline.

Source	Investment	Proceeds	COM	P&L	Return
Power Scan	12,900	13,300	10.45	389.55	3.02%

Daily (Left) RSLC - RSL COMMUNICATIONS A Bar Volume
2000

As I closed my position in CLRN, I noticed that RSLC might have found some support. If you remember, RSLC was on my watch list for a potential trade yesterday.

Buy 300

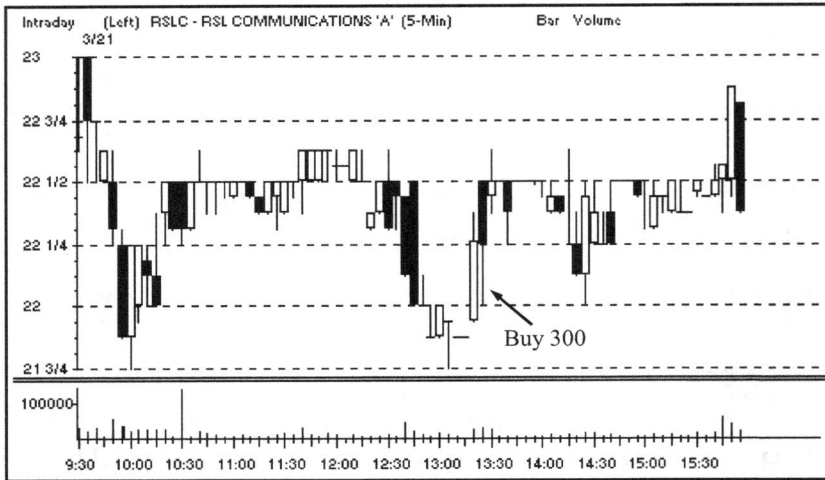

What I liked about this setup was that the stock made two bottoms at 21.75. The stock was trading at 22 and if a bounce was to take place, RSLC could go up to 23.75- 26.75. I thought this setup presented me with a great risk/reward trade. My plan was to buy 300 shares at 22.06. I would place a stop loss at 21.62, which is 0.12 below the low of the day. I will be risking 0.44 trying to capture 1.75- 4.75 in reward. The fact that the 21.75 price level held twice was very encouraging, so I bought 300 RSLC at 22.06. I placed my stop loss at 21.62, and I held it into the announcement of the Fed.

The moment we have been waiting for all day was near. Finally, the Fed announced 0.25% rate hike in both the federal funds and discount rate. This is exactly what everyone expected, so there were no adverse surprises. Party time!

The initial reaction to the announcement was the predictable panic selling. I was watching RMBS free falling. The stock was trading at 293 prior to the announcement, and now it was down to 275. The stock dropped as low as 269 before bouncing back in a violent way.

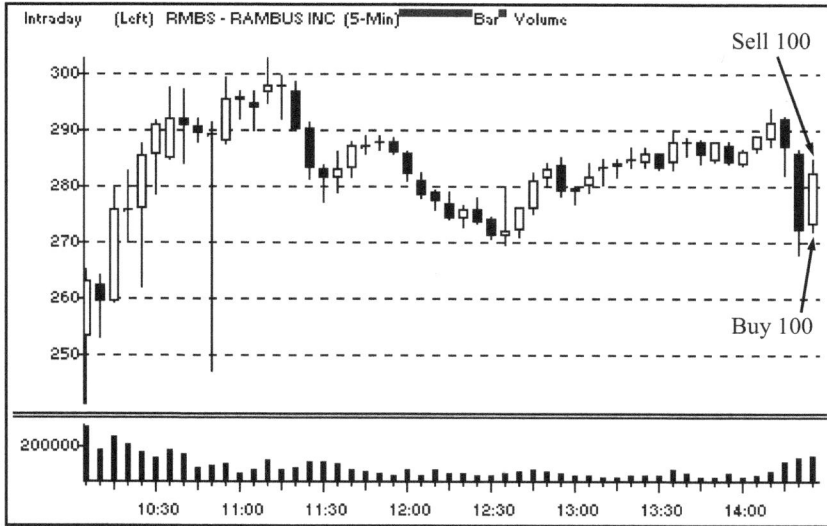

Intraday (Left) RMBS - RAMBUS INC (5-Min) Bar Volume

Sell 100

Buy 100

Reprinted with permission of Townsend Analytics, Ltd.

I expected the stock to bounce at 270, which was the previous low set at 12:30 PM, but there was no way I was going to try and catch a falling knife. I wanted to see it bouncing first. The problem is that when almost any volatile momentum stock, like RMBS, trades, supply and demand are pretty much one sided. There are either a lot of sellers or a lot of buyers. When the shift from panic selling to buying frenzy takes place, the price swing is very violent. When RMBS started bouncing at 269, the offer instantly jumped directly to 271.25. I then entered my buy order; however, there was no way I was going to get a fill at that price, because the stock was already printing 274 on the ticker. Momentum traders were sending SelectNet Preference orders to Market Makers and ECNs at higher prices out-of-market to guarantee themselves a fill. I was forced to do the same thing. I entered a buy order for 100 shares of RMBS at 275 on the Island ECN. There was a seller on Island at 275 and our orders were crossed and executed immediately. My price target was 285 - 288. I was in the trade for four minutes as RMBS hit the price target of 285. It started to show some weakness, so I entered a sell order. I was out at 283.25.

Source	Investment	Proceeds	COM	P&L	Return
Constant List	27,500	28,325	10.95	814.05	2.96%

Once the initial reaction to the Fed's announcement was over and buyers stepped in, the market gained momentum and traded higher. At this point, I was monitoring my Constant watch list for buying opportunities. I was also watching the candidates which my scanning software was generating.

33

MRVC came up on my Pullback Swing Trade Scan, and it was just about to make an attempt at breaking out through resistance at 112 to make a new intraday high. At the same time, I was following CIEN, which resides on my Constant watch list. It was forming an ascending triangle and was also just about to possibly penetrate through resistance and move higher.

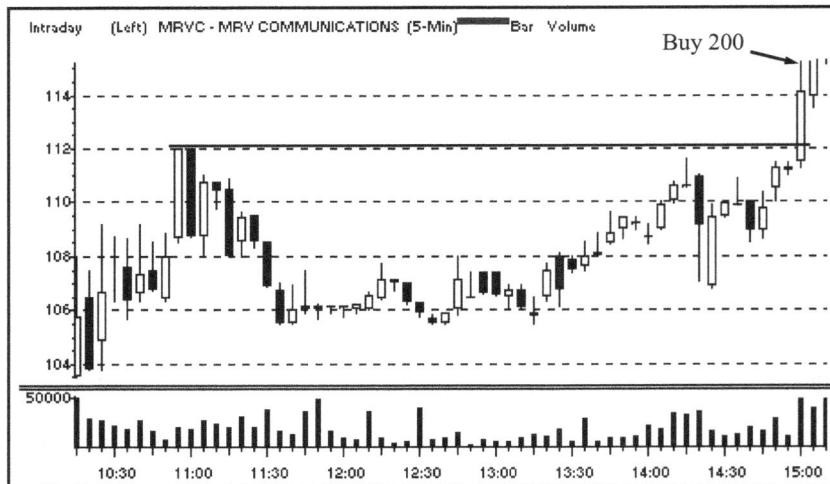

Reprinted with permission of Townsend Analytics, Ltd.

MRVC broke out over the 112 resistance level. I entered a buy order on ARCA for 200 shares at 113.50. I didn't get a fill because the stock was running up fast. It was printing 114.75. I cancelled my order and sent another order to buy 200 shares at 115 on Island. I got a fill for 100 shares and the rest of my order was cancelled for the reason that it would have locked or crossed the market. If there is no one selling at the price that you enter a buy order on an ECN, and the price is higher than the inside offer, the order gets cancelled, because you cannot bid for a stock at a higher price than the best offer. This is a NASDAQ rule*, so the order will be kicked back in these scenarios. Since I wanted another 100 shares, I sent another order to buy 100 shares on Island at 115. My order was cancelled again. I sent the same order a few times more and finally there was a seller at 114.94, and I got a fill. My price target was somewhere between 122 - 126, which were resistance levels from the previous two trading days. I placed my stop loss at 111.75, which was below the 112 level. Unfortunately, I didn't have the best entry on the trade. I tried to buy it at 113.50 and missed it; however, I had to manage my position as if I did buy it at 113.50, because the logical stop loss would be at 111.74.

*This rule has changed and depending on which ECN you trade with your order may sit on the ECN at a crossed market price without automatically canceling itself, but it will not be displayed on Level II.

CIEN also broke out to a new daily high over 138. I had better success entering this trade at a price close enough to the breakout. I bought 100 shares at 138.50. My price target was 144.75 - 149, which was resistance for the stock a few days back. My stop loss was placed at 136.75, which was 0.50 below the lower trendline of the ascending triangle.

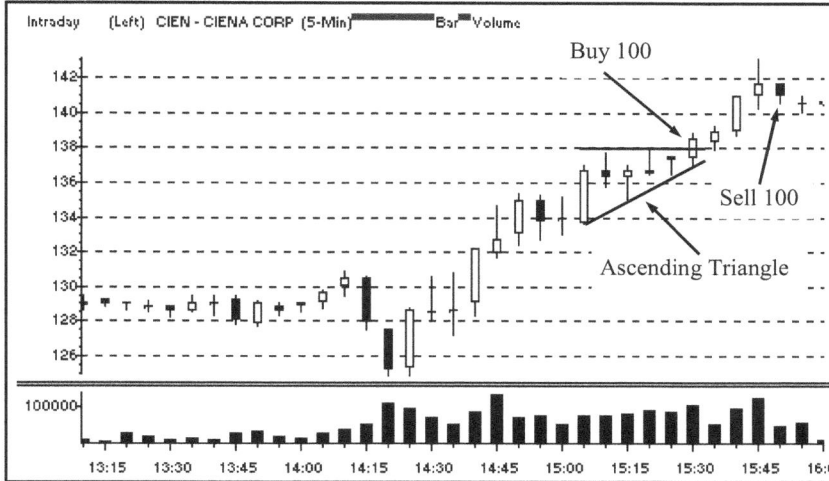

Reprinted with permission of Townsend Analytics, Ltd.

CIEN traded as high as 143.18 before pulling back. I had a mental trailing a stop behind the stock. When it hit 143, it was 1.75 away from my price target. At this point, I raised my stop loss to 141.75. CIEN turned around and traded at 141.75, activating my stop loss, but I didn't get executed until 140.50, as the stock fell down fast. This is a good reminder that you can always lose more than you anticipate even if you have a stop loss in place. No one knows where their order will finally get executed. In fact, I have heard of, and seen, horrifying incidents in which stocks were in a total free fall. There was this one stock, ONSL, that was trading at 104. Many of the traders in the stock had their stop loss at 99.75, 99.50, 99.25 etc., which was just under 100. The stock broke through 100 and fell sharply. It dropped all the way down to 44 in a matter of 14 minutes. Traders who had stop losses at 99 and above were executed at 50! Another incident was with QCOM late in 1999. The stock opened for trading at 740 and went down to 639 within 24 minutes. That was more than a 100 point move in 24 minutes. Trades were executing at 30 points below best bid. I had to go out of market almost 20 points myself to get out of QCOM at 720.94, right at the open. **It is extremely important to understand that a stop loss order doesn't necessarily mean that you will get out of your position once the stop triggers at the stop price. It could be executed at a much lower price.**

Source	Investment	Proceeds	COM	P&L	Return
Constant List	13,850	14,050	11.97	188.03	1.36%

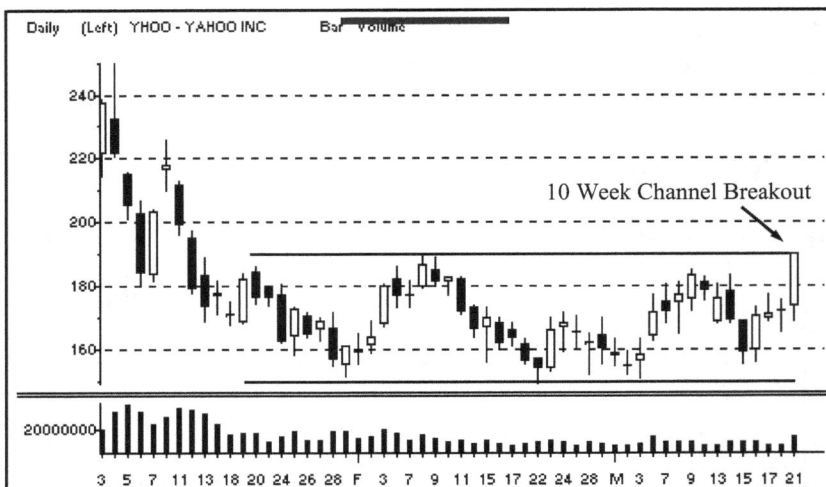

Daily (Left) YHOO - YAHOO INC   Bar Volume

10 Week Channel Breakout

Reprinted with permission of Townsend Analytics, Ltd.

While I was in both MRVC and CIEN, YHOO showed up on my Power Trader Scan. The stock was racing up as it just broke out over 188.

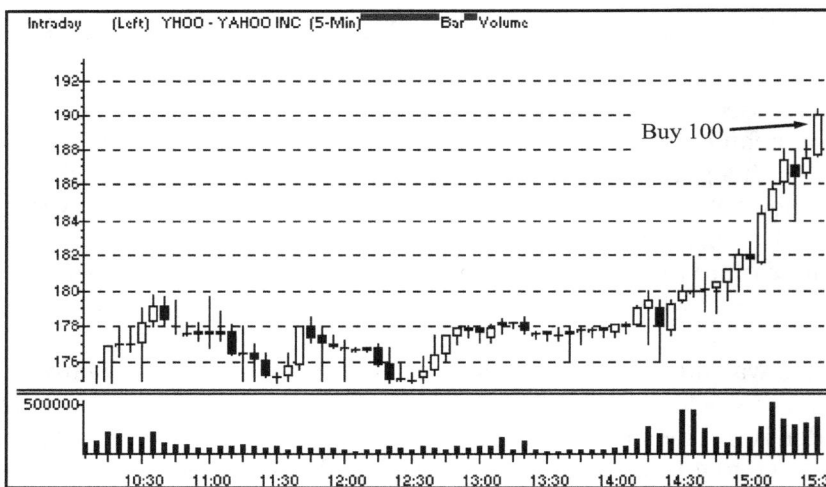

Intraday (Left) YHOO - YAHOO INC (5-Min)   Bar Volume

Buy 100

Reprinted with permission of Townsend Analytics, Ltd.

I bought 100 shares at 189.97. My price target was 195. I placed a stop loss at 187.75. The stock went up as high as 193.25. I noticed that the stock could fall hard if things were to turn around, so I sold on the first sign of weakness. I sold 100 shares at 192.50.

Source	Investment	Proceeds	COM	P&L	Return
Power Scan	18,996.87	19,250	10.65	242.47	1.28%

I had two open positions left which I liked for a possible overnight hold: RSLC and MRVC. RSLC was not doing much. On the other hand, MRVC was approaching the price target of 122.

Reprinted with permission of Townsend Analytics, Ltd.

The stock hit 121 and pulled back. I really thought that MRVC could go much higher the next day, so I was trying to give it some wiggle room. The stock went down to 119.50, so I sold 100 shares. I wanted to lock in some profit and give the rest of my position a chance; however, the stock went down to 118, which was the trigger of the stop loss on the remainder of the position, so I sold the last 100 shares at 118.

Source	Investment	Proceeds	COM	P&L	Return
Oz Pullback	22,993.75	23,750	22.30	733.95	3.19%

The final bell rang and the second day of the challenge was now officially over. The Nasdaq was up 101 points from yesterday's close. It was a great day for the bulls. The driving force behind the rise in stock prices was the completion of the FOMC meeting, and the announcement that followed shortly after. I felt very good about my trading, and a potential upward bias for the next few days. However, I did not want to take a big overnight risk.

Open positions: 300 Shares of RSLC
Total profit for 3/21/00: $2,470.11

Day Two Lessons

The market tends to overreact to news.

Look to buy intraday breakouts on reversal days.

A stop loss order does not guarantee an exit at the trigger price.

*Please note that you can get the proprietary stock scan formulas I used in day two, as well as my *Stock Market Calculator* at the SFO Academy website. *www.sfoacademy.com.* If you are having difficulty finding them, please email *info@tonyoz.com* and we will email you a direct link.

6

Working on My Golf Swing

DAY THREE

Wednesday, March 22, 2000

The market gapped up at the open and pulled back. I was watching both MRVC, which opened at 125, and CIEN, which opened at 141. I had both these stocks on my watch list, because I traded them yesterday.

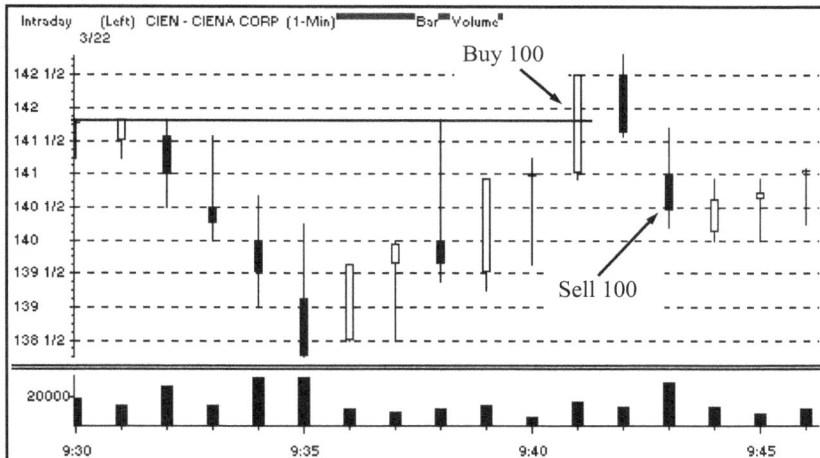

Reprinted with permission of Townsend Analytics, Ltd.

CIEN took out its morning high, after a very early bounce, and I bought 100 shares at 142. What happened next was a classic breakout play. The stock pulled back, and I dumped it at 140.50 for a loss. This is one of the problems of trading a breakout. More often than not, the stock will pull back and stop you out. The solution is to try and buy the pullback or give the stock more wiggle. In hindsight, if I placed my stop loss at 138.12, which was just below today's low, I would have been very fortunate, since it ended the day much higher. Nevertheless, a point and a half was all I was willing to lose on this trade.

Source	Investment	Proceeds	COM	P&L	Return
Watch List 1	14,200	14,050	10.47	-160.47	-1.13%

I just took my first loss in this challenge. It is important to put losses behind you quickly and to be ready for the next opportunity. I was now in my sniper position and my target was MRVC. I was waiting for the right time to take my shot.

Reprinted with permission of Townsend Analytics, Ltd.

MRVC held 119.25 and turned back up. I was carefully studying the ticker tape once the stock hit 121.18 around 10:17 AM EST. The stock pulled back a little and was able to hold 120.50. What I am looking for at this point is for the stock to trade higher than 121.18. This will confirm a new uptrend with rising bottoms and rising tops. The stock traded higher than 121.18, and I bought 100 shares at 121.25. My price target was 128 - 135 if it could break out over 125 (morning high). I placed my stop loss at 119.87.

Reprinted with permission of Townsend Analytics, Ltd.

40

The stock went up to 124.37 and pulled back a little. There were a lot of buyers at 124 - 124.31. All of a sudden, the Dow broke through the low of the day and sellers showed up on MRVC. I sold 100 shares at 123.87 with the intent to buy it back if it breaks over 125. I was very quick on the trigger, after beginning my day with a losing trade on CIEN.

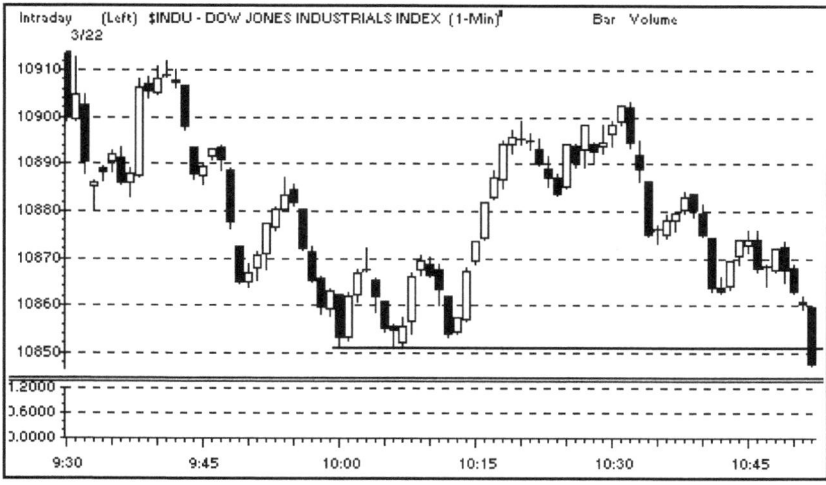

Reprinted with permission of Townsend Analytics, Ltd.

I always watch the indexes very carefully when I am in a trade. Although stocks can trade against the indexes, and the indexes themselves can trade inversely to each other, I like to exit positions if one of the indexes breaks down through support to make an intraday low. It is a part of my risk management philosophy. In this case, it was the Dow that crumbled, so I cashed in my chips and took my profits of the table.

Source	Investment	Proceeds	COM	P&L	Return
Watch List 1	12,125	12387.50	10.42	252.08	2.08%

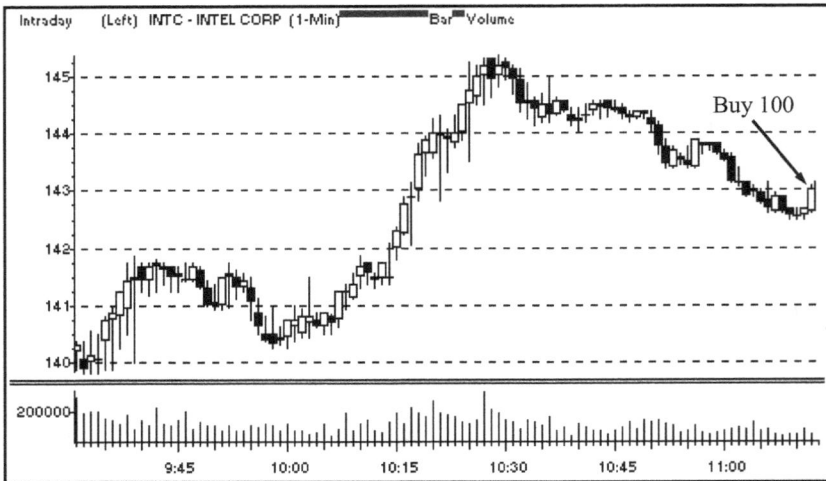

Reprinted with permission of Townsend Analytics, Ltd.

I was watching INTC, which just made a 52-week high at 145.37, this morning. It ran very strong from the opening price of 140.37, and I was looking to buy a pullback. INTC hit 142.50 on its pullback and started bouncing up. I bought 100 shares at 143.

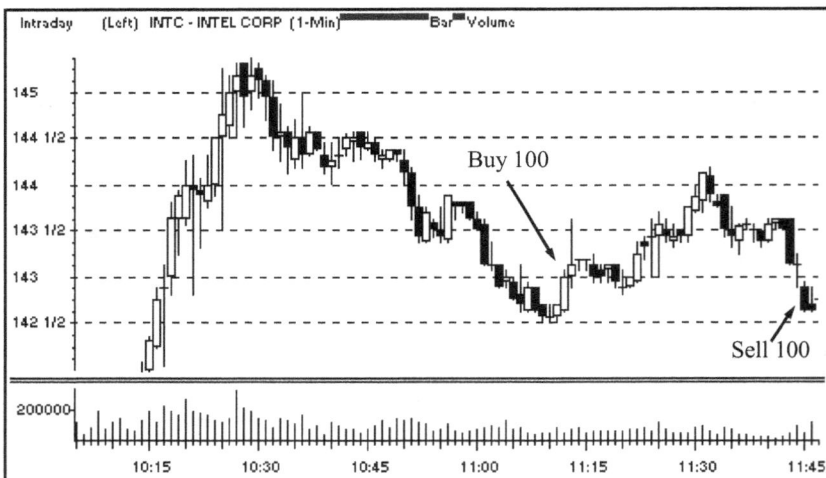

Reprinted with permission of Townsend Analytics, Ltd.

The stock went up as high as 144.18. Since it was trading in all-time high territory, I wanted to give the stock a chance to move higher, or at least a retest. My stop loss was initially set at 142.37, which was below the 142.50 level the stock hit at 11:10 AM EST. Once I was in the money, I moved my stop loss up to 143.25. The stock dropped to 143 1/4 and activated my stop loss order, before trading down some more, and I got my fill at 142.62.

Source	Investment	Proceeds	COM	P&L	Return
Constant List	14,300	14,262.50	10.48	-47.98	-0.34%

The All Mighty Ax

The Ax is the leading Market Maker. Market Makers make their money from trading profits. This causes competition, which is good for the general investor. This competition also brings in another element that is important to understand. They all want to be on the right side of the market. In many cases, a stock can be controlled by a leading Market Maker, who is well capitalized. He can sell or buy a very large number of shares. He can stand in the face of a rally or support a stock during panic selling situations.

The important thing is to learn how to locate the leading Market Maker, the Ax, and avoid getting caught on the wrong side of the trade. The Ax will normally spend more time on one side of the inside market (best bid or best ask), than on the other side of the inside market. They will *appear* to do both selling and buying, but the key thing is to pay attention to how much they are buying versus selling. When you look at a Level II montage for a while, you will be able to see and follow the movement of Market Makers. Pay attention to which side each Market Maker is spending most of his time.

Using the Time & Sales Print Report will help in pointing out the Ax. The easiest way to spot an Ax is when he is present on the best offer or best bid with a size of 1000 shares, yet the print report shows several 1000 shares trading at his price, as he is continually refreshing his size, and he does not leave his position at the inside bid or offer. I have seen situations where 100,000 shares or more traded at that price, yet the Market Maker never left the inside bid or offer.

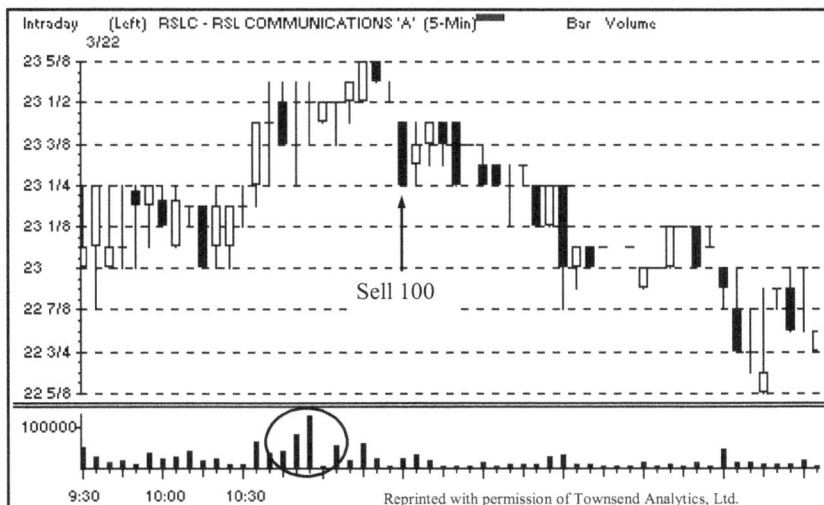

Reprinted with permission of Townsend Analytics, Ltd.

RSLC broke out over 23.25 at 10:30 AM. Volume increased and the stock hit a ceiling at 23.62. *DLJP* was the only visible seller on the Level II montage. He was the Ax. I didn't like the fact that the stock was not progressing in price on the big spurt in volume. That is what I would call a

43

waste of effort. The bid strength started to deteriorate and sellers came in on the offer using the ECNs at 23.50. *DLJP* was not going to be denied from being at the inside market and he down-ticked his offer to 23.43. The bid was 23.25 at the time. I decided to enter a sell order immediately. I sold 300 RSLC at 23.25. I was not going to stand in the way of the Ax.

Source	Investment	Proceeds	COM	P&L	Return
Watch List 1	6,618.75	6,975	10.24	346.01	5.23%

It was lunchtime in New York, and I was playing around with a my Power Trader Scan. I was changing the price criteria to see if I could find a low-priced stock that had an attractive setup. I don't normally trade low-priced stocks, but I wanted to see if there is a "new kid on the block" that was making a move. This is how I spotted AMBI.

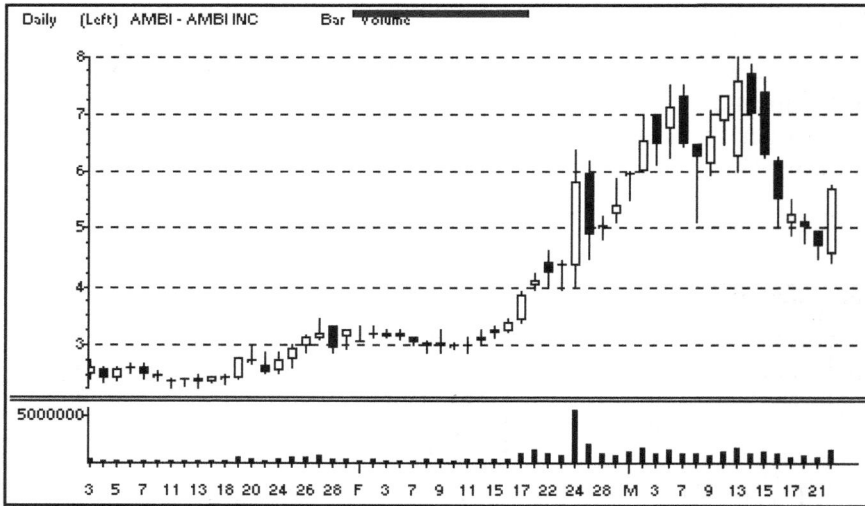

Reprinted with permission of Townsend Analytics, Ltd.

AMBI had a nice run from 2.50 to 8, where it topped on 3/13/00. The stock pulled back to 4.43, which was the low today, and then reversed on strong volume.

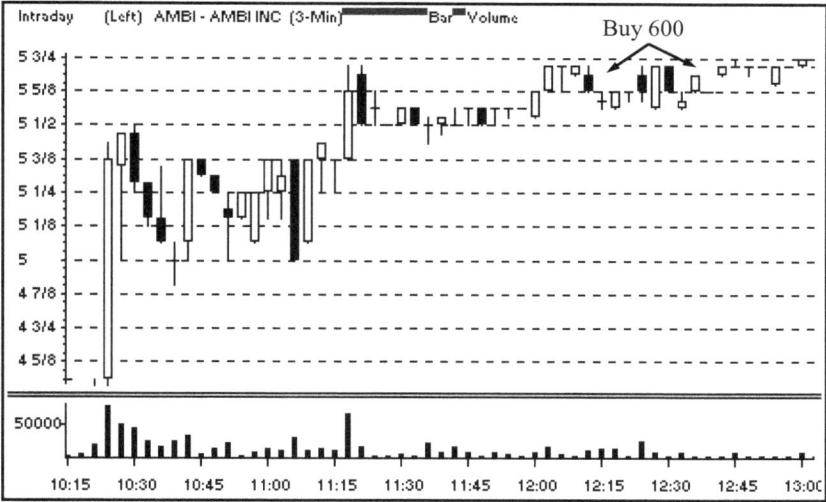

The stock was consolidating and looked ready to breakout. I bought 300 shares at 5.59. The stock looked good, and I bought another 300 shares at 5.72. I placed a stop loss at 5.31. My price target was 7 - 8.

What to do When Frustration Strikes?

You will hear many traders tell you stories of how they bought a stock at 20, sold it at 25, and watched the stock go up to 300. This is the devil of Wall Street – looking back. How do I know when to sell a stock? The truth is that I don't know. I don't think anyone does. I do know one thing, though. I must manage all risks in accordance with my trading system. This means that if a stock triggers a sell price, I have to execute it.

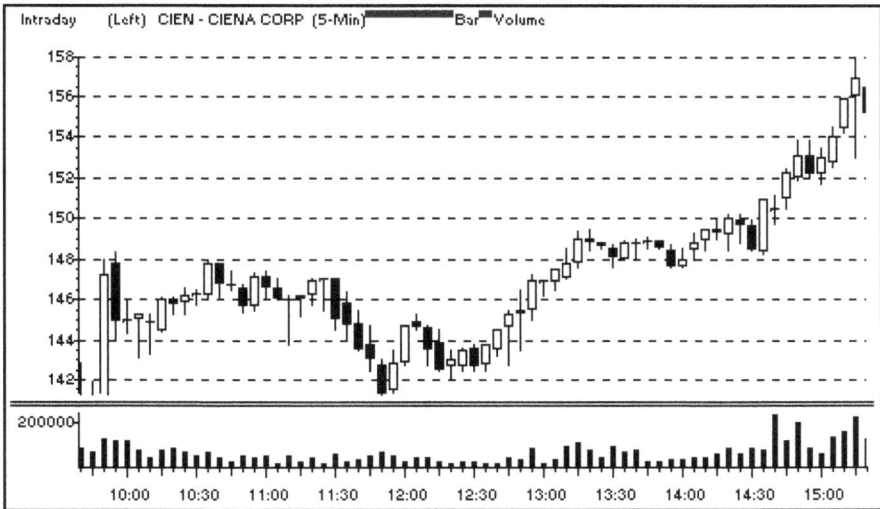

Today was a very frustrating day for me. As you recall, I sold CIEN earlier for a loss at 140.50. The stock was at 148.50 now, and it would go all the way up to 158 before day's end, as seen on the chart on the previous page.

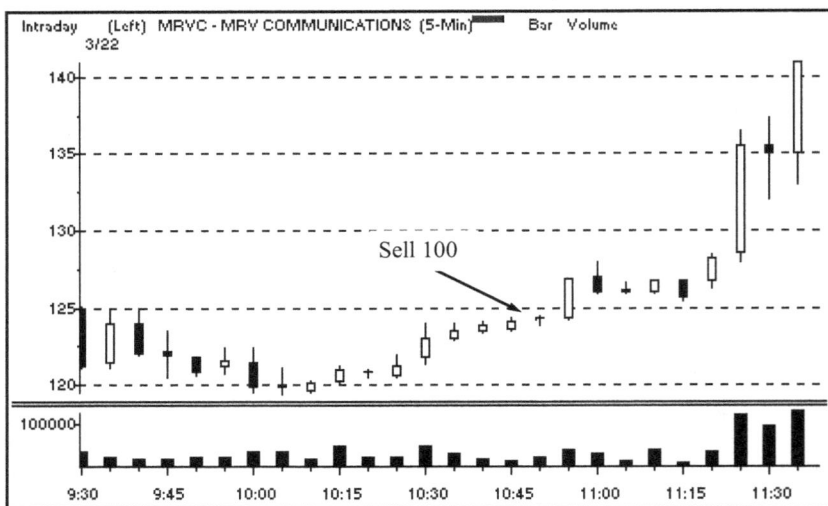

Reprinted with permission of Townsend Analytics, Ltd.

I sold MRVC at 123.87, at resistance. Shortly thereafter, the stock went up to 141. I tried to buy it when it broke over 125, but I didn't want to pay more than 125.50 for it, so I missed it. I waited for it at 125.50 when it started pulling back around 11:20. I missed the entry there as well. It wasn't the end of the world, just frustration, so I decided to do what I always do in this case – call it a day. I have found that it's best to walk away from situations like this, so that I may recharge my emotional energies and be in a positive frame of mind for the next battle.

I called the local golf course and got a tee time. I had a stop loss in place for my open position on AMBI, so my risk was being managed. It was off to the golf course to work on my swing.

I didn't hear the final bell ring today, but when it was all done and finished, it was another strong day for the bulls. The Nasdaq closed the day up 153 points from yesterday's close. My stop loss on AMBI was never activated.

Open positions: 600 Shares of AMBI
Total profit for 3/21/00: $389.64

Day Three Lessons

Try to wait for a pullback when buying a breakout, or you must be willing to let it wiggle.

Stocks may trade against the indices.

Stay out of the Ax's way.

Step away when frustration reaches extreme levels.

Tony needs to take golfing lessons before he embarrasses himself on the golf course again. ☺

7

The Running of the Bulls

DAY FOUR

Thursday, March 23, 2000

　　Following a frustrating day in the market, and an even more frustrating day at the golf course yesterday, I was looking forward to the market open today. I really liked the strong showing the Nasdaq had yesterday. My strategy for today is to manage my open position in AMBI effectively. I also wrote some intraday support and resistance levels for the stocks in my Constant watch list. I am looking to enter long positions in some of these stocks should they show continued strength. Sipping my cup of coffee, I was making my way upstairs to my trading desk preparing myself for today's battle.

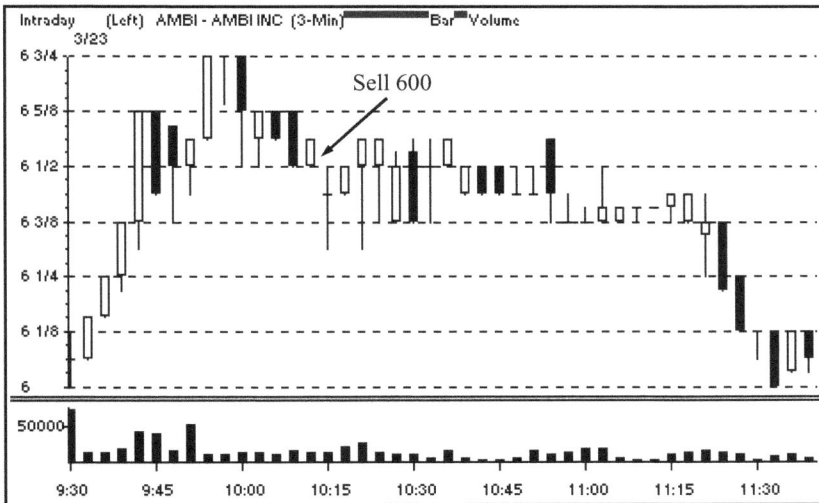

Reprinted with permission of Townsend Analytics, Ltd.

　　AMBI had a nice run from the open and it hit 6.75. *HRZG* was the Ax. I sold 300 AMBI at 6.50 when the stock pulled back from 6.75. I was going to give the other 300 shares some wiggle room. However, *HRZG* would not let AMBI go up higher. I decided to sell the remaining 300 shares at 6.50.

Source	Investment	Proceeds	COM	P&L	Return
Power Scan	3,393.75	3,900	20.15	486.10	14.32%

Although this trade does not look like a major home run when you look at the dollars and cents, it was actually a very profitable trade on a percentage basis. The reason I only allocated about $3,400 to this trade was because AMBI is a low price stock. I feel that there is an added risk to trading low price stocks, so I chose to be very defensive in this trade. I was very happy with the rewards; however, the stock could have just as easily gone down in price one point or more from where I entered it, and caused me a big loss. Keep that in mind!

The market is very strong today. In fact, the Nasdaq-100 Index is making new all time highs. I was looking to buy the tracking stock for the Nasdaq-100 Index (QQQ). The Nasdaq-100 Trust Series 1 is a pooled investment designed to closely track the price and yield performance of the Nasdaq-100 Index. It allows you to buy the entire index (actually pooled investment in the stocks which make the index) in one single security. The way it is calculated, more or less, every 40 points on the index are about one point on the tracking stock.

Reprinted with permission of Townsend Analytics, Ltd.

QQQ broke out to an intraday high (all time high), and I bought 200 shares at 116.25. I placed a stop loss at 114.37. Since we just broke out to an all time high, my price target was at 122.

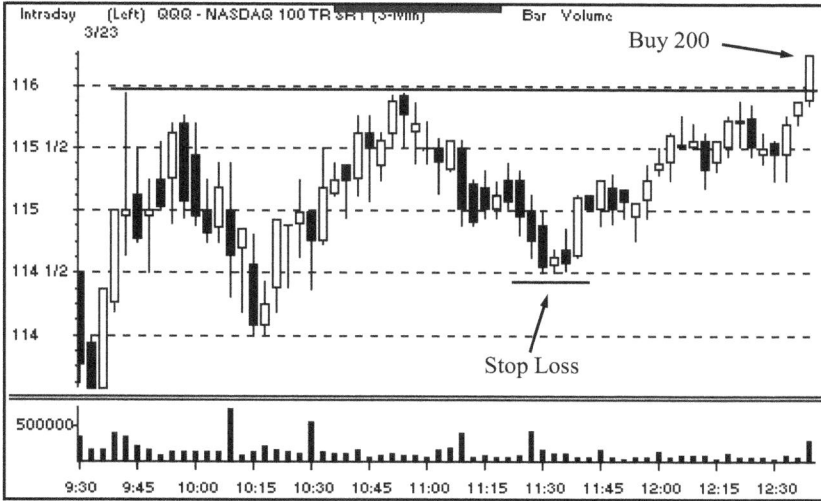

Reprinted with permission of Townsend Analytics, Ltd.

Since the index of the biggest 100 non-financial stocks on the Nasdaq was at an all-time high, I was monitoring the big blue chip companies which make the index. These blue chip companies are on my Constant watch list on a daily basis.

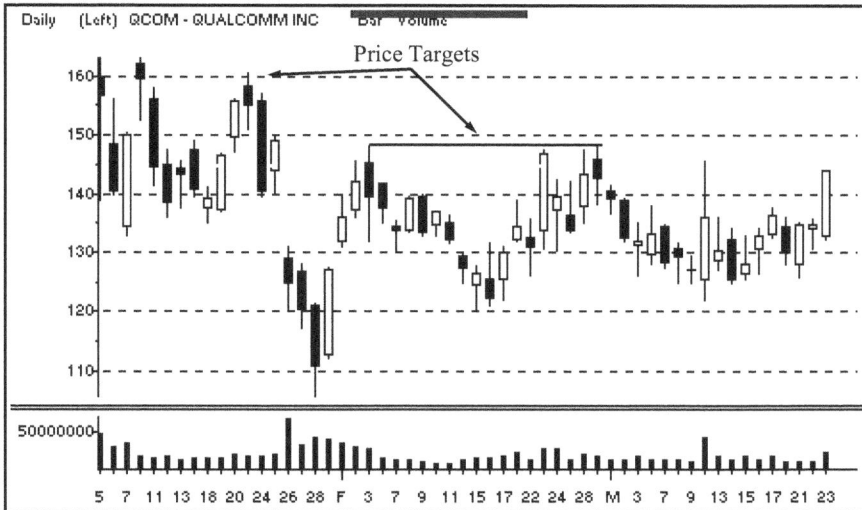

Reprinted with permission of Townsend Analytics, Ltd.

QCOM was moving up with the market on higher than average volume. I thought the stock could possibly go to 148 which is the next resistance level and possibly 160 if it broke out, as seen in the chart above.

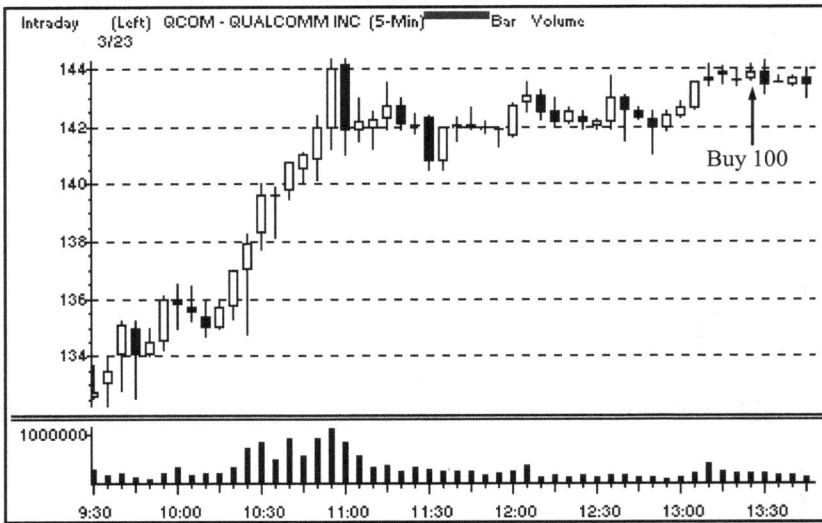

Reprinted with permission of Townsend Analytics, Ltd.

The stock was consolidating after the big run it had earlier in the day. I felt that a powerful breakout might take place, and I entered a buy order for 100 shares on ISLD ECN at 143.81. I got a partial fill of 50 shares, and my order was cancelled for the reason it would lock or cross a market. I wanted 100 shares, so I entered another order for 50 shares and got a fill at 144.06. I placed a stop loss at 142.50. My price target was 148 –160.

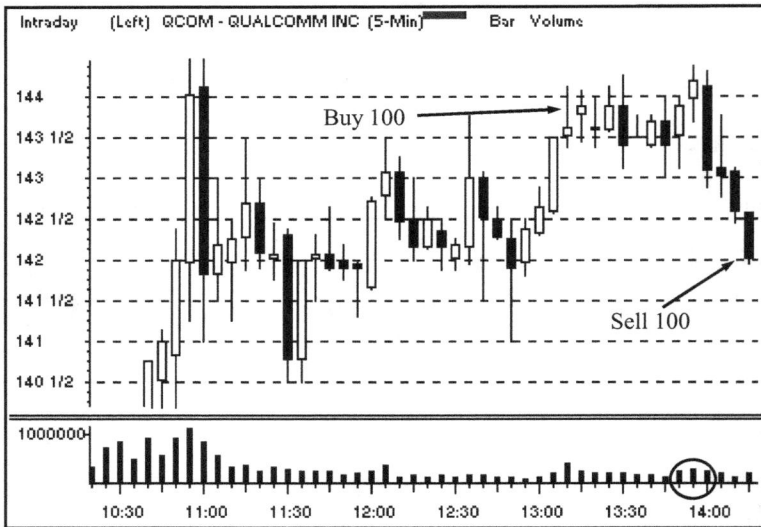

Reprinted with permission of Townsend Analytics, Ltd.

QCOM tried to breakout again as volume came in just before 2:00 EST. However, *SBSH* was axing the stock and the stock lost momentum and started falling down. It hit 142.50 and triggered my stop loss. I sold 100 shares at 142.06.

Source	Investment	Proceeds	COM	P&L	Return
Constant List	14,393.75	14,206.25	15.48	-202.98	-1.41%

Reprinted with permission of Townsend Analytics, Ltd.

INTC was lagging the index most of the day; however, as soon as the index broke out, INTC started to move as well. It broke out over resistance at 141 and went vertical. I tried to buy the breakout, but I couldn't get a fill. I started chasing it, and I finally got a fill. I bought 200 shares at 142.12. The stock broke out to an intraday high and went up to 142.94. It then pulled back to 141.50. The next rally attempt was very weak, and the stock peaked at 142.43. It then traded down to 141.75 where it found support (shown by horizontal line on chart). The next rally attempt took out the top at 142.43, and the stock traded as high as 142.56. INTC was starting an uptrend. I moved my stop loss up to 141.62 from 141.37. I felt that if INTC were to drop below the 141.75 level, it would be reversing its trend. INTC started selling off and it took the 141.75 support level out. My stop loss was triggered, and I sold 200 shares at 141.50.

Source	Investment	Proceeds	COM	P&L	Return
Watch List 1	28,425	28,300	10.95	-135.95	-0.48%

53

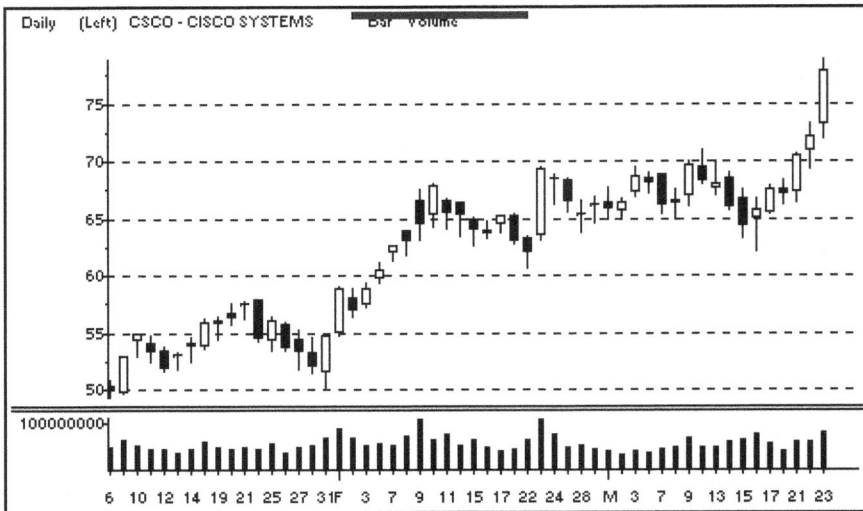

Reprinted with permission of Townsend Analytics, Ltd.

CSCO broke out to a 52-week high as well. I had learned my lesson and decided to wait for a pullback this time.

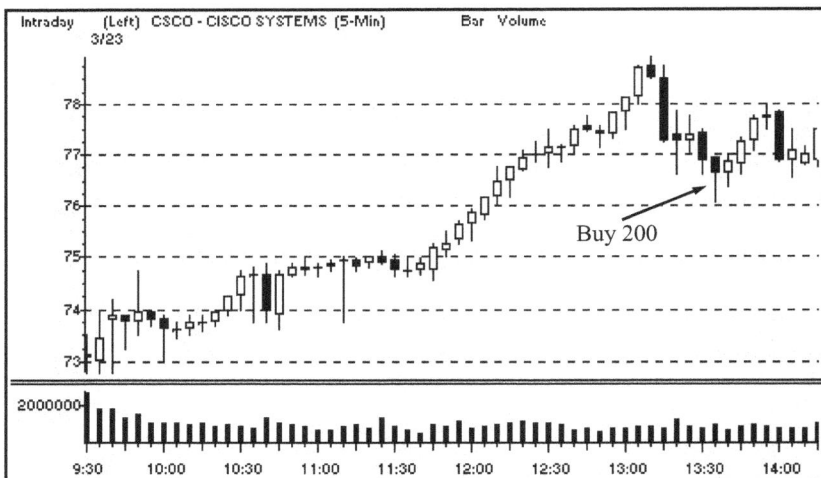

Buy 200

Reprinted with permission of Townsend Analytics, Ltd.

CSCO ran from a breakout at 75 at 11:30 to 78.87. It then pulled back to 76 .12 and started moving back up. I entered an order to buy 200 shares at 76.43, and I got a fill of only 10 shares! This was very frustrating. I entered another order to buy 190 shares and I got a fill of only 80 shares at 76.62. I couldn't believe it. I entered another order to buy 110 shares, and this time, I was able to complete my position. I got 110 shares at 76.75. I placed a stop loss at 75.87. My price target was 80.

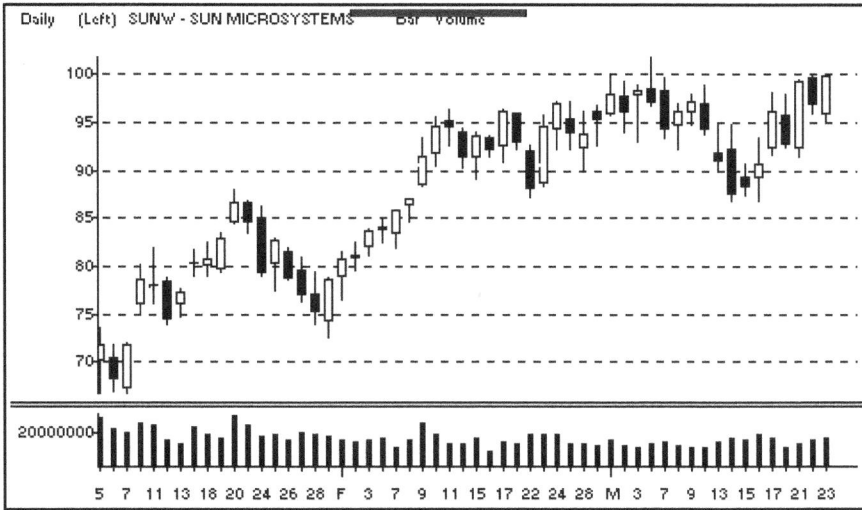

Reprinted with permission of Townsend Analytics, Ltd.

SUNW was close to breaking out to an all time high as well. I had prepared notes to keep a close eye on it today when I studied the stocks on my Constant watch list last night. I was looking for a potential swing trade.

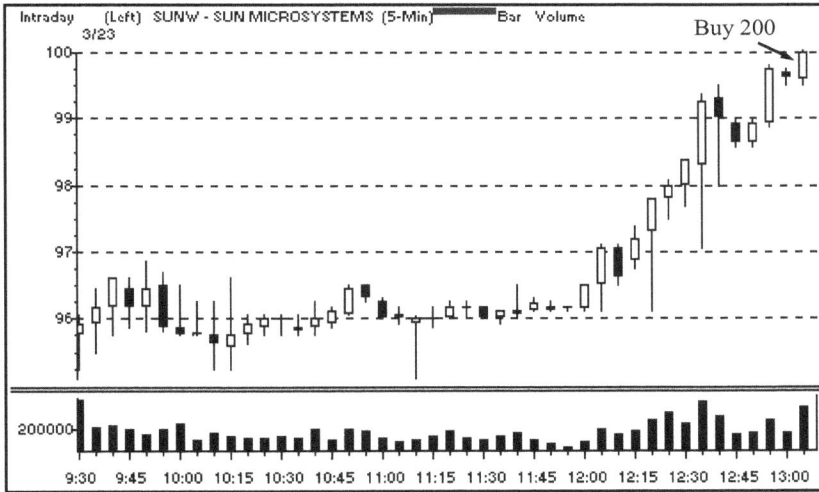

Reprinted with permission of Townsend Analytics, Ltd.

SUNW took out the high of the day and was now flirting with 100. I bought 200 shares at 99.87.

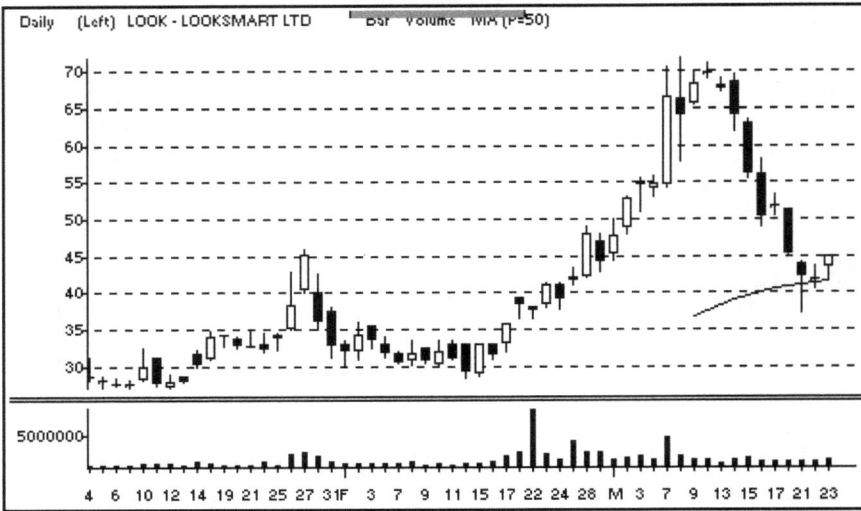

Daily (Left) LOOK - LOOKSMART LTD   Bar Volume MA (P=50)

I found LOOK on my Bottom Fisher Scan. The stock peaked at 72 on 3/8/00. Then, it had traded down to 37.25 three days ago and was bouncing back up. It was trading near the high of the day (44) when I first saw it.

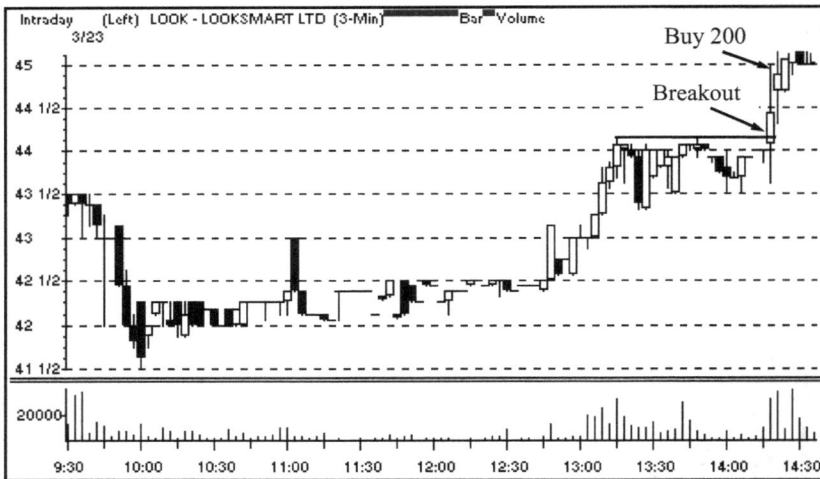

Intraday (Left) LOOK - LOOKSMART LTD (3-Min)   Bar Volume

Buy 200

Breakout

Around 2:18 PM, LOOK broke out of the consolidation pattern it was in, with increasing volume. I bought 200 shares at 44.87. I placed a stop loss at 43.87, and my price target was 48.25, which was the support level that was penetrated successfully four days ago.

Reprinted with permission of Townsend Analytics, Ltd.

The stock traded up to 46.50. Then it quickly pulled back and I got scared and sold 200 shares at 45.

Source	Investment	Proceeds	COM	P&L	Return
Pullback Scan	8,975	9,000	10.30	14.70	0.16%

The stock stabilized and started trading up again. I bought 200 shares again at 45.25. I added another 100 shares at 45.50 and 100 shares at 45.87.

Reprinted with permission of Townsend Analytics, Ltd.

ORCL broke out to an all time high. Again, remembering my lesson about jumping in too soon, I waited for a pullback.

ORCL did pull back, and I bought 300 shares at 87.15. If there was more time in the day, I would have placed a stop loss below support, illustrated by the horizontal line on the chart; however, there was only one minute left to the closing bell. I was buying ORCL for a swing trade.

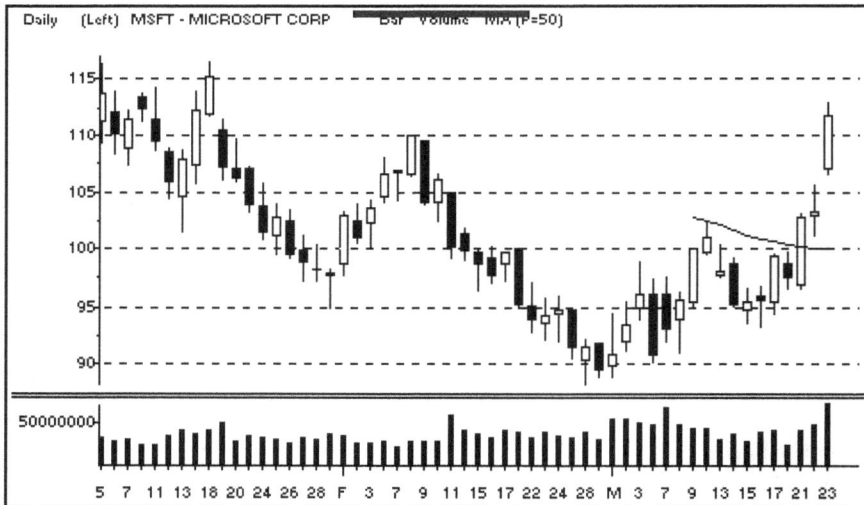

MSFT looked really strong. I was watching it most of the day. I was going to buy it for an overnight hold if the stock closed strong.

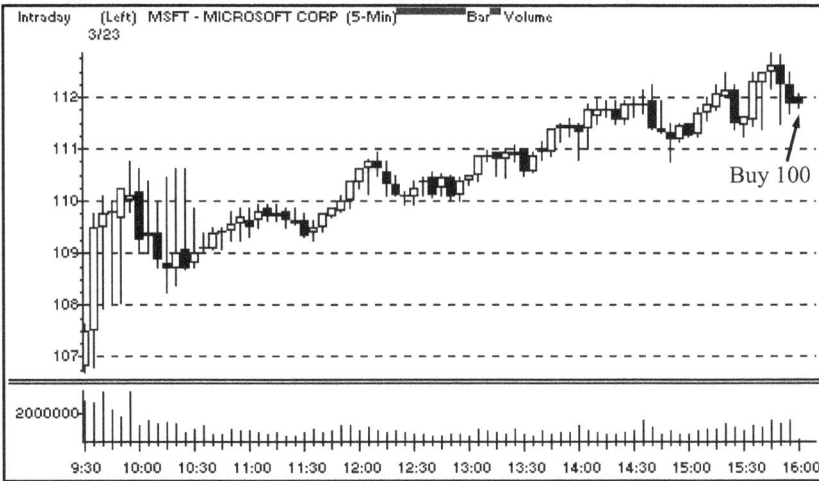

Reprinted with permission of Townsend Analytics, Ltd.

MSFT closed very strong and I bought 100 shares at 112.06 for an overnight hold. I felt that the stock would attempt to make it to 115 tomorrow.

The trading day was over. I had six open positions, and I felt somewhat over extended, but the stocks I was in were trading higher in after-hours trading. I was assessing my overnight risk and decided to sell CSCO. The stock closed at 77.81, and there was a bid on Island at 78.25. I took another look at the CSCO daily chart, and I decided to sell it.

Reprinted with permission of Townsend Analytics, Ltd.

As you can see in the chart above, CSCO ran up from 62.18 to 79 in the last five days. This is not a normal price appreciation for a stock like CSCO, so I felt the risk/reward in holding the stock overnight was not worth it. I sold 200 shares at 78.25.

Source	Investment	Proceeds	COM	P&L	Return
Constant List	15,336.87	15,650	20.54	292.59	1.91%

Once the final bell rang and the final sell ticket was stamped, the bulls were celebrating again. The Nasdaq closed up 75 points from yesterday's close. I felt that I traded well, and I felt comfortable holding five positions overnight.

Open positions: 200 QQQ, 300 ORCL, 200 SUNW, 400 LOOK, 100 MSFT. Total profit for 3/23/00: $454.46

Day Four Lessons

Wait for a pullback before buying a breakout setup .

You can trade an index tracking stock such as QQQ.

Don't be afraid to buy back a stock which you have sold earlier at a lower price.

Do not chase stocks!

CHAPTER 8

Oakland Here I Come

DAY FIVE

Friday, March 24, 2000

I slept real well last night even though I was holding five open positions. When I did my research last night, I was trying to determine how greedy I was going to be today. In my notes, I wrote down strategies for both a gap-up open and a gap-down open on any of my positions. If my positions are to enjoy the same momentum today that they did yesterday, I will simply place trailing stops. I did not study any new setups for potential entry this morning, because my basket was full. Instead, I evaluated each stock I owned in order to make things easy at the open. It is very challenging to manage five positions simultaneously, so I must follow the guidelines I have outlined in my plans for today.

I woke up extra early this morning, and I was pumped up for today's action. The Nasdaq looked strong early in the morning, as most of the stocks I held overnight were trading higher pre-market. MSFT was trading at 114.50. I placed a stop loss order on MSFT at 111.94.

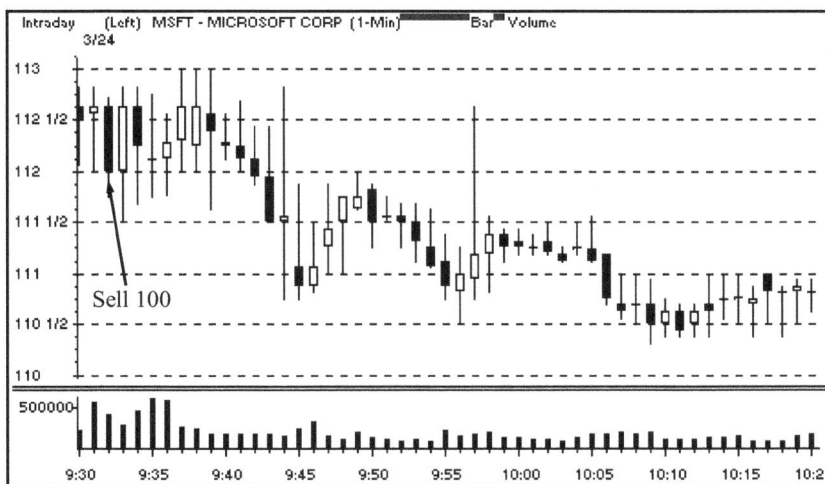

Intraday (Left) MSFT - MICROSOFT CORP (1-Min) Bar Volume
3/24

Sell 100

Reprinted with permission of Townsend Analytics, Ltd.

MSFT opened for trading at 112.50, after it traded as high as 115 pre-market, and then tanked from there. My stop loss was triggered and I sold 100 shares at 111.94.

Source	Investment	Proceeds	COM	P&L	Return
Constant List	11,206.25	11,187.50	10.38	-29.13	-0.26%

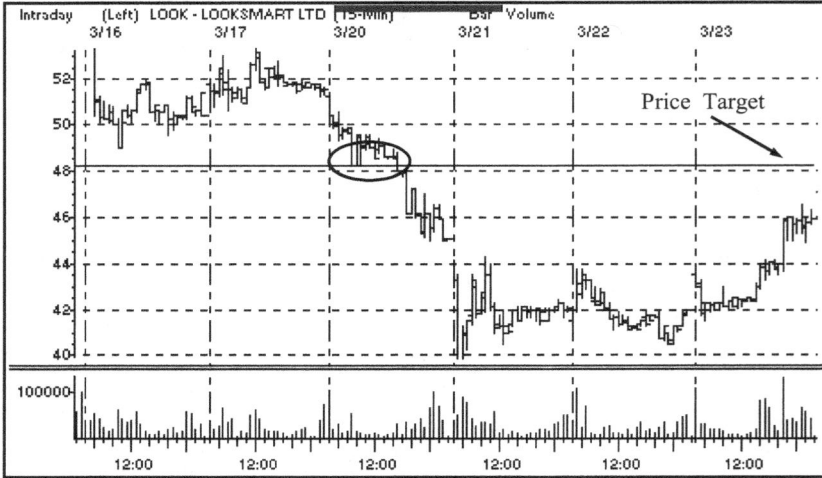

Reprinted with permission of Townsend Analytics, Ltd.

LOOK gapped up to 47.12. I placed a stop loss for 200 shares at 46.87, and I also placed a sell limit order for 200 shares at 48.25, which was my price target, as seen in the chart above.

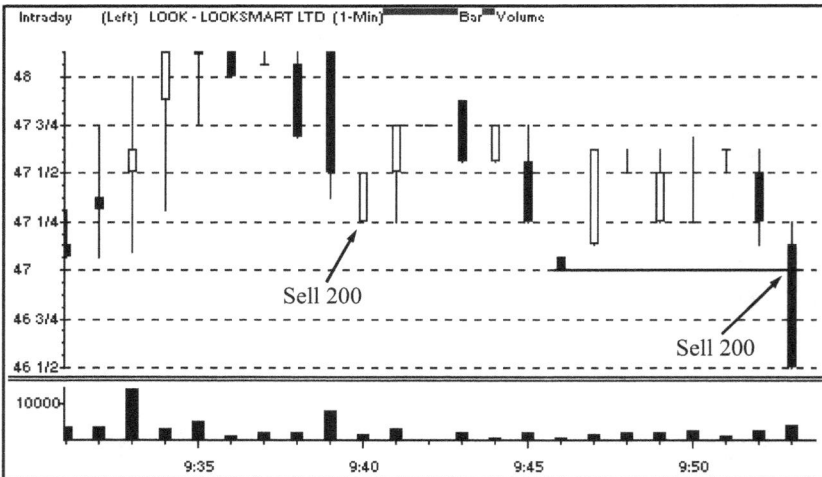

Reprinted with permission of Townsend Analytics, Ltd.

The stock ran up and hit 48.12. It was trading there for about 3 minutes. I thought that my sell order at 48.25 was going to get executed for sure, but it didn't. The stock was being axed by an anonymous party using Instinet. The size on *INCA* (Instinet) kept refreshing. I cancelled my sell limit order at 48.25, and I sold 200 shares at 47.25. At 9:53, the stock broke down through 47, and my stop loss triggered. I sold the remaining 200 shares at 46.87.

Source	Investment	Proceeds	COM	P&L	Return
Pullback Scan	18,187.50	18,825	27.14	610.36	3.36%

ORCL went up from 87.37 to 89.62. It was in all time high territory. I was trailing a stop on 200 shares, and as ORCL hit 89.50, I placed my stop at 88.94. The stock turned around and traded lower than 89. My stop was triggered, and I sold 200 shares at 88.94.

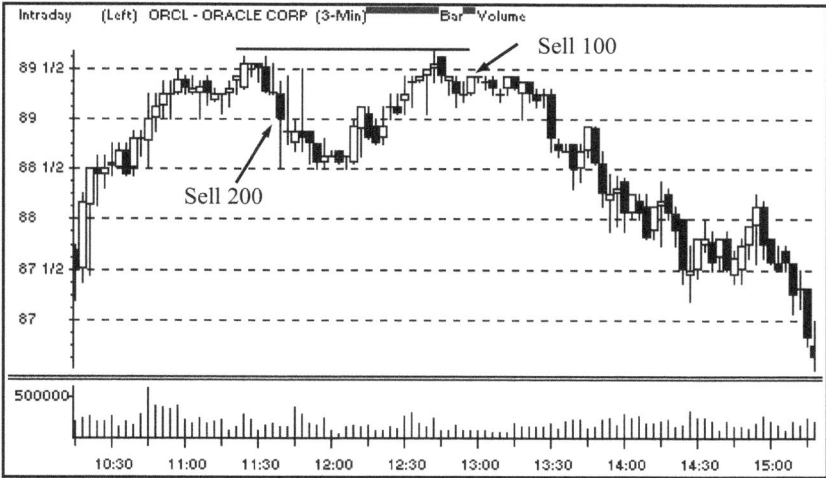

Reprinted with permission of Townsend Analytics, Ltd.

ORCL hit 88.50 and started to make another attempt to go higher. It traded as high as 89.69 before turning back down. *SBSH* was the Ax. He was selling it all the way to the top, and he down-ticked his offering price on the way down. I decided to sell. I sold my remaining 100 shares at 89.37.

Source	Investment	Proceeds	COM	P&L	Return
Constant List	26,147	26,725	20.65	557.35	2.13%

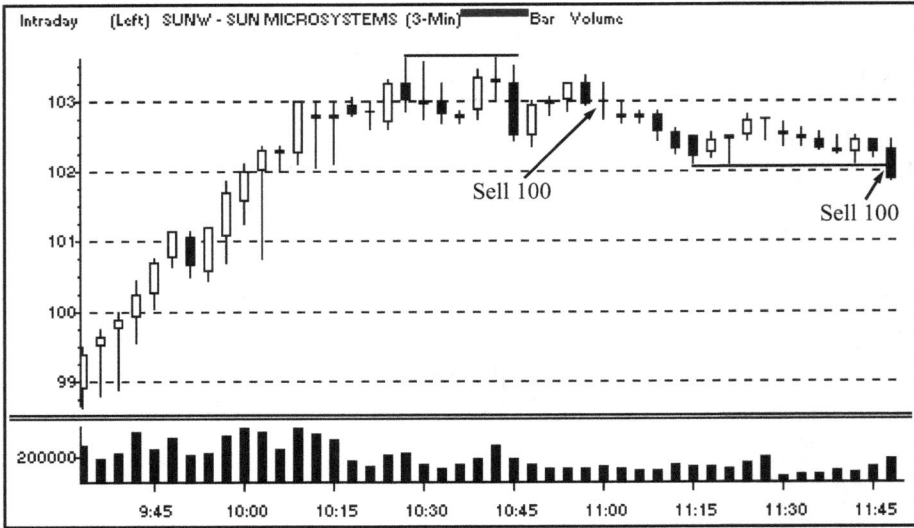

Reprinted with permission of Townsend Analytics, Ltd.

SUNW ran from 99 to 103 5/8 where it topped. It came down a little and then rose to attempt a breakout above that price level, but failed to do so. It looked like a double top had formed, so I sold 100 shares at 102.87. SUNW traded down to 102.12 and bounced back up to 102.75. I placed a stop loss for the remaining 100 shares at 102. The reason I placed it at that mild support level was that if SUNW was to break down, it would suggest a trend reversal confirmed by lower highs and lower lows. The stock penetrated through 102.12 and my stop was triggered. I sold 100 shares at 102.

Source	Investment	Proceeds	COM	P&L	Return
Constant List	19,975	20,487.50	15.69	496.81	2.49%

SUNW sold off and went as low as 99 as seen in the chart below.

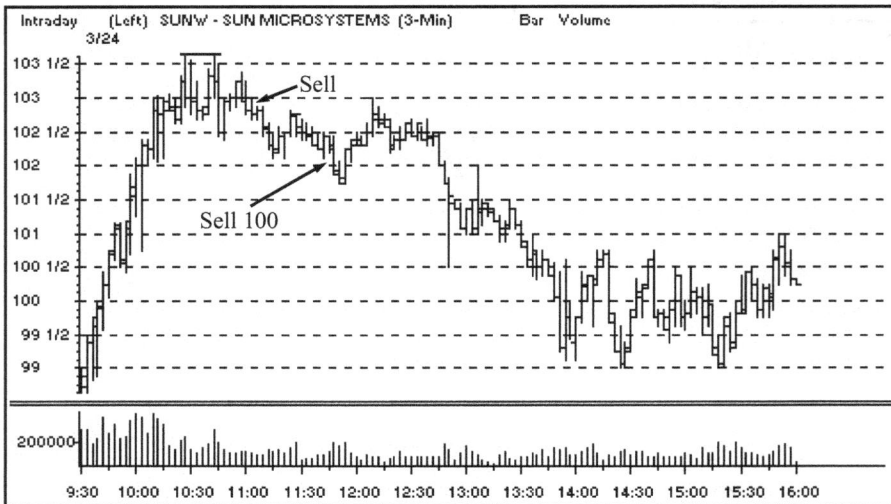

Reprinted with permission of Townsend Analytics, Ltd.

64

Reprinted with permission of Townsend Analytics, Ltd.

QQQ topped at 120.50 and started trending down at a slow, sadistic pace. I placed a stop loss at 118.94. The stock went lower than 119 and triggered my stop loss. I sold 200 shares at 118.94.

Source	Investment	Proceeds	COM	P&L	Return
Market Play	23,250	23,787.50	10.80	526.70	2.26%

The Market sold off hard as seen in the QQQ chart below.

Reprinted with permission of Townsend Analytics, Ltd.

65

The final bell rang, and the bulls managed a small victory. The Nasdaq closed up 22 points from yesterday's close. However, the Nasdaq seemed to have topped out as it closed 115 points off the day's high and 23 points below the open. It had a reversal day, which was a sign of weakness. I didn't like this weakness, so I did not enter any new long positions.

Open positions: None
Total profit for 3/24/00: $2,162.09

The first week of the challenge was over. It was a great week in which I was able to capitalize on many of the opportunities presented to me. I started the week sitting tight on the sidelines without executing one trade for the entire day. I think this was the key point for the success I have had this week. My total profits for week one were $5,476.19. I faxed my broker a request for a check in the amount of $5,000.00. After all, Friday is payday!

Southwest Securities 1201 Elm St. Suite 3500. Dallas, TX 75270	SIPC	88-88 1113 209490
	DATE	AMOUNT
PAY ********5,000DOLLARS 00CENTS Pay To	3/24/00	$*****5,000.00
TONY OZ LAGUNA HILLS, CA 92654		

The reason I like to order checks rather than electronic transfers of any kind is because I get to see something that represents a reward for my hard work. It also makes my "better half" very happy when she opens the mail. I have also found it to be very encouraging on those days when I am struggling. Let's say I had a very bad day, and I lost a few thousand in the market. When I check my mail that evening, I find a check for a few thousand that I ordered last week. This puts a smile on my face and helps me get ready for the next trading day.

After I ordered my paycheck from my broker, I made my way to John Wayne Airport to catch a plane. I was going to attend the Online Trading Expo, which was taking place in Oakland this weekend.

Day Five Lessons

Hold only as many positions as you can manage effectively.

Manage multiple positions with trailing stops.

Do not look to enter new positions when your basket is full.

Sell when things don't look right.

Friday is a payday, don't you forget that!

Learning from Beginner Traders

DAY SIX

Monday, March 27, 2000

I returned from Oakland late on Sunday night, and I was very tired; however, I wanted to write a summary of the most valuable things I have learned at the conference. On Friday night, I attended the reception party given by the host of the event. I sat at a table with six other individuals, who were discussing trading methodologies. I soon found myself participating in a round table conversation, or should I say debate. The beauty of the debate was that there were green traders at the table, professional traders, and trader wannabes.

One of the traders was telling us how he has been writing naked put options, successfully. This got my attention very quickly. Anytime I hear this strategy, I quiver. I remember stories of those who lost all they had, and then some, using this technique. When someone writes (sells) a naked put option, he commits to buy the stock at a certain price, over a certain period of time, from the person who buys this option. He receives a premium payment up-front for entering this contract. Let's try to simplify it.

XYZ is trading at $150. Using the above strategy, I can give someone the option to sell me 1000 shares of XYZ anytime over the next two months at 150. For this right, the purchaser of this contract will pay me $6.00 today. This will be my profit (maximum reward). This strategy is very bullish and extremely risky. My trading philosophy is to always manage risk properly. The first thing I take into consideration is what happens if things go wrong. The following table will illustrate the risk and reward for this trade.

How much money will I make or lose if XYZ traded at the following prices two months from now?

As you can see, my reward is limited to $6,000. My risk is not lim-

50	70	90	110	130	150	170	190	210	230	250
-95K	-75K	-55K	-35K	-15K	+6K	+6K	+6K	+6K	+6K	+6K

ited, and I can lose a lot of money if something went wrong. This is not what I look for in a trade. I'd like to capture a great reward when I am right, and I'd like to lose the minimal amount when I am wrong. There isn't one right way to trade, and I don't discourage anyone from trading the way they like to; however, what made this debate so unique was the fact that I felt the trader who was using this strategy did not really understand the risk he was taking. And I wasn't alone on this one.

The argument about selling naked options started a discussion about risk management, which I felt was very valuable, especially, because we were discussing risks that are sometime out of our control. How can we be prepared for power outages, network downtime, slow Internet connection, etc., were the questions we were trying to answer. These are the behind-the-scenes risks of doing business online that everyone should be aware of. You could write more than a handful of books on the various subjects that were discussed at the conference.

Now, that I was home, much of the information I gathered in Oakland started to sink in. I was very concerned with much of what I saw at the show. There were many traders who were going to take on Wall Street with inferior tools, little knowledge, and a lot of money to lose, and no one was going to stop them from doing so. I don't know if it is a special quality or simple human nature, but these soon-to-be traders believe they know better than everyone else, and they are going to prove to the world they have what it takes to break the code to the Wall Street vault.

The reason I am bringing this up is because, what I am presenting in this book in an easy-to-understand way, is much more complex in real life, especially, if you have not experienced any of the pain that stock trading via the Internet inflicts. I don't want to deceive you and make you believe that it is easy. It is not. It is, however, doable! That is what I hope to be able to show in this book. I need to be able to trade as well as I did last week over the next three weeks in order to do so.

Beep! Beep! Beep! My alarm clock goes off. It is 4:45 AM and time to get up. I was so tired that I couldn't open my eyes. I hit the snooze button, trying to steal another six minutes of sleep. Beep! Beep! Beep! I hit the snooze button again. Another six minutes go by, and the alarm clock goes off again. It was one of those mornings where I had a million-mile-an-hour argument in my head, where I would list all the pros and cons to determine if I should get out of bed or sleep in. This, of course, happens almost every morning that I am not holding positions overnight. When I don't hold any positions overnight, turning on the TV in the bedroom will be the first step in getting up. I turn the TV on, and I jump back into bed. I raise the pillows somewhat and put on my glasses. My eyes are still shut. The alarm clock is still in snooze mode in case I fall into deep sleep again. I hold the alarm clock in the palm of my hand with my thumb on the snooze button. It takes me a fraction of a second to press the button should the alarm go off again. Every once in a while, I will open one eye and take a quick peek at Mark Haines, Joe Kernen, David Faber, and the ticker that runs at the bottom of the screen on CNBC. This process repeats itself for the next 20-30 minutes until I finally get out of bed; however, there are days, like today, in which I will stay in my cozy warm bed for a longer (much longer) period of time. The cons win the argument today, and I am sleeping in. I turned the alarm off.

It was 8:30 AM PST, when I finally woke up. The market had been open for two hours already, and I didn't care. I made my way to the bathroom and took an extra long shower. What a luxury. Another hour went by, and I finally made it upstairs to my trading desk. I started RealTick and my scanning program. I was catching up to what I have missed over the last three hours. I was very relaxed, and I was waiting for a good setup to show up on my scan.

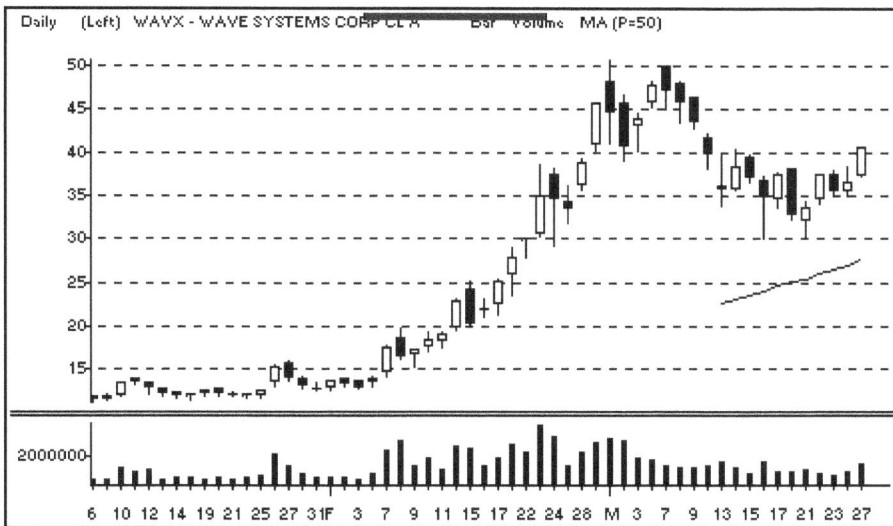

Reprinted with permission of Townsend Analytics, Ltd.

WAVX was the sniper's first target of the day. It showed up on my Power Scan. The stock had a nice run from 12 in February, and it topped at 50.75 on 3/1/00. It then traded down to 39, where it bounced. It made another run at the high and topped at 50, testing the top again on 3/7/00. Once it failed to make a new high, the stock sold off and went down to 30 on 3/16/00, where it found support. The stock traded back up to 38.18 on 3/18/00. The following day, it traded back down to 30, which was the price level that held on the 16th. The stock held that price level again and traded back up. The two tops at 50 suggested a double top pattern, which was confirmed. The two bottoms set at 30 were a positive sign of good support. The

71

resistance level is at 38.25. If the stock is able to trade higher than that level, it should test 40, where resistance should be stronger. If the stock can penetrate that level, then it should try and test the highs at 50.

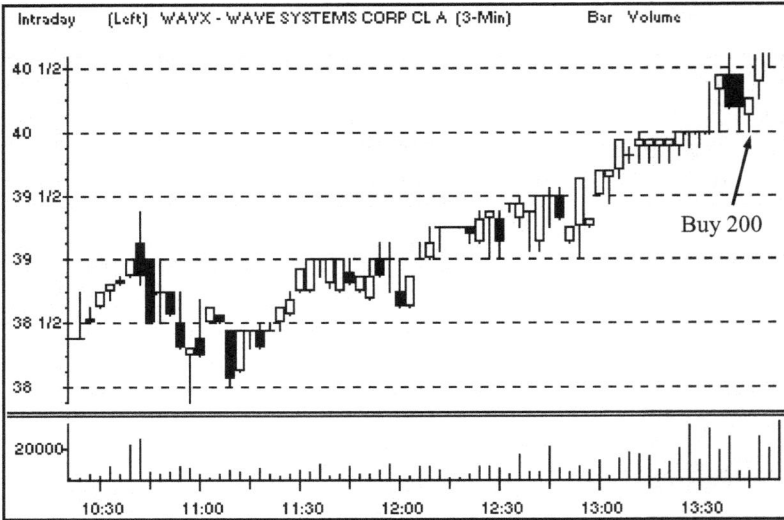

Reprinted with permission of Townsend Analytics, Ltd.

WAVX traded over the 40 level as it broke out from an ascending triangle. It traded as high as 40.62 and pulled back on relatively low volume. I bought 200 shares at 40.12. I placed a stop loss at 39.62. My price target was 42 - 45.

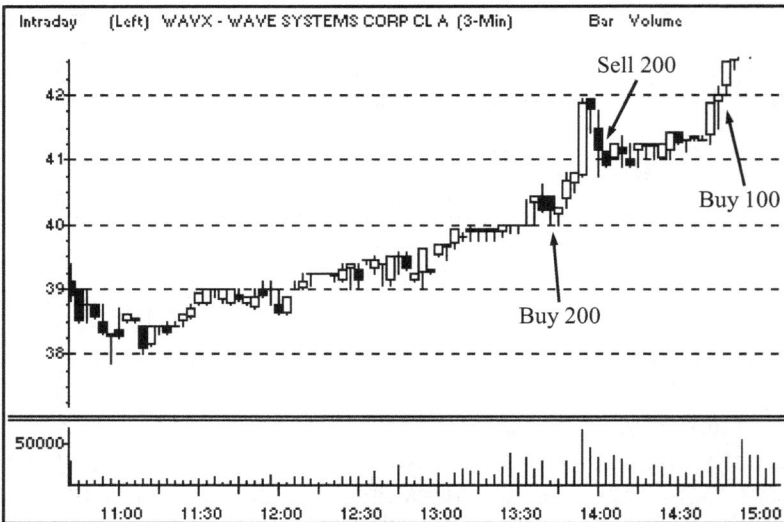

Reprinted with permission of Townsend Analytics, Ltd.

WAVX went as high as 42 then sold off quickly. I sold 200 shares at

41.18. The stock found good support at the 41 level, consolidated and started to move back up. I tried to buy 200 shares again, but only got 100 shares filled at 41.87.

Source	Investment	Proceeds	COM	P&L	Return
Power Scan	8,025	8,237.50	10.28	202.22	2.52%

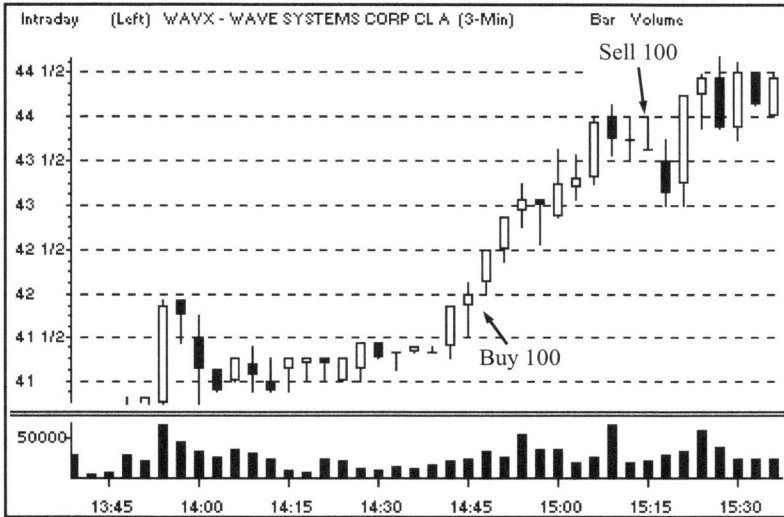

Reprinted with permission of Townsend Analytics, Ltd.

WAVX broke out over 42. I tried to add to my position, but the stock was very strong, and I couldn't get a fill. The stock hit 44.18 and was having problems there. It kept banging its head against 44 for the next 11 minutes, so I decided to sell. I sold 100 shares at 43.94, and I entered a buy order for 200 shares at 42.18, where it would sit on the ISLD ECN, waiting for a pullback to occur down to the point of the original breakout.

Source	Investment	Proceeds	COM	P&L	Return
Power Scan	4,187.5	4393.75	10.15	196.10	4.68%

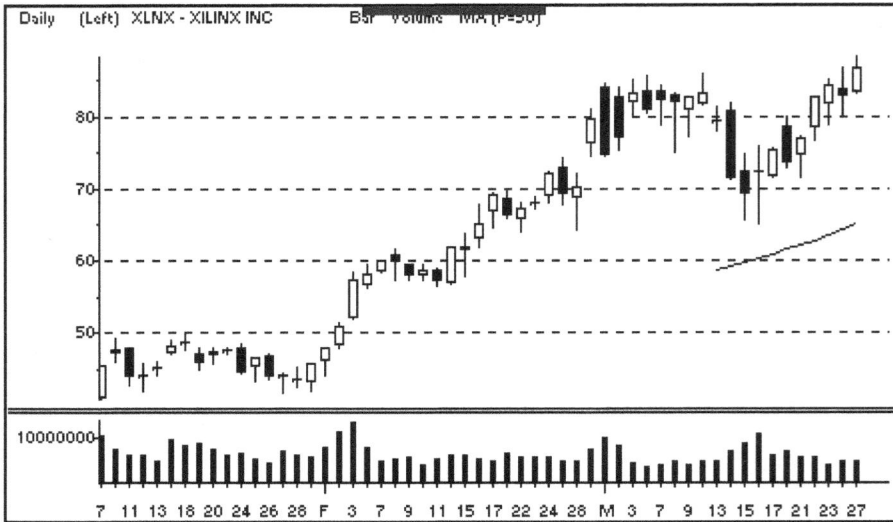

Reprinted with permission of Townsend Analytics, Ltd.

XLNX showed up on my 52-Week High Scan. It had been moving up nicely over the last eight days. I was looking to capitalize on continued strength in the stock.

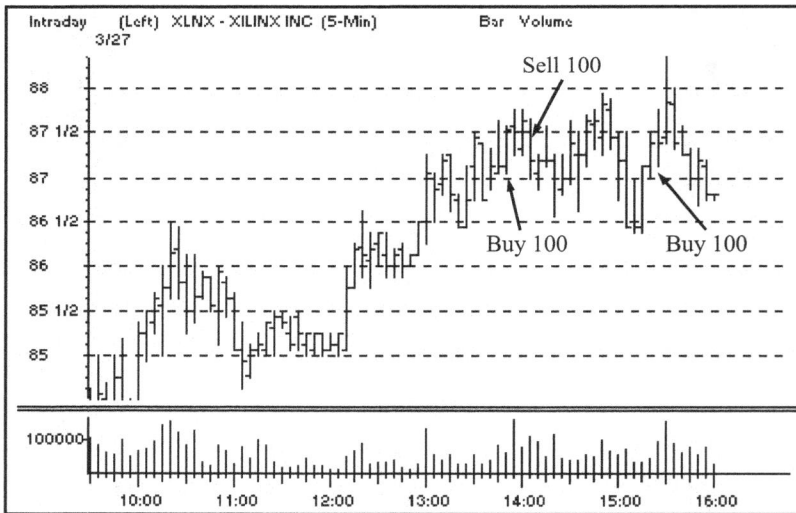

Reprinted with permission of Townsend Analytics, Ltd.

I bought 100 shares of XLNX at 87.25. The stock went as high as 87.69. *BEST* was the Ax, and he was not letting it go any higher. I sold 100 shares at 87.43. The stock went down to 86.31 and traded back up. I bought 100 shares at 87.06 and decided to hold it overnight.

Source	Investment	Proceeds	COM	P&L	Return
52-week High	8,225	8,243.75	10.30	8.45	0.1%

My love affair with WAVX was not over. The stock wouldn't trade back down to 42.18, and was actually very strong. I entered a stop buy order for 200 shares at 45.25.

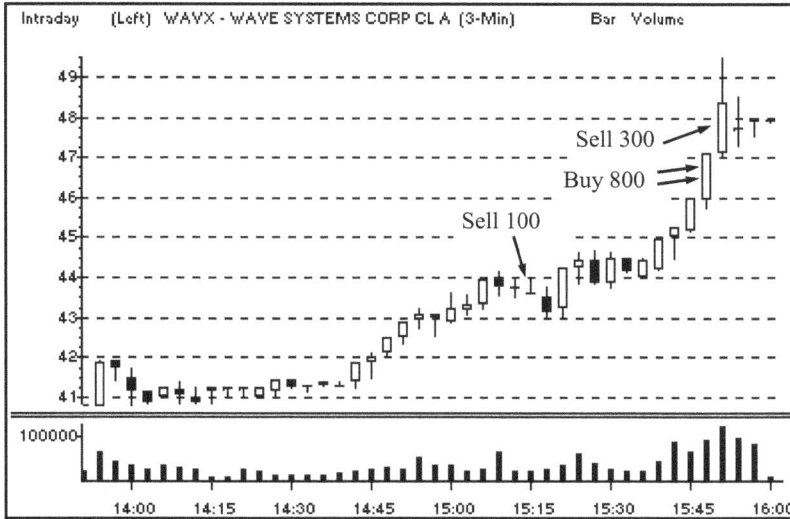

Reprinted with permission of Townsend Analytics, Ltd.

WAVX broke out over 45.25, and my stop buy was activated. The volume increased drastically, and I was having problems getting a fill. The stock was flying! I wanted to get into the stock badly enough that I decided to cancel my buy stop order. Then, I sent out a SelectNet Preference order, out-of-market. I sent out three orders in rapid succession for 200 shares each at 46.81. I got 200 shares at 46.81 from one Market Maker, another 200 shares at 46.81 from a second Market Maker, and yet another 200 shares from ISLD at 46.86. Now I had 600 shares. About 30 seconds went by, and the stock was trading at 48. It was a wild ride, and in the midst of all the frenzy, I didn't realize that my stop-buy order, which I tried to cancel, was still open. Before I could sneeze, I got a confirmation that my order for 200 shares was filled at 46.62. This is not very common, but in fast moving markets, it's very possible to get delayed confirmations. Since my stop buy order was on ARCA, cancellations can take a while, because ARCA breaks down the order and preferences Market Makers, who hang on to the order for 30 seconds and sometimes longer. Since I only wanted 600 shares, and the stock was at 48, as soon as I realized I had more shares than I wanted, I entered a sell order for 300 shares. I got a fill at 47.75.

Source	Investment	Proceeds	COM	P&L	Return
Power Scan	14,006.25	14,325	10.30	308.45	2.20%

75

The market closed, and WAVX was moving higher in after-hours trading. I decided to sell another 100 shares to manage risk more effectively. I expected WAVX to take the 50.75 top out tomorrow, based on the strong momentum it had today. However, I wanted to lock in more profits, so I sold 100 shares at 49.69.

Source	Investment	Proceeds	COM	P&L	Return
Power Scan	4,681.25	4,968.75	10.75	276.75	5.91%

The market was mixed today, but the bears were showing more teeth. The Nasdaq lost four points since Friday's close. I wasn't so crazy about the market overall, but I did like the two stocks I was in.

Open positions: 100 XLNX, 400 WAVX.
Total profit for 3/27/2000: $991.97

Day Six Lessons

Learn all the behind-the-scenes risks.

Interaction with other traders can be very beneficial.

Selling naked options is very risky.

There is nothing wrong with sleeping in if you have no open positions.

CHAPTER 10

When the Guru Speaks, We Should All Listen

DAY SEVEN

Tuesday, March 28, 2000

I had no problem getting out of bed this morning. In fact, I was looking forward to the opening of the stock market. I turned off my alarm as soon as it went off, and jumped into the shower. I took a quick shower this morning as I was anxious to get to my trading desk, and watch the pre-market action on my overnight positions, WAVX and XLNX. I turned on the computer and saw that trades on WAVX were taking place north of 50. It is going to be a great day, I thought to myself. I then turned on the TV and noticed that the futures were trading down sharply. This was a warning sign. The reason they were trading down was because Abbey Joseph Cohen from Goldman Sachs recommended that investors reduce their asset allocation to stocks from 70% down to 65%. The Guru who has been famously bullish on the market is recommending a reduction of exposure to stocks. This was not a good sign at all.

WAVX started to trade down, and I sold 400 shares pre-market at 49.12. My reasoning was that the market will be weak at the open, because those who cannot sell pre-market will have their market sell order go live at the opening bell. This will create selling pressure, which will also trigger many stop loss orders. I call it the domino effect. I was not going to take that risk. I had profit in the trade, and I took it.

As you can see on the chart on the next page, when WAVX finally opened for trading, the first trade took place at 48.12. The stock then tanked really hard, and it went all the way down to 42 in seven minutes. It would have been impossible to get out at a decent price had I waited for the open. My analysis was right on the money. It was nothing more than common sense.

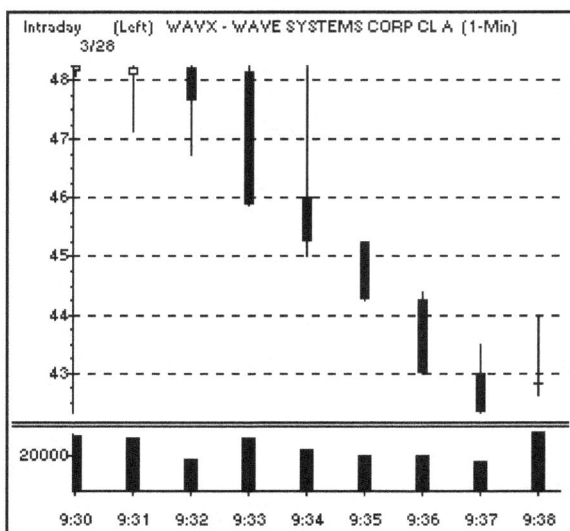

Intraday (Left) WAVX - WAVE SYSTEMS CORP CL A (1-Min)
3/28

Reprinted with permission of Townsend Analytics, Ltd.

Although it sounds like common sense to me today, I didn't understand this concept in the past. The reason was that I was often in love with a stock or with the setup I was trading. I just "knew" the stock was going to make a big move, and that I was going to make a killing on it. I would be counting the money and spending it before the market would even open. This was my subjective point of view, where the obvious is disregarded. However, after I paid my tuition, I learned a few valuable lessons, and one of them was to always analyze my positions and the market in an objective way. I would let the market guide me regarding what it wants to do, rather than me trying to dictate to the market what to do.

Source	Investment	Proceeds	COM	P&L	Return
Power Scan	18,738	19,650	31.54	880.46	4.70%

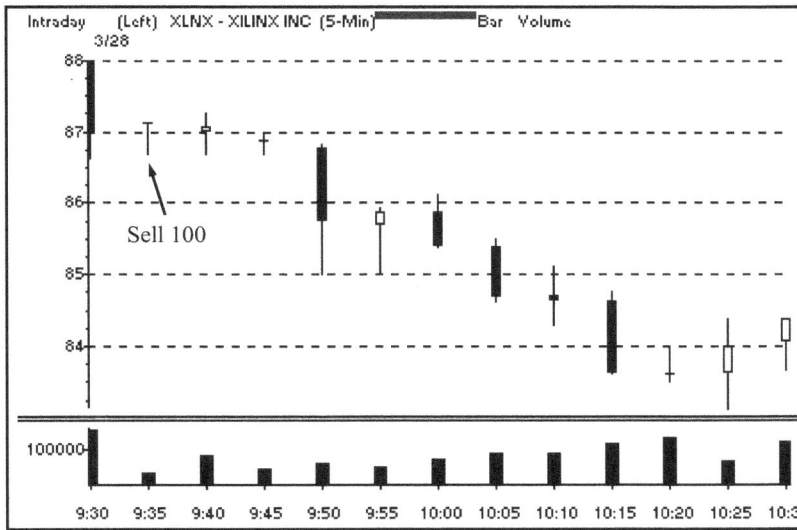

Intraday   (Left) XLNX - XILINX INC (5-Min)   Bar Volume
3/28

Sell 100

Reprinted with permission of Townsend Analytics, Ltd.

I was so preoccupied with managing the risk on my 400 share position of WAVX that I was not paying too much attention to XLNX. As soon as it opened, however, I entered a sell order, and was able to get out of my 100 shares at 86.75.

Source	Investment	Proceeds	COM	P&L	Return
52-Week High	8,706.25	8,675.00	10.29	-41.54	-0.48%

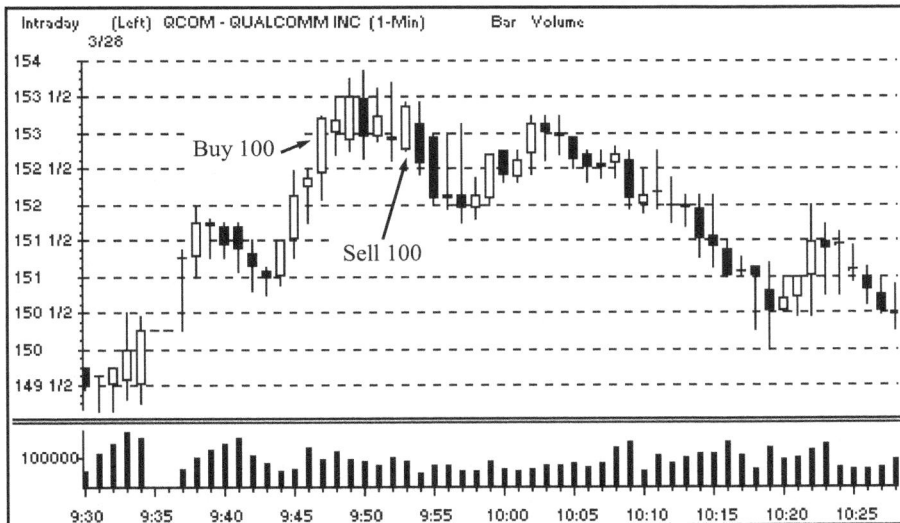

Intraday   (Left) QCOM - QUALCOMM INC (1-Min)   Bar Volume
3/28

Buy 100

Sell 100

Reprinted with permission of Townsend Analytics, Ltd.

I was watching my Constant watch list and noticed that QCOM had a strong showing this morning. I bought 100 shares at 152.94. The stock went as high as 153.87 and pulled back. My price target was 160; however, the market was weak, so as QCOM traded down, I sold it at 152.69.

79

Source	Investment	Proceeds	COM	P&L	Return
Constant List	15,293.75	15,268.75	10.51	-35.51	-0.23%

Reprinted with permission of Townsend Analytics, Ltd.

I couldn't resist a great setup when I noticed MRVC sitting at its 50-day moving average. I tried to buy 100 shares but got a partial fill of 50 shares at 110.50. I bought an additional 100 shares at 110.87. My price target was 118 - 140, and my stop loss was placed at 108.87, 0.25 below today's low.

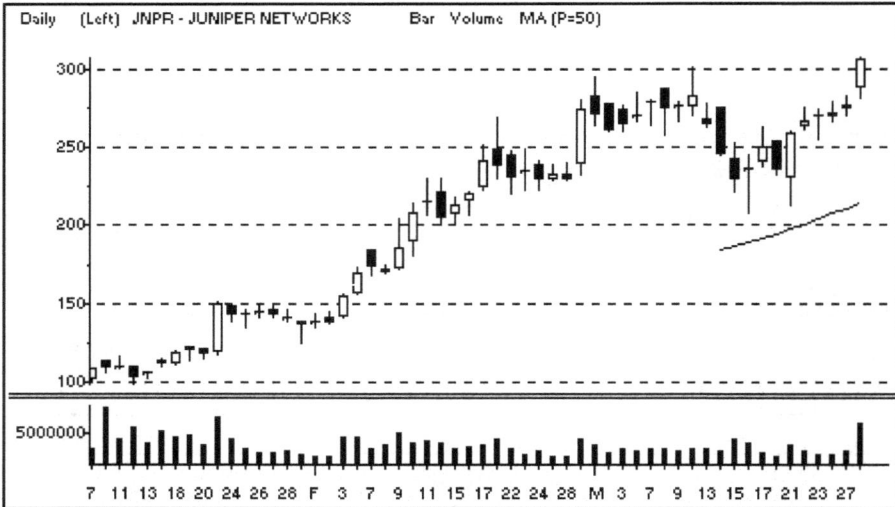

Reprinted with permission of Townsend Analytics, Ltd.

JNPR had a strong day. It broke out to a 52-week high on higher than average volume. I found the stock using my Power Scan. I tried to buy it a few times during the day at intraday support levels; however, I was never successful in getting a fill. JNPR was closing the day on a strong note, and I bought 100 shares at 307.72. The stock closed at 307.

JNPR was trading higher after-hours. Trades were going by at 312. I entered a sell order at 314.94 on the Island ECN and went to the dentist. My logic was that if I was going to be able to sell the stock almost eight points higher than its closing price, it wasn't worth taking the overnight risk. I can always buy it back the next morning if I still like it. While I was getting my teeth cleaned, someone bought my 100 shares, so I sold 100 shares at 314.94.

Source	Investment	Proceeds	COM	P&L	Return
Power Scan	30,771.88	31,493.75	11.05	710.82	2.31%

The bears won the battle today. The Nasdaq lost 124 points from yesterday's close. I had a great day, because I got out of my WAVX pre-market. I felt that my MRVC open position was very risky; however, I felt that my small relative position should not get me into a deep hole. But you never know what can happen the next morning ...

Open positions: 150 MRVC
Total profit for 3/28/00: $1,514.23

Day Seven Lessons

Learn how to manage risk pre-market and after-hours.

Let the market tell you what it wants to do.

Be objective when you manage your positions.

CHAPTER *11*

The Market is Always Right

DAY EIGHT

Wednesday, March 29, 2000

After the 125-point decline on the Nasdaq, I didn't know what to expect. The futures were trading up, so we should have some strength at the open. The newscasters are still talking about Abbey Joseph Cohen's recommendation to decrease exposure to the equity market, so I am going to be very cautious today. I was remembering the time when Ralph Acampora, a long time bull, made bearish comments about the Dow in 1998, sending stocks prices down sharply. Is it going to happen again? Time will tell. In the meantime, my strategy for the day is to manage my open position in MRVC effectively, and to monitor my Constant watch list for potential trades. Since I was not sure about market direction, I was not going to trade stocks I do not know.

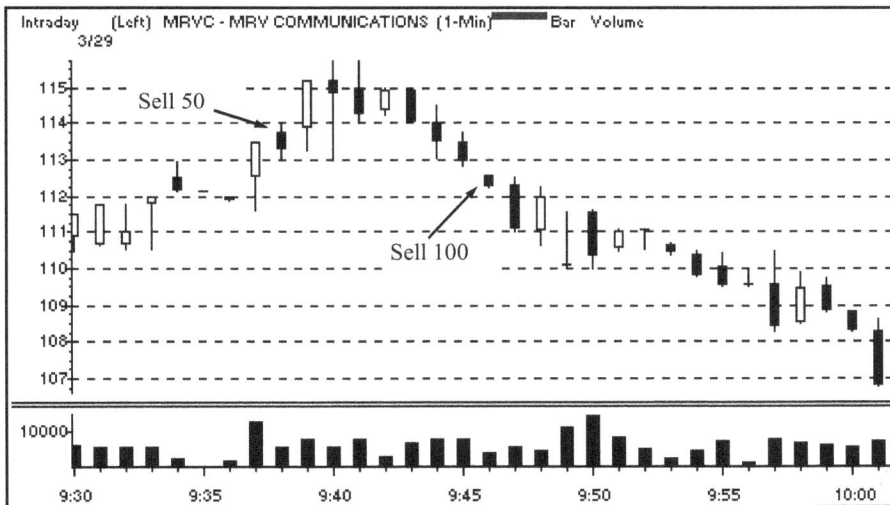

Reprinted with permission of Townsend Analytics, Ltd.

My overnight position, MRVC, traded up from the open, but the Nasdaq was trading lower. I decided to sell 50 shares into the strength in order to eliminate my odd-lot position of 150. The reason I was doing that is because most ECNs only trade in round lots. Since my order entry window is set to automatically enter the number of shares equivalent to my open position in a stock, I will have to adjust the number of shares prior to entering an order, and then I will have to enter another order to sell the remaining shares.

83

This can be time consuming, and very dangerous. Also, I can only enter a stop loss order in round lots on ARCA. I sold 50 Shares at 113.94. The stock traded as high as 115.75. I placed my stop loss at 113.50. The stock traded down through 113.50, and my stop was triggered. I wasn't able to get out of 100 shares until the price fell to 112.43.

Source	Investment	Proceeds	COM	P&L	Return
Constant List	16,612.48	16,940.62	20.57	307.57	1.85%

Reprinted with permission of Townsend Analytics, Ltd.

INTC pulled back from its 52-week high and found support around 135. It then traded higher, and was just about to breakout to a new intraday high.

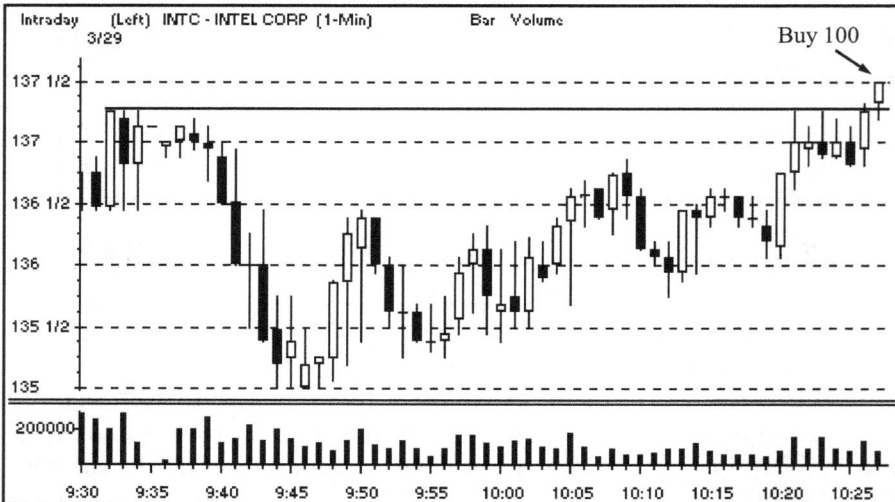

Reprinted with permission of Townsend Analytics, Ltd.

The stock did break out successfully, so I bought 100 shares at 137.56.

84

Yikes! How classic is this? I buy the high of a breakout and the stock tanks. My price target for INTC was 140, and my stop loss was placed at 136.50. The stock traded down to 136.50, and my stop loss was triggered. I sold 100 shares at 136.

Source	Investment	Proceeds	COM	P&L	Return
Constant List	17,756.25	17,600	10.46	-166.71	-0.94%

While I was in INTC, ORCL was breaking out of an ascending triangle. The pattern earlier looked like a double bottom around 84.75, and a trend reversal with a possible test of 86, and maybe even a breakout passing 86.12 to an intraday high. I bought ORCL at 85.50, placing a stop loss at 85.12.

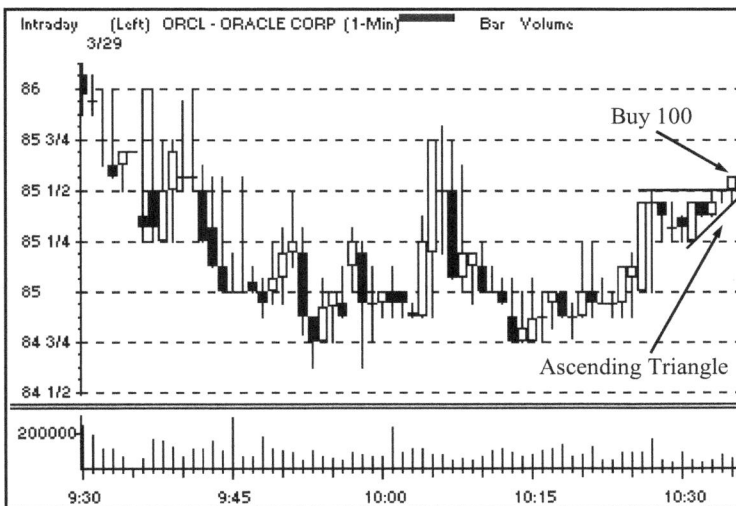

85

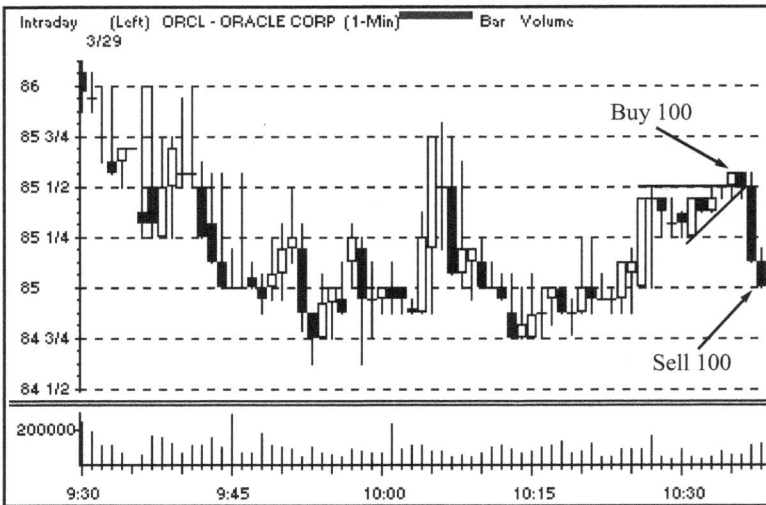

Reprinted with permission of Townsend Analytics, Ltd.

It looks like it is going to be a very long day. ORCL pulled back and my stop loss triggered. I sold 100 shares at 85.

Source	Investment	Proceeds	COM	P&L	Return
Constant List	8,550	8,500	10.29	-60.29	-0.70%

It wasn't like I was loosing a lot of money, but it certainly felt that way. I was making all these breakout plays, and I was getting slapped. I was very upset, and the market was starting to look very ugly, so I took a little break.

I wanted a breath of fresh air, so I went out on the balcony. We live on top of the mountain overlooking the saddleback valley. Things are so peaceful when you are up high enough. I can see all the cars on the main streets, yet I can't really hear them. Once in a while, I will hear the kids playing at the school down the mountain. On a clear winter day, I can see snow on top of the San Bernardino mountains, which are more than sixty miles away, and on the 4th of July, I can see fireworks go off in as many as 11 different places. I have spent many crucial moments in my trading career right here on this balcony.

When I feel like I am struggling, yet, I feel there is a good opportunity to make money in the market, I take a break. I go downstairs to our balcony and try to regroup. While standing on my balcony, I close my eyes and listen to the sounds coming across from various places. Sometimes I hear the kids playing, sometimes I hear a big truck, sometime the wind blowing through the pine trees, and sometimes, I hear the birds singing. I try to relax. I take a big deep breath, and I blow the air out slowly. I then tell myself, "Tony! It is a great day. Put everything behind you. Go up there and take money out of the market!" I have found this method to be very powerful. It has worked really well for me on days when I held large positions overnight and something went wrong the next morning.

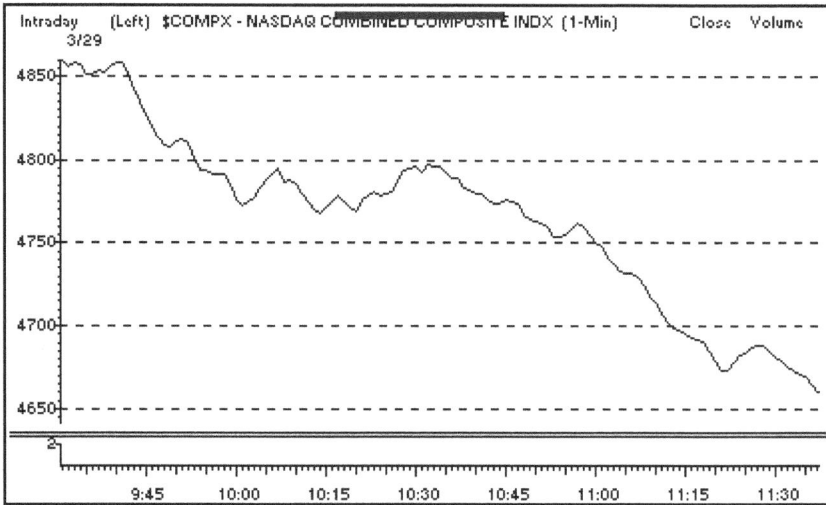

I went back upstairs and went into shock, seeing what the Nasdaq was doing. It was down almost 200 points from the morning highs.

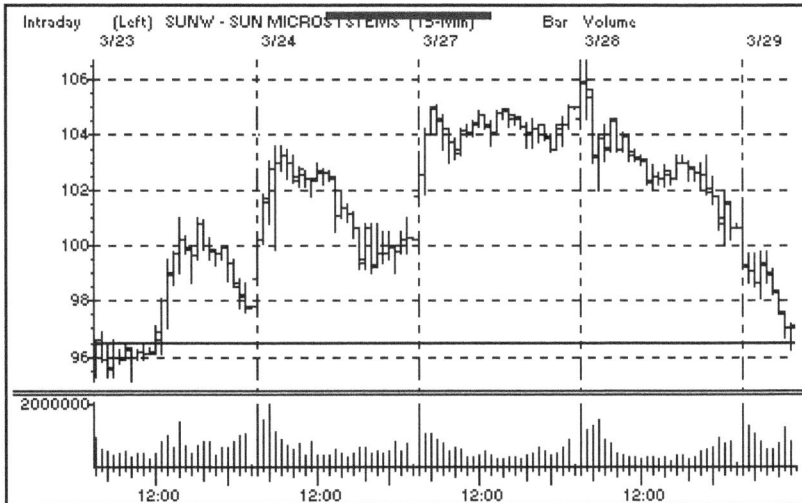

I needed a low risk trade to get back on track, so I was looking for a possible trade at support levels. SUNW was trading at support levels around 96.50, which was the top of the early morning trading range on 3/23/00.

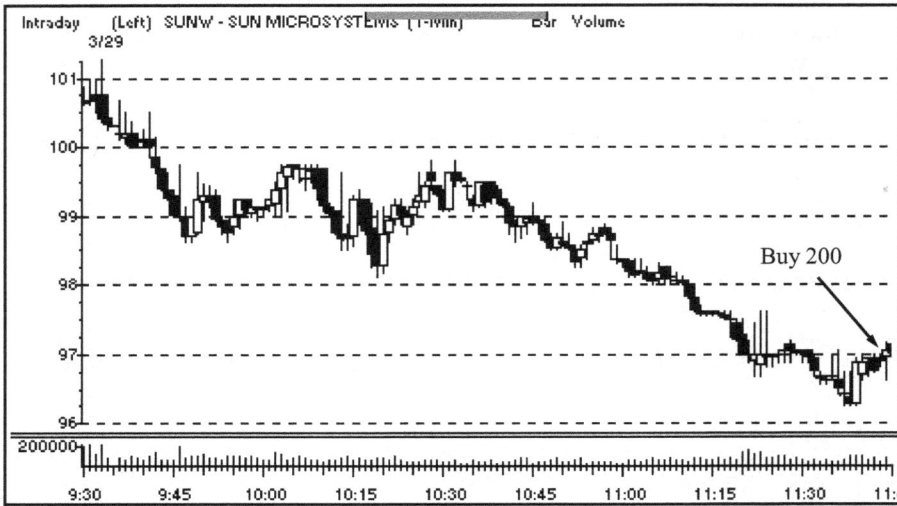

Intraday (Left) SUNW - SUN MICROSYSTEMS (1-Min)   Bar Volume
3/29

Buy 200

Reprinted with permission of Townsend Analytics, Ltd.

SUNW bottomed at 96.37 and started trading higher. I bought 100 shares at 96.94, and 100 shares at 96.93. I placed a stop loss at 96.25, which was just below today's low. My price target was 98.75 - 99.50.

Intraday (Left) SUNW - SUN MICROSYSTEMS (1-Min)   Bar Volume

Buy 200

Sell 200

Reprinted with permission of Townsend Analytics, Ltd.

SUNW soon traded as high as 98. I raised my stop loss to 97.25. The stock turned back down and my stop was triggered. I sold 200 shares at 97.25.

Source	Investment	Proceeds	COM	P&L	Return
Constant List	19,387.05	19,450	18.70	44.25	0.23%

88

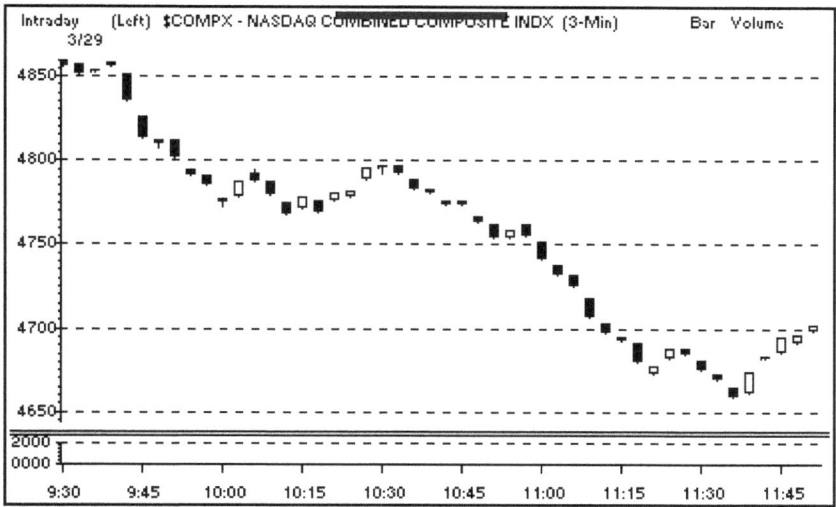

Reprinted with permission of Townsend Analytics, Ltd.

The Nasdaq was trying to bounce and move over 4700, at which point I was looking at ORCL.

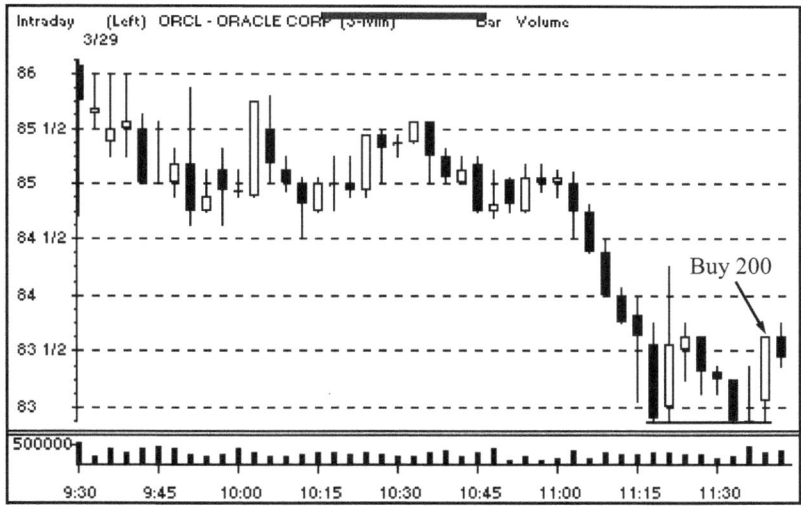

Reprinted with permission of Townsend Analytics, Ltd.

ORCL seemed to have found support at 82.75. It was in the process of confirming a double bottom pattern. I bought 200 shares at 83.65. I placed a stop loss at 82.69, which was just below the double bottom lows. My price target was 85.50.

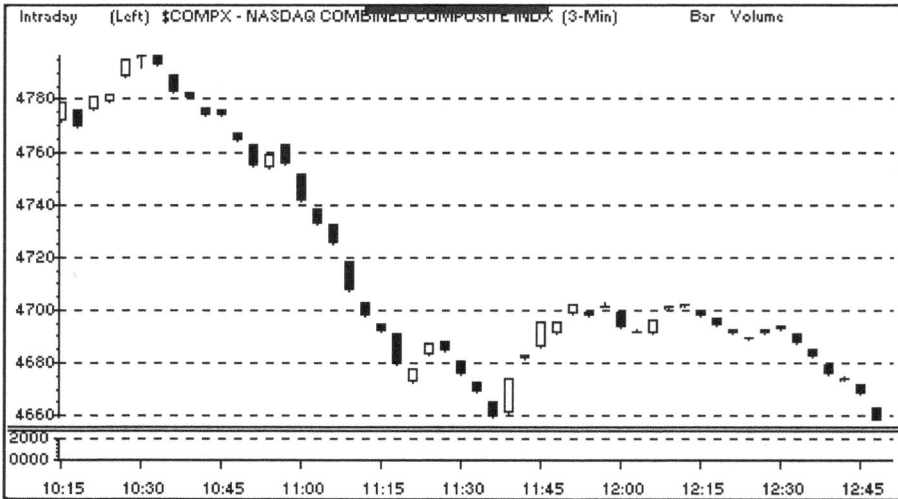

Reprinted with permission of Townsend Analytics, Ltd.

After a feeble attempt at a rally, the Nasdaq turned down again and was on the way to test the previous lows at 4660.

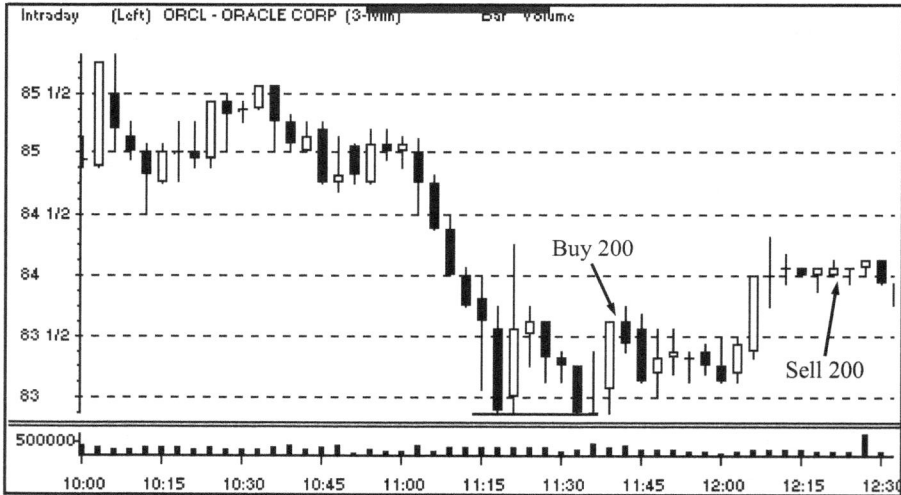

Reprinted with permission of Townsend Analytics, Ltd.

I was nervous about the weakness in the Nasdaq, so I sold 200 shares of ORCL at 84.

Source	Investment	Proceeds	COM	P&L	Return
Constant List	16,731.25	16,800	10.56	58.19	0.35%

90

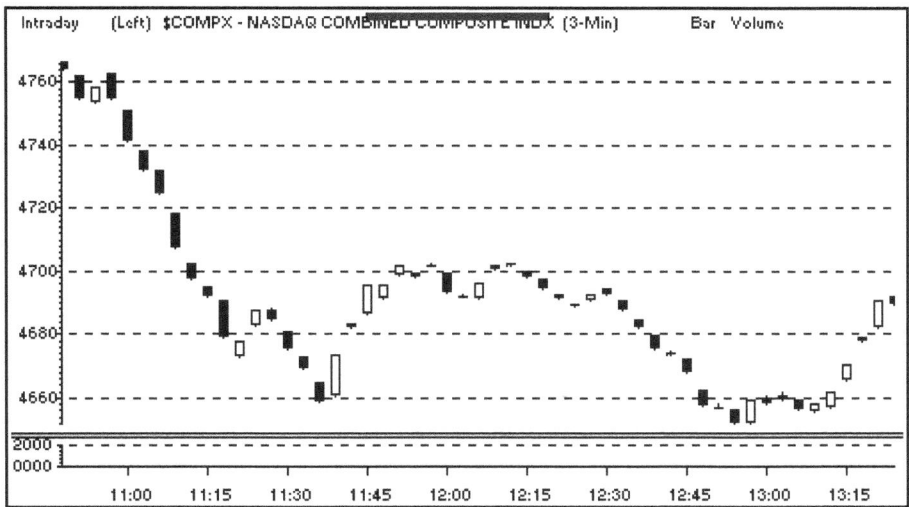

Reprinted with permission of Townsend Analytics, Ltd.

The Nasdaq made a slightly lower low at 12:50, and started moving back up. I was looking at MRVC for a possible bounce play.

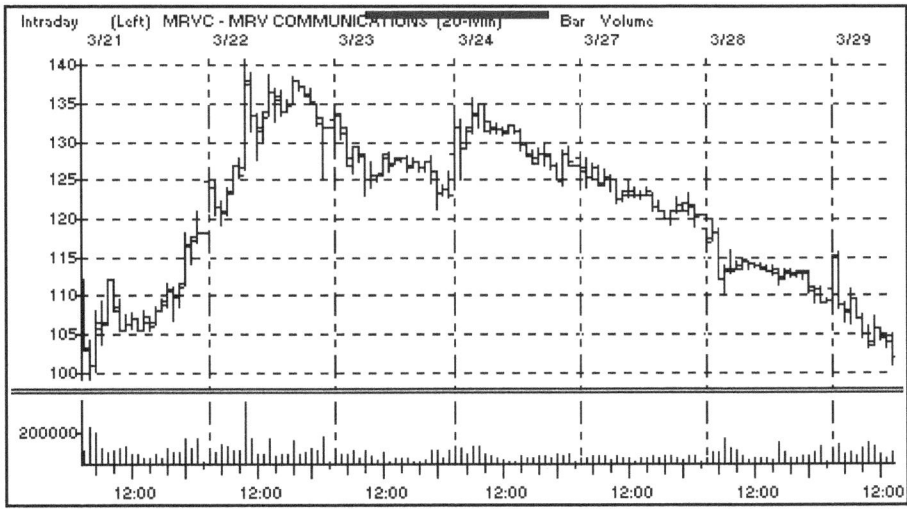

Reprinted with permission of Townsend Analytics, Ltd.

MRVC was trading around the lows made back on 3/21/00. It looked like it had good support at 100 or so.

Reprinted with permission of Townsend Analytics, Ltd.

The stock had traded as low as 101, and after bouncing to around 102, was trading in a tight range for 15 minutes or so. The volume started to rise and the stock moved up a bit, so I bought 100 shares at 103. My price target was 106 - 108. I placed a stop loss at 101.87. The stock traded up to 105, but just couldn't make it any higher. It looked weak, so I sold 100 shares at 104.38.

Source	Investment	Proceeds	COM	P&L	Return
Constant List	10,300	10,437.5	10.35	127.15	1.24%

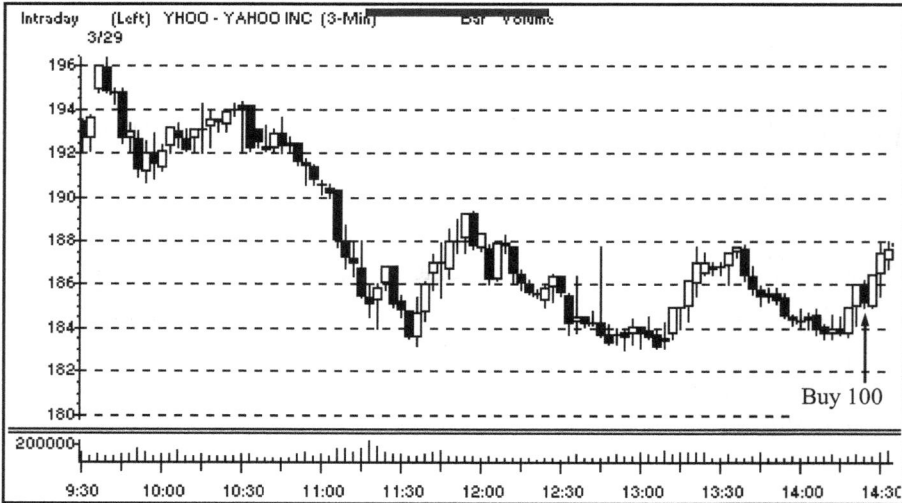

Reprinted with permission of Townsend Analytics, Ltd.

YHOO held the 184 level and was trading in a tight trading range. I bought 100 shares at 185.50. My price target was 194–191 (the top at 10:30 and the bottom at 10:00). I placed a stop loss at 183, just below today's low.

92

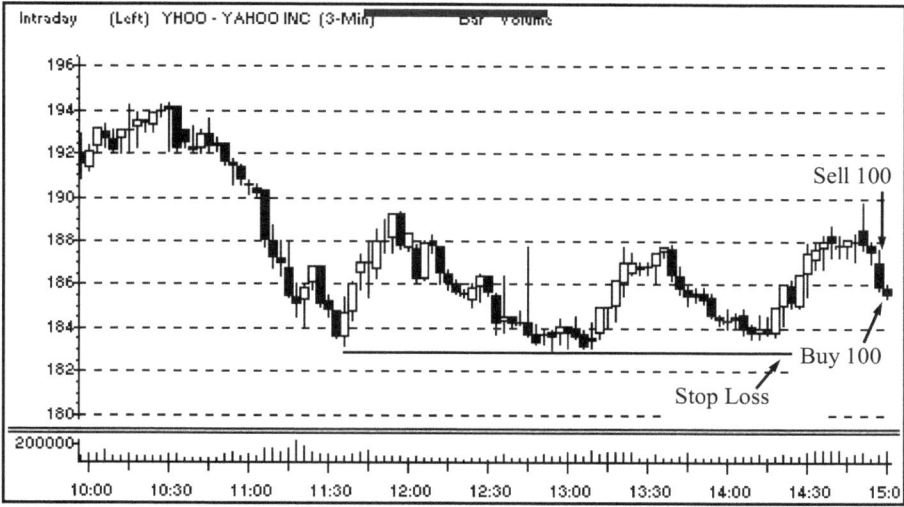

Reprinted with permission of Townsend Analytics, Ltd.

YHOO hit resistance at 188.75 and turned back down. I sold 100 shares at 187.67. I was looking to buy YHOO again if it pulled back. YHOO pulled back to 185.50 , and I bought 100 shares again at 185.50.

Source	Investment	Proceeds	COM	P&L	Return
Constant List	18,550	18,767	11.94	205.06	1.1%

While I was in the YHOO trade, I bought 100 SUNW at 97.50 and sold it at 99.18*.

Source	Investment	Proceeds	COM	P&L	Return
Constant List	9,750	9,918.75	10.34	158.41	1.62%

Although I had five winners in a row following my balcony-break, I wasn't making much money, and I still felt there was a struggle going on. I wanted to give my YHOO trade a chance. I saw that it was getting weak, and I was in the money, but I didn't move my stop loss up.

*In the flurry of all the activity, the charts for this trade did not get captured, sorry.

YHOO broke down hard and broke the low of the day. My stop loss triggered, and I sold 100 YHOO at 182.06.

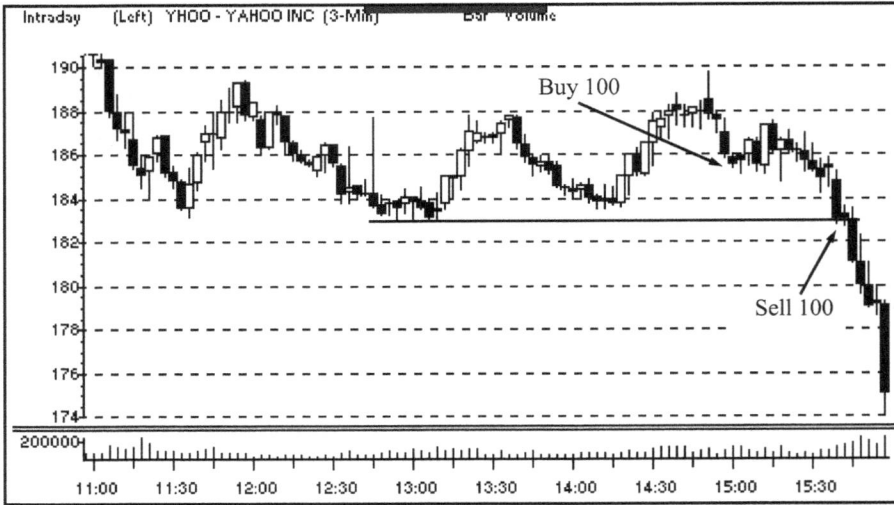

Reprinted with permission of Townsend Analytics, Ltd.

Source	Investment	Proceeds	COM	P&L	Return
Constant List	18,550	18,206.25	10.61	-354.36	-1.91%

This last trade was a devastating blow to my confidence. In the first nine days of the challenge, my biggest loss was $202. I just lost $354 on YHOO to close the day, but what was demoralizing about it was that the total profit I made on the previous five trades, which were all winners, was $593. I just gave back more than half of it on my last trade. The break I took to regroup earlier helped me turn the day around. Now, I have to take another break and regroup again. Although my exit wasn't all that bad considering YHOO dropped another 8 points over the next 15 minutes from where I got out, I felt I should have seen it coming and bailed out of the trade earlier, somewhere around 185.50. My critical blunder was to argue with the tape. And when you do that, you lose! The market is always right.

When the final bell finally rang, the bears were in total command. The Nasdaq was down a whopping 189 points from yesterday's close. If you haven't guessed it by now, there were no high probability setups for a long position. I went to bed flat.

Open positions: None
Total profit for 3/29/00: $319.27

Day Eight Lessons

When and if you are struggling, learn to take a break and regroup.

The market is always right. The prints don't lie, so don't argue with the tape!

CHAPTER 12

Awakening of the Bears

DAY NINE

Thursday, March 30, 2000

Following the 189-point decline the Nasdaq had yesterday, the futures were indicating a very weak opening for the market. I wanted to take the day off, but I was thinking that I might find some bargains if I traded today. At the opening bell, the Nasdaq gapped down 109 points and opened at 4540, which was right at the 50-day moving average. It was down 10.6% from the intraday high it set on Day Five of this challenge. The Nasdaq is officially in correction territory, the fourth time this year.

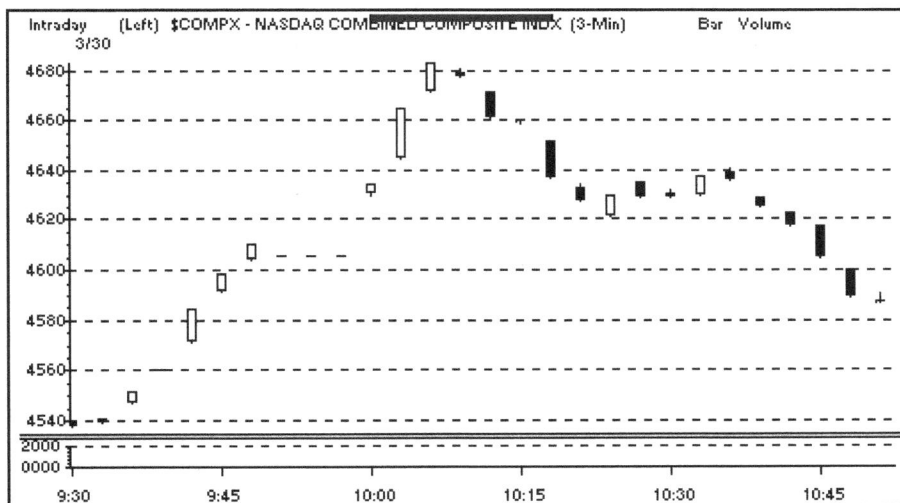

Reprinted with permission of Townsend Analytics, Ltd.

Bargain hunters were all over the place and the Nasdaq shot up more than 140 points in the first 35 minutes of trading on big volume. I tried to buy SUNW, ORCL, and CSCO, but they were flying, and I missed all entries. I decided not to chase any of the stocks. I was going to wait for a pullback.

What took place next was very painful to watch. I saw a small fortune that could have been made, had I gotten those fills earlier, grow bigger and larger with every tick. I knew that the top was near, and I took my sniper

97

position, waiting for the pullback. I had not yet gotten over my frustration, so I wasn't as focused as I should have been. In hindsight, it would have been a perfect time to go out to my balcony and regroup. But, how could I? I was a ravenous animal smelling blood. I couldn't afford to miss my meal. I already did that once today.

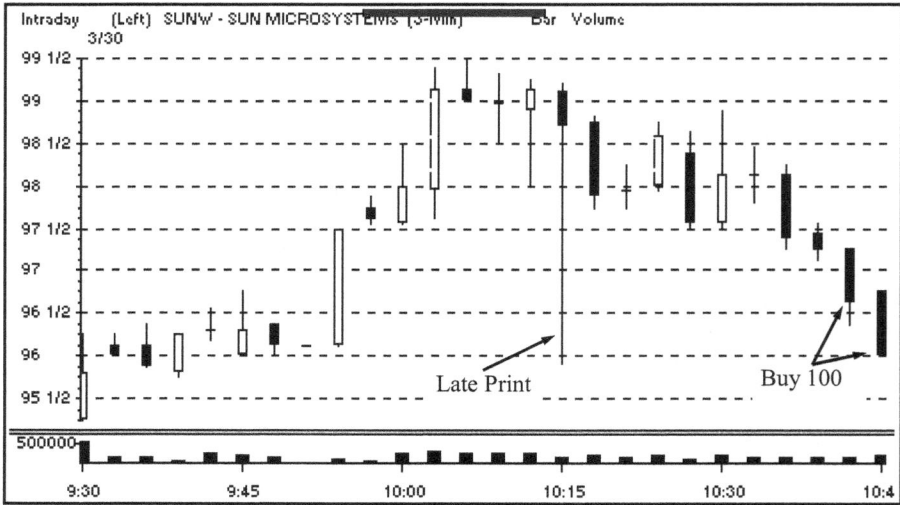

Reprinted with permission of Townsend Analytics, Ltd.

I got the pullback I was looking for, and I bought 100 shares of SUNW at 96.69 and another 100 shares when it dropped lower to 96. I placed a stop loss at 94.94, which was below the 95 support level for the stock. My price target was the high of the day, 99.50.

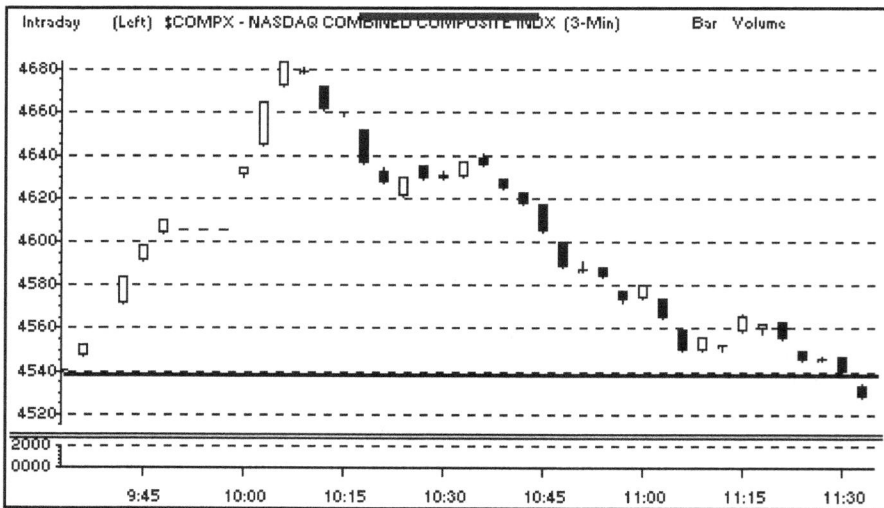

Reprinted with permission of Townsend Analytics, Ltd.

Oh, oh. The Nasdaq took out the low of the day, which indicated a reversal pattern. The street was once again flooded with sellers.

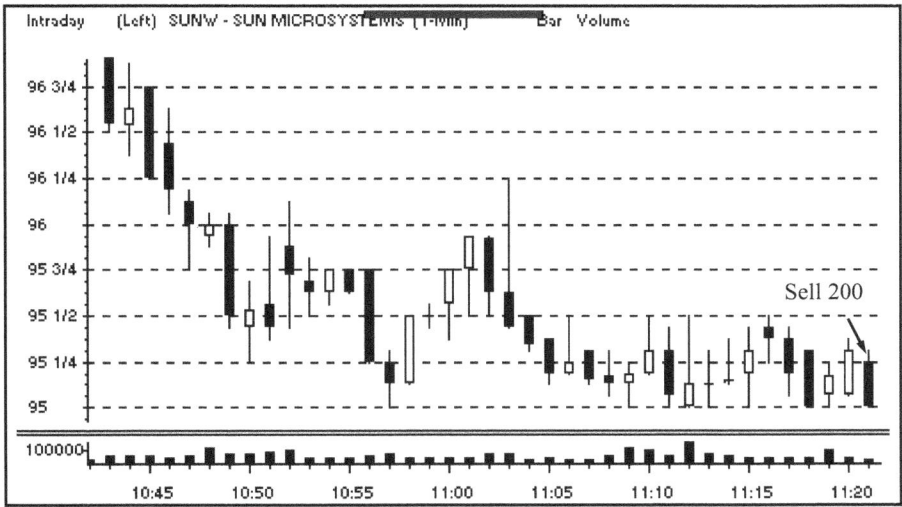

Reprinted with permission of Townsend Analytics, Ltd.

SUNW bounced at 95 numerous times. The support level was holding; however, with the Nasdaq breaking down, I was afraid SUNW was going to tank hard and that my stop at 94.94 could possibly not get executed until dropping to 94. I decided not to ignore the tape, and I sold 200 shares at 95.06.

Source	Investment	Proceeds	COM	P&L	Return
Constant List	19268.75	19,012.50	15.64	-271.89	-1.41%

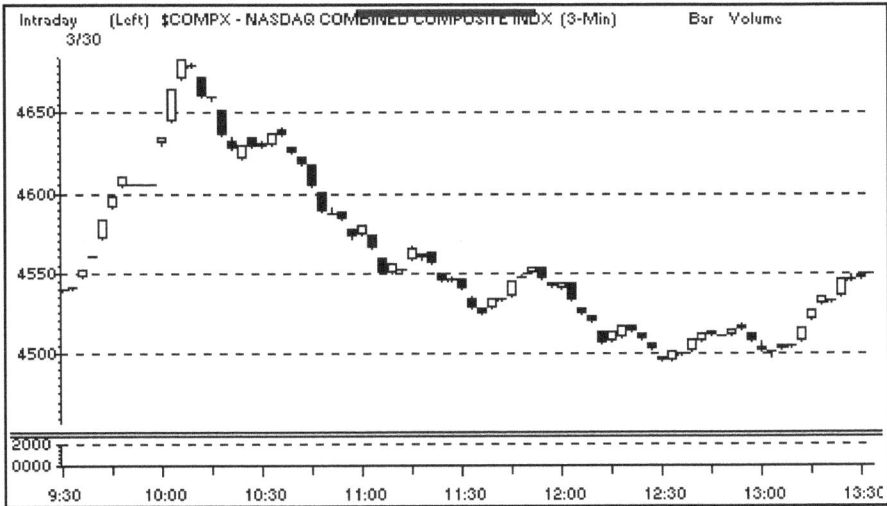

Reprinted with permission of Townsend Analytics, Ltd.

The Nasdaq kept declining and it found some support at 4500, where it formed a double bottom pattern. At about 1:15, it started to trade back up and was again at 4550.

99

Buy 300

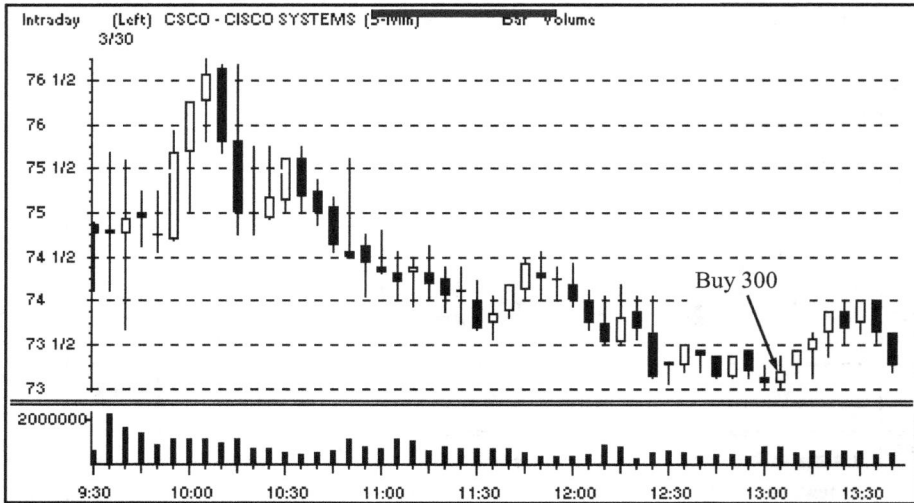

CSCO followed the same pattern and it bounced at 73. I bought 300 CSCO at 73.25. My price target was 75. I placed a stop loss at 72.94, which was just below the 73 support.

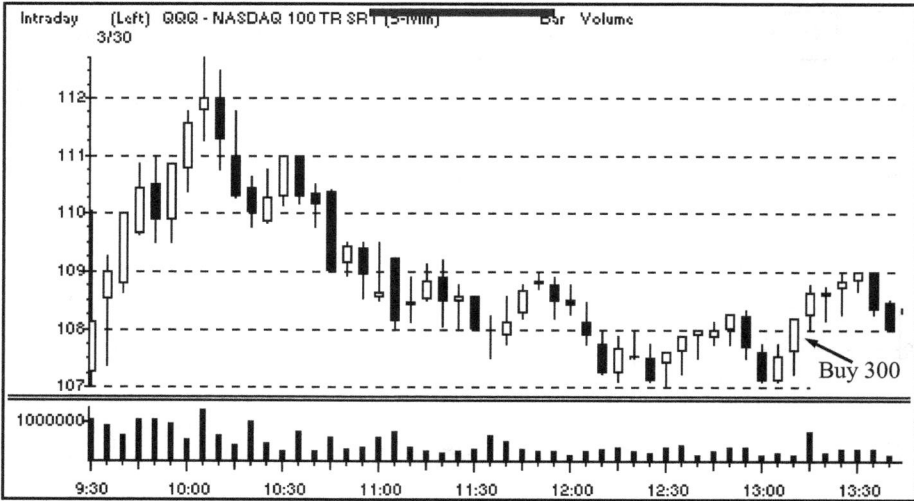

Buy 300

QQQ also had a double bottom pattern at 107. I entered a market order to buy 300 shares, and I got taken advantage of by the Specialist. I bought 300 shares via a market order and it got executed at 107.87. I placed a stop loss at 106.87, which was below the 107 support level. My price target was 111.

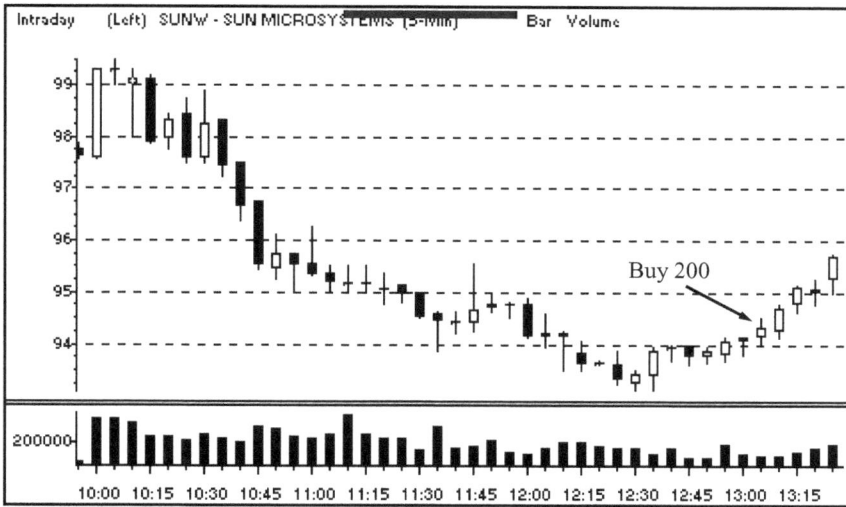

Whew! SUNW went as low as 93 after I sold it at 95.06. I was following it closely for a possible reentry. The stock started trading higher and I
bought 200 shares at 94.50. I now had three open positions. I felt good being
in my positions as they were all showing me some profit. My P&L was over
$800. I decided to let my positions wiggle. I had Jesse Livermore words in
my head, "*Men who can both be right and sit tight are uncommon.*" I felt
that the market was oversold, and that I might have just bought the bottom. I
was willing to bet my profits on that.

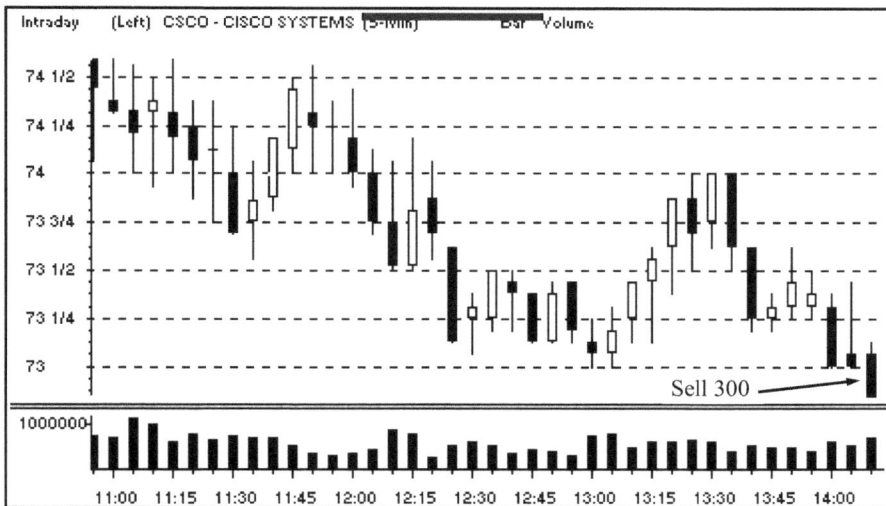

CSCO broke down and triggered my stop loss. I sold 300 shares at 72.94.

Source	Investment	Proceeds	COM	P&L	Return
Constant List	21,975	21,882	10.31	-103.31	-0.47%

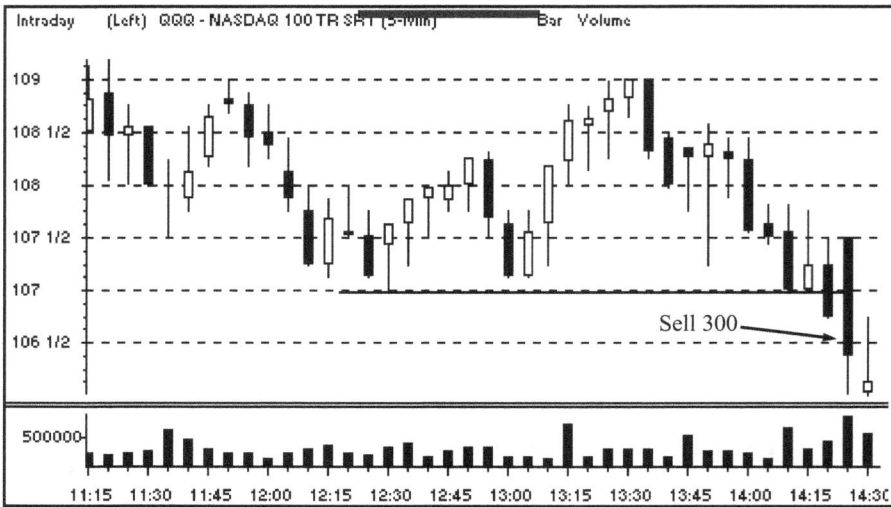

Reprinted with permission of Townsend Analytics, Ltd.

QQQ broke down as well, and I got taken advantage of again by the specialist on the execution of my stop loss. I sold 300 QQQ at 106.52.

Source	Investment	Proceeds	COM	P&L	Return
Constant List	32,362.50	31,954.67	11.07	-418.88	-1.29%

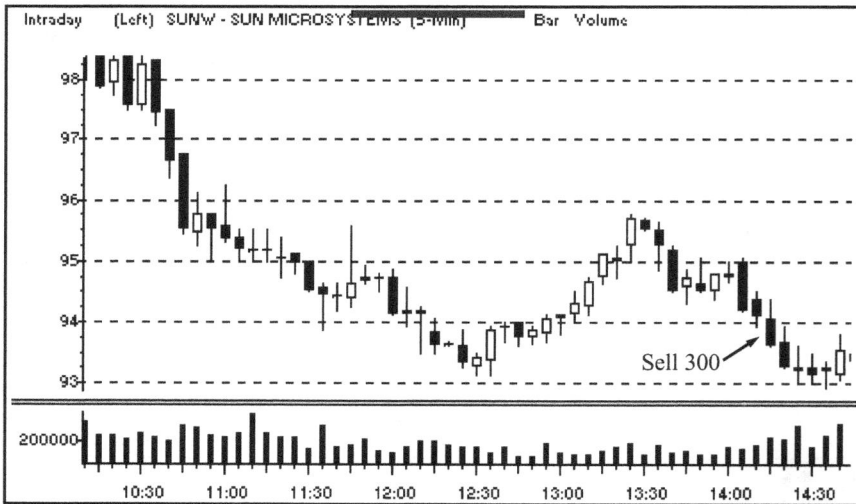

Reprinted with permission of Townsend Analytics, Ltd.

As the market disintegrated, my stop loss on SUNW was triggered as well. I sold 200 shares at 93.63.

Source	Investment	Proceeds	COM	P&L	Return
Constant List	18,900	18,725	10.63	-185.63	-0.98%

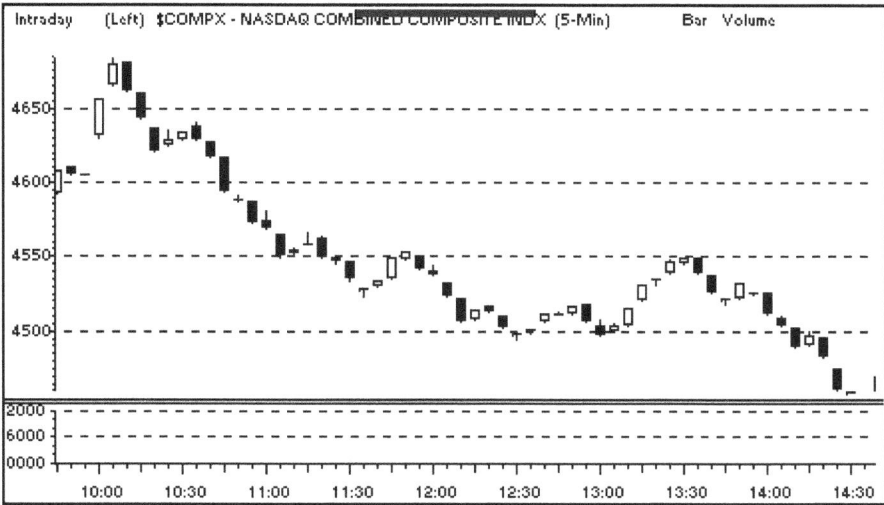

The Nasdaq took out the low of the day, and I sold my positions for a total loss of $708. I was thinking about Livermore's famous words again, *"Men who can both be right and sit tight are uncommon."* I was sitting tight, but I wasn't right. I was WRONG! I let an open profit of $812 turn into $708 loss. I went from having a profitable day to having a losing day. I wasn't very happy about that. I lost on each of the four trades I made today, so I needed a good trade to make a little bit of money to build my confidence back up.

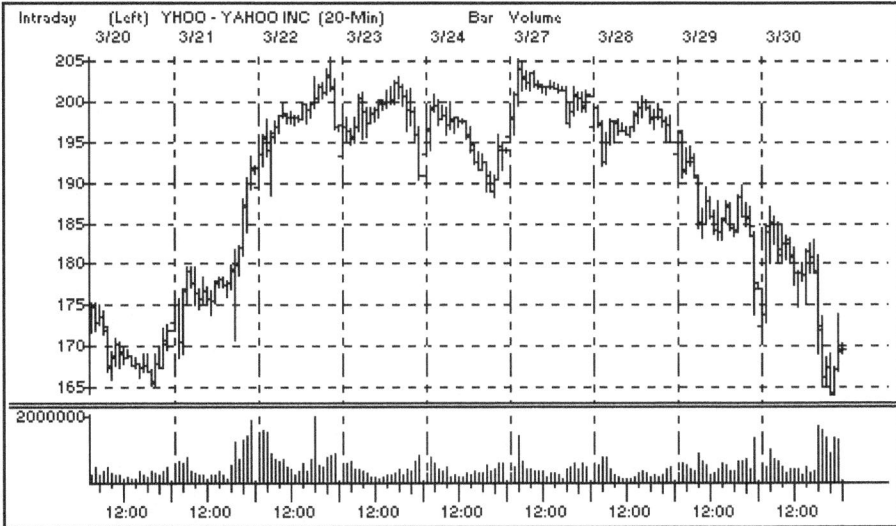

YHOO had an interesting setup where the stock was trading around 165, which was the support level on 3/20/00.

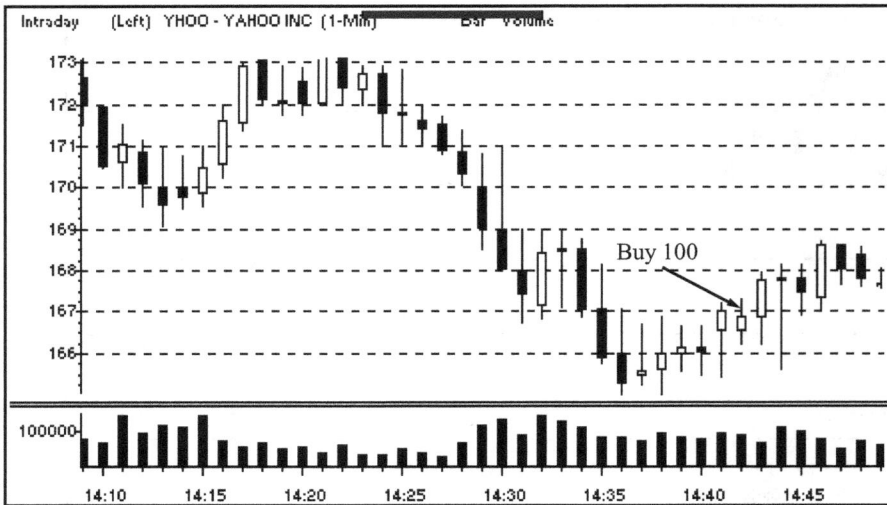

YHOO bounced at 165 and looked strong. I bought 100 shares at 167.09. I thought the stock could go to 169.50. I was trading strictly off the Level II activity, and I was ready to sell at the first sign of weakness.

YHOO went up as high as 168.50, but was getting weak, so I sold 100 shares at 168.19. This was no home run, but it made me feel good. It was the first trade of the day in which I actually cashed in profits.

Source	Investment	Proceeds	COM	P&L	Return
Constant List	16,721.87	16,818.75	10.58	86.30	0.52%

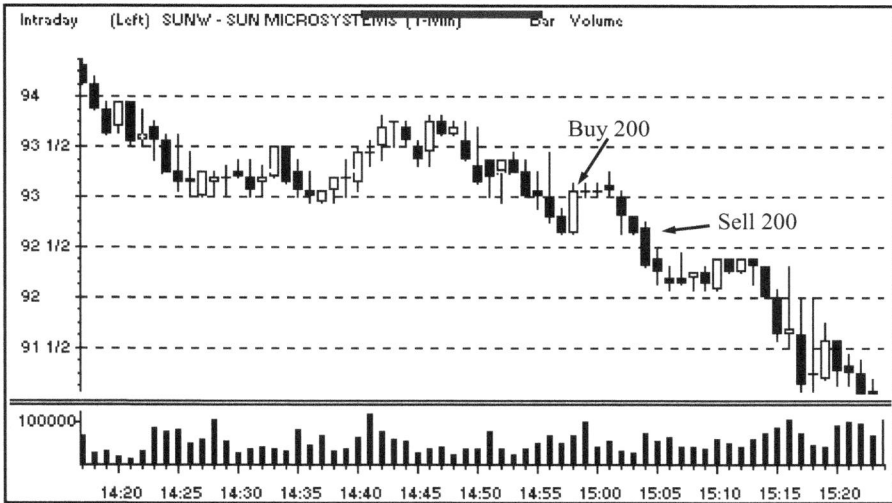

My love affair with SUNW was not over. After penetrating through support at 93. The stock traded as low as 92.62. It then snapped back up and took out the 93 level. Little did I know it would be a perfect fake-out, merely there to mock me. I bought 200 SUNW at 93.06. The stock lost steam and went below 92.62. It triggered my stop loss, and I sold 200 SUNW at 92.38.

Source	Investment	Proceeds	COM	P&L	Return
Constant List	18,612.50	18,475	10.62	-148.12	-0.79%

SUNW traded all the way down to 90. I really wanted to buy it there, but I was having a bad day and was getting gun-shy.

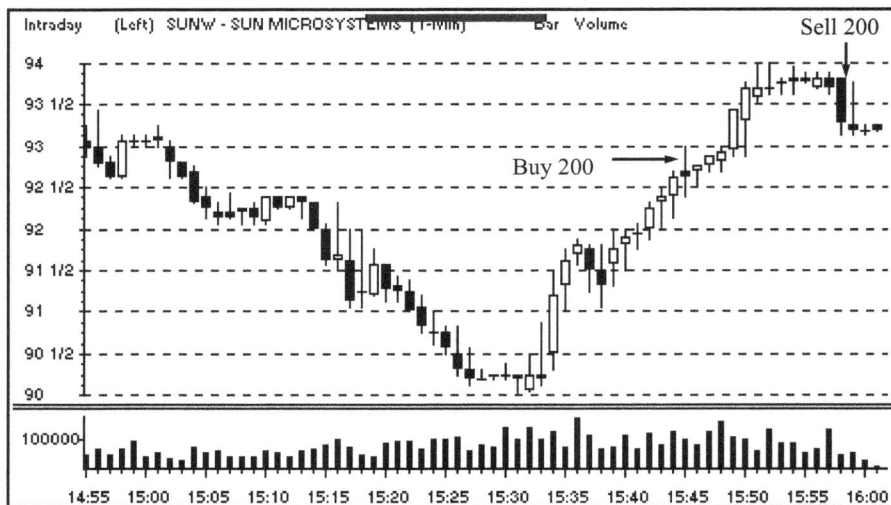

Intraday (Left) SUNW - SUN MICROSYSTEMS (1-Min) Bar Volume   Sell 200

Buy 200 →

Reprinted with permission of Townsend Analytics, Ltd.

I watched SUNW go up 2 1/2 points from the low. It was running. The momentum players were jumping on board, and the shorts were getting squeezed. I liked what I saw, and I wanted to finish the day on a positive note, so I threw my hat in the ring and bought 200 shares at 92.92. My plan was to sell the stock near the close. SUNW hit 94 with only eight minutes left in the trading day. The bears were growling and the stock could not go any higher. I sold 100 shares at 93.75. Another two minutes went by without any price progress, so I sold the remaining 100 shares at 93.69.

Source	Investment	Proceeds	COM	P&L	Return
Constant List	18584.37	18743.75	15.65	143.73	0.77%

Ding! Ding! The final bell rang as the bears were now completely awake. It was another brutal day for the bulls as the Nasdaq dropped 186 points from yesterday's close. It has been very difficult to call things in this sharp decline. I will need to evaluate things in more depth tonight.

Open positions: None
Total profit for 3/30/00: -$897.00

Day Nine Lesson

Sitting tight only works when you are right!

106

CHAPTER *13*

Sitting on My Hands

DAY TEN

Friday, March 31, 2000

Yesterday was my first losing day of the challenge, and I wanted to look back and examine what I did wrong. It wasn't that I expected to make money everyday when I accepted the challenge, but I believe it is always a good idea to take a step back and study your trading, especially on losing days, and I was looking for something I may have been missing. I wanted an answer for what happened yesterday, so I spent a lot of time going over my trades. I finally reached the conclusion that I had managed risk properly, even on the three positions that were in-the-money and were given a wide wiggle room. Those positions did become losers and were the difference between having a winning day to having a losing day; however, the $1,500 turnaround was only 2% draw down on the entire position. If I had been correct in my assessment at the time, my entry would have been the bottom, and the rewards could have been as much as seven times the money I lost. If I had to do it all over again, I probably would play it the exact same way.

I have spent most of last night studying charts. I was looking at each and every stock that is in my Constant watch list, and I wrote down support and resistance levels for each one of these stocks. Then, I studied the Nasdaq chart in greater depth.

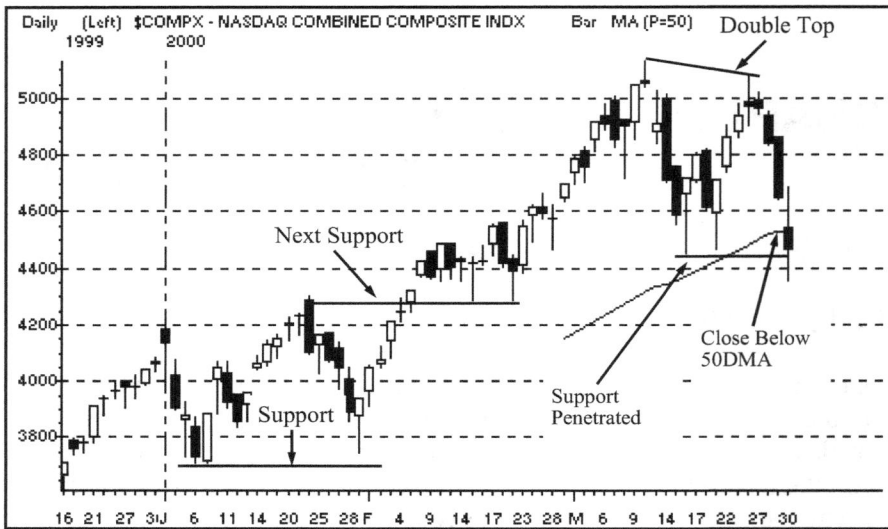

Reprinted with permission of Townsend Analytics, Ltd.

The Nasdaq chart was telling me that the market may have topped. We closed below the 50-day moving average for the first time since October 19, 1999. We possibly formed a double top pattern, which was confirmed yesterday once we traded lower than the low price made on 3/16 and 3/21. The next support level I see on the chart is at 4290, and the next support after that is at 3715. If we have in fact topped and the double top pattern is confirmed, we could go as low as 3700. This chart was a legitimate reason to be apprehensive.

Following the 186-point decline in the Nasdaq yesterday, I expected the futures to be down big this morning. I thought that we were going to open low, sell even harder at the open, then bounce somewhere around 4290 and completely reverse. I felt there was going to be some serious panic selling in the morning. I was ready to pick up all the bargains! I brought out my wish list from last Christmas, and I had my shopping bag ready to be filled with goodies.

Then, once my bag is filled up to the top with the best stocks in North America, I would sit tight and let the institutions push the market back up. Today is the end of the quarter, and I expect fund managers to support the big name stocks, so their portfolios look somewhat better.

But it wasn't so. The gap down open I anticipated didn't happen at all. Instead the market gapped up! The Nasdaq was up 93 points at the open! Only then, did it start trading down. And down. And then, down some more. By lunch time, the Index was down more than 100 points from the open.

There were no high percentage trades that I could see unless I wanted to play with fire, so I sat on my hands the entire day. When the Nasdaq made a new intraday low at 12:00 PM, I closed everything up, and I got a head start on the weekend. I felt very fortunate to be all in cash. I thought that the market looked very ugly.

When the final bell rang, I was at the park flying a kite with my son. While my son, Jordan, was singing the tunes "Let's go fly a kite" from the classic movie, *Mary Poppins*, and I was trying to figure out how you get the kite in the air when there is no wind, the Nasdaq managed to rally and close the day up 114 points from yesterday's close (21 points from the open).

Open positions: None
Total profit for 3/31/00: $0.00

The second week of the challenge was over. It was a decent week in which I had mixed results. I started the week with four winners on Monday. I had two decent winners in JNPR and WAVX on Tuesday giving me a comfort cushion for the remainder of the week. I executed a lot of trades on Wednesday making a little profit at the end. Thursday was my first losing day, in which I was trying to catch the market bottom and sit tight. I was proven to be wrong time and time again, but I didn't lose too much, even though I gave back all my gains. On Friday, I did not execute even one trade. I was way off in my expectations for the day, so I sat on the sidelines and observed the action from the passenger's seat.

My total profits for week one were $1,928.47. I faxed my broker a request for a check in the amount of $2,000.00. After all, Friday is payday!

Southwest Securities	SIPC	88-88
1201 Elm St. Suite 3500. Dallas, TX 75270		1113

	DATE	AMOUNT
PAY ********2,000DOLLARS 00CENTS	3/31/00	$*****2,000.00
Pay To		

TONY OZ
LAGUNA HILLS, CA 92654

Day Ten Lessons

If what you planned is not there the next day, don't force any trades.

In depth analysis the night before can save you a small fortune.

It's nice to have wind when you go fly a kite. ☺

CHAPTER 14

Free Willy

DAY ELEVEN

Monday, April 3, 2000

I did a lot of research over the weekend, and I had a handful of candidates for potential long positions. I was very excited, because I thought I had some high percentage setups and trading plans. I had my alarm set to 5:30 AM, and I got up without hitting the snooze button. I took a quick shower and went upstairs to my trading desk. It was 30 minutes to the market open. I turned on my computer, and saw that the futures were down sharply. Stocks were trading much lower pre-market and my candidates were no different. They were all trading lower than where I was planning to enter them. I turned on the TV and found out that Microsoft failed to settle their case with the justice department over the weekend. This was very bad news. Suddenly, all my trading plans were tossed out of the *Windows*, or should I say out through the *Gates*. I was now expecting a major sell off. This has changed my current strategy for the day. My new strategy will be to find high percentage bounce plays. The Nasdaq gapped down 78 points, and Microsoft gapped down 12.69.

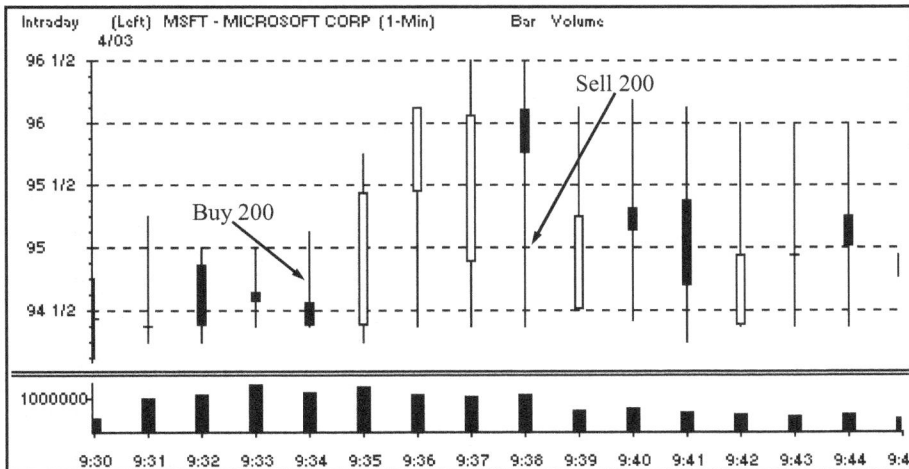

Reprinted with permission of Townsend Analytics, Ltd.

I was trying to play the opening bounce on MSFT. The market tends to overreact to bad news, so I expected a nice little bounce. I bought 200 shares of MSFT at 94.75. The stock went up as high as 96.50, but then

111

turned and tanked very fast. I sold 200 MSFT and barely got out at 95.

Source	Investment	Proceeds	COM	P&L	Return
Constant List	18,950	19,000	10.94	39.06	0.21%

     ORCL bounced at 77. I bought 300 ORCL at 77.62. My price target was 80. My stop loss was at 76.94, just below today's low. ORCL never made it to 80, but topped at 78.25. I entered a sell order and got a partial fill. I sold 100 shares at 78.12. The stock went lower and I sold 200 shares at 77.43.

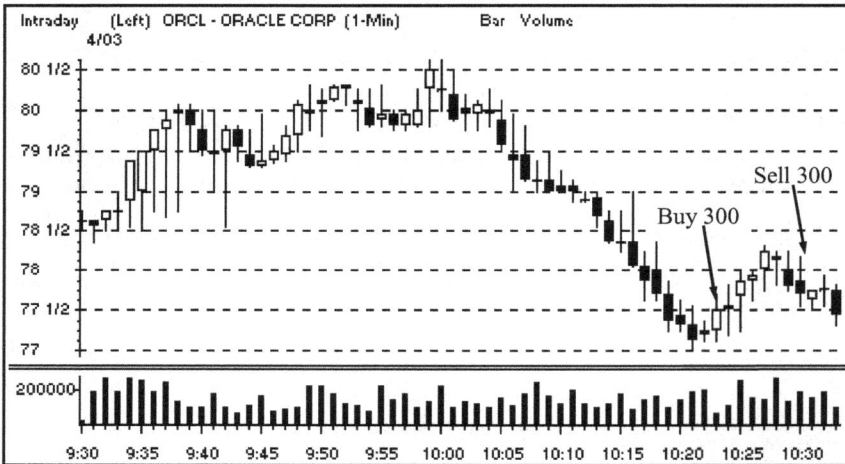

Reprinted with permission of Townsend Analytics, Ltd.

Source	Investment	Proceeds	COM	P&L	Return
Constant List	23,287.50	23,300	15.79	-3.29	-0.01%

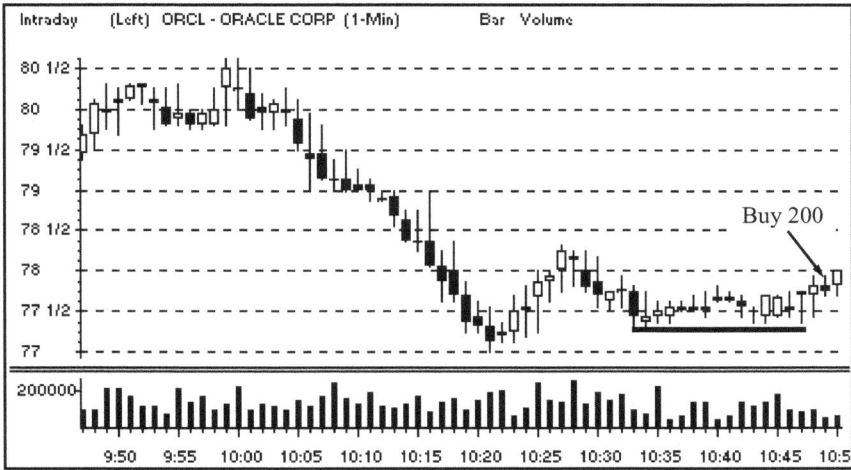

Reprinted with permission of Townsend Analytics, Ltd.

ORCL held 77.38 and started to move higher again, so I bought 200 shares at 77.87. I was still looking for 80. I placed a stop loss at 77.25.

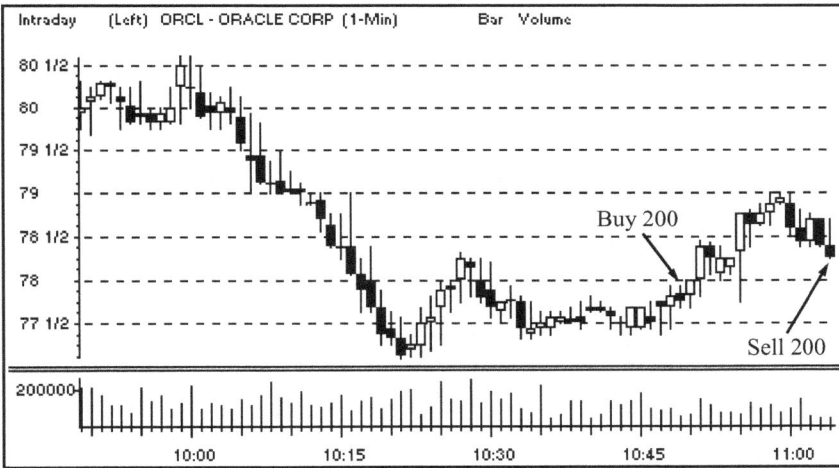

Reprinted with permission of Townsend Analytics, Ltd.

This time ORCL traded as high as 79, before turning back down. I sold 200 shares at 78.25.

Source	Investment	Proceeds	COM	P&L	Return
Constant List	15,575	15,650	10.53	64.47	0.41%

113

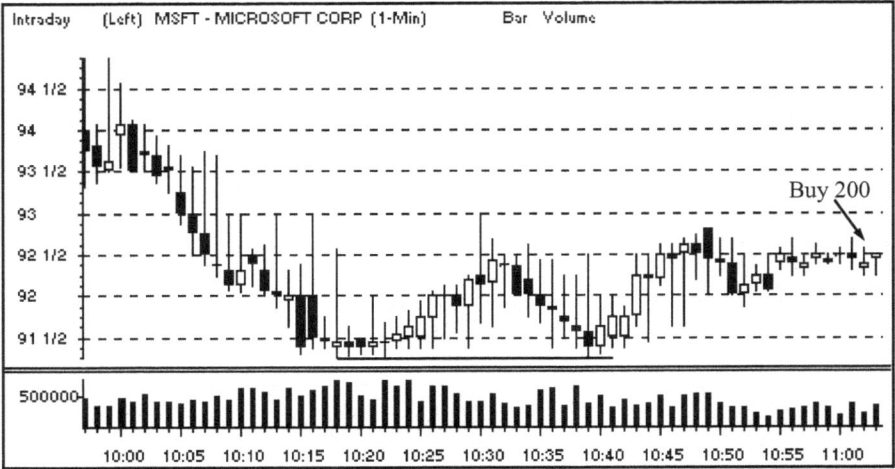

MSFT setup a double bottom and was now trading higher. I thought it had a chance to pop 93 and run, so I bought 200 shares at 92.44.

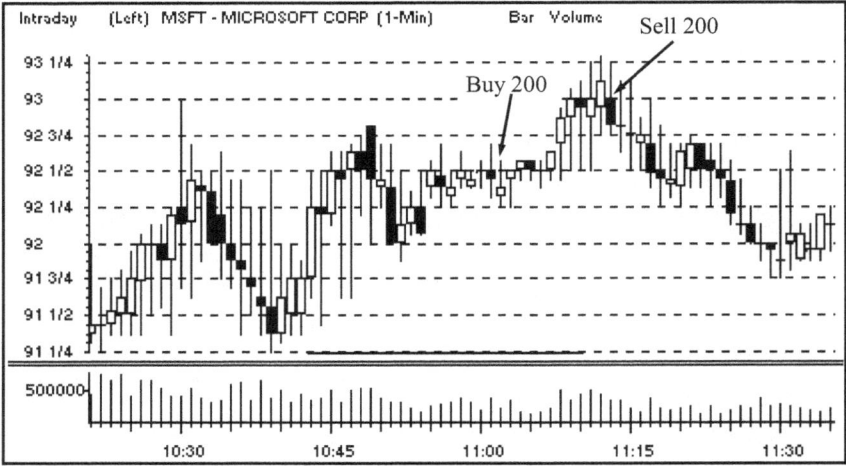

MSFT went as high as 93.31, then lost steam. I sold 200 shares at 92.94.

Source	Investment	Proceeds	COM	P&L	Return
Constant List	18,487.50	18,587.50	10.62	89.38	0.48%

114

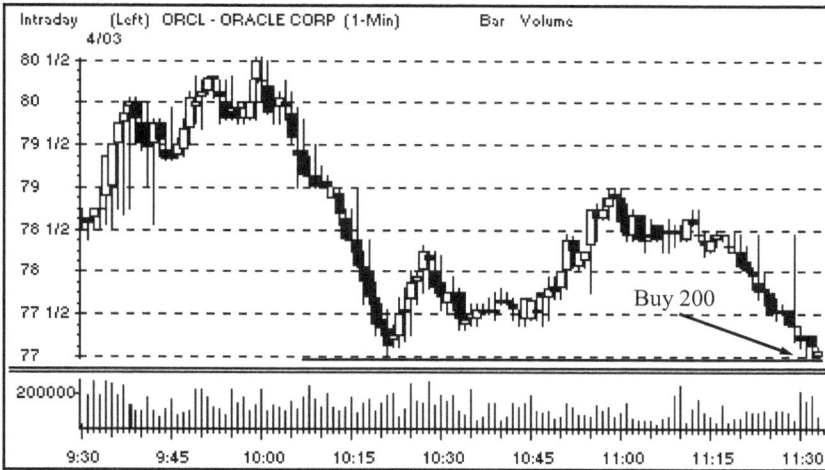

Reprinted with permission of Townsend Analytics, Ltd.

ORCL was back to the 77 level, and I thought it might be forming a double bottom. I bought 200 shares at 77.07. My price target was 79 - 80. My stop loss was at 76.75, which was 0.25 below the lows of the day.

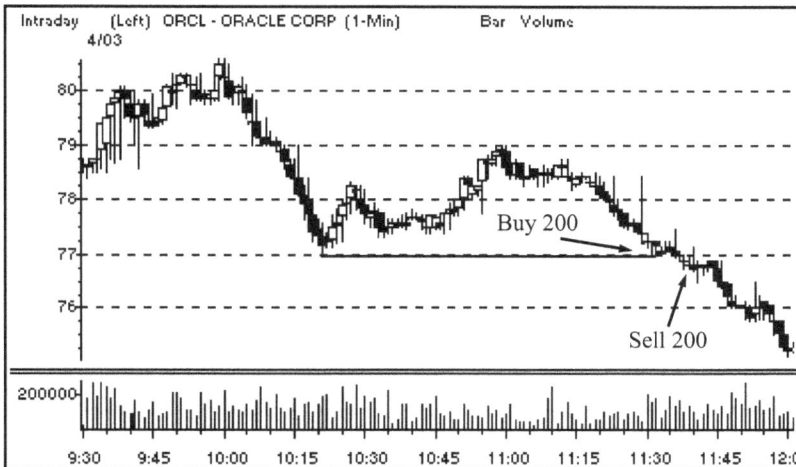

Reprinted with permission of Townsend Analytics, Ltd.

Ouch. ORCL breaks down through support, and my stop loss is activated. I sold 200 ORCL at 76.75. Again, the chart shows the importance of being disciplined about keeping a stop.

Source	Investment	Proceeds	COM	P&L	Return
Constant List	15,414	15,350	15.15	-79.15	-0.51%

115

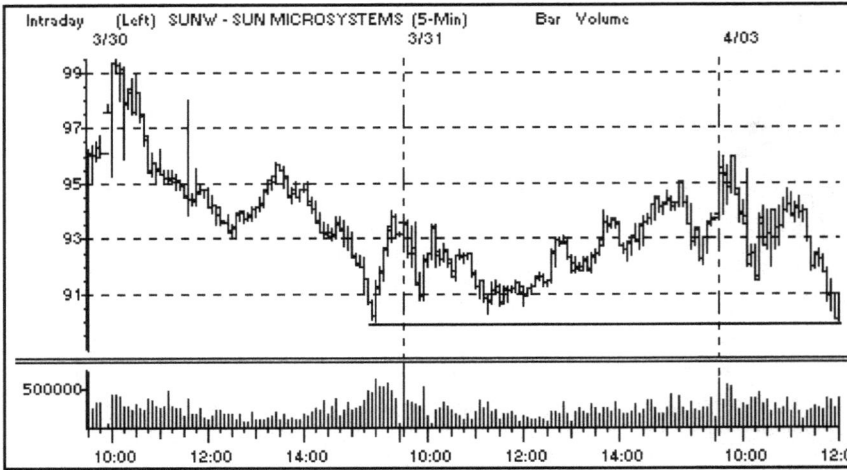

Reprinted with permission of Townsend Analytics, Ltd.

SUNW has support at 90, which were the lows several days back on 3/30/00. I traded it numerous times that day, and I remembered how the 90 level held, and the stock ran up to 94 from there.

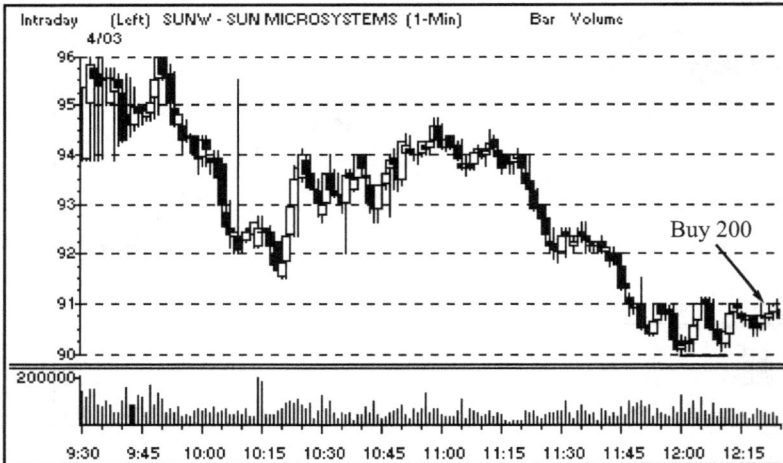

Reprinted with permission of Townsend Analytics, Ltd.

To make things somewhat more comforting, SUNW had also formed a double bottom and was working on forming a reverse head and shoulders. I bought 200 shares at 90.94. I placed a stop loss at 89.94, which is 0.06 below today's low. My price target was 94 - 96.

116

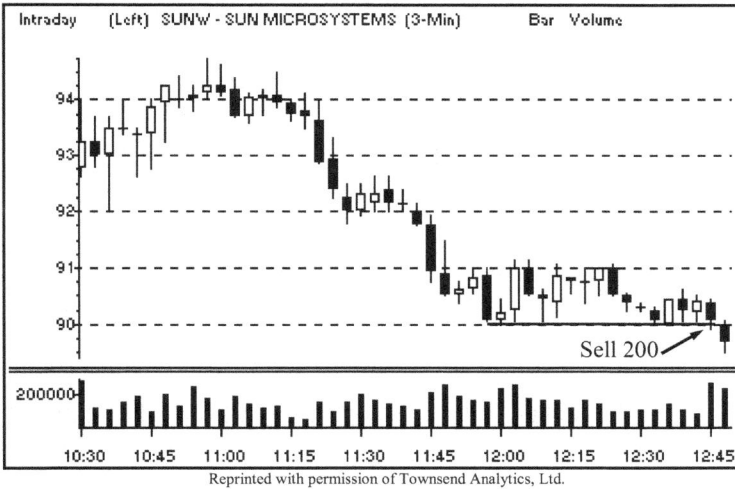

Reprinted with permission of Townsend Analytics, Ltd.

Then the "unthinkable" happened and SUNW actually broke down through 90. My stop loss was activated, and I sold 200 shares at 90. I got a price improvement on my stop loss order, which is not very common.

Source	Investment	Proceeds	COM	P&L	Return
Constant List	18,187.50	18,000	10.6	-198.10	-1.09%

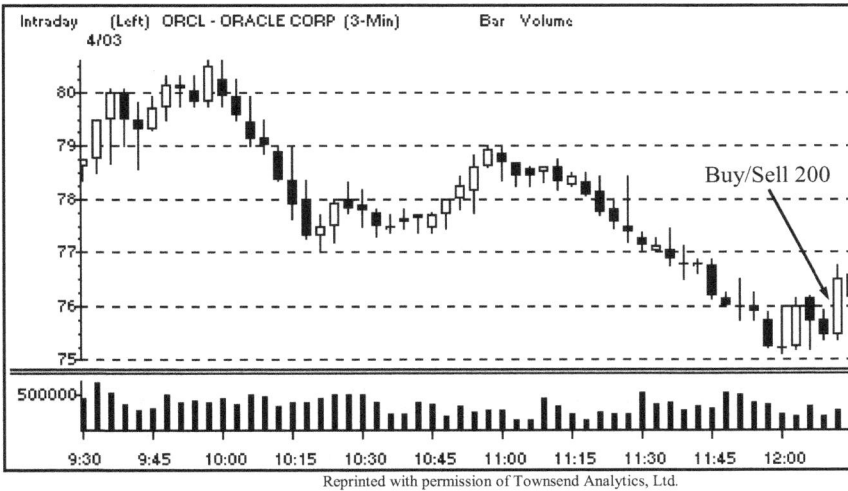

Reprinted with permission of Townsend Analytics, Ltd.

ORCL went as low as 75.12 and started to bounce. As it came back up I bought 200 shares at 76.19. *SBSH* was axing the stock. I didn't like the fact that he would not tick-up in the face of buying pressure, so I immediately sold the stock on the bid. I sold 200 shares at 76.12.

Source	Investment	Proceeds	COM	P&L	Return
Constant List	15,237.50	15,225	10.51	-23.01	-0.15%

117

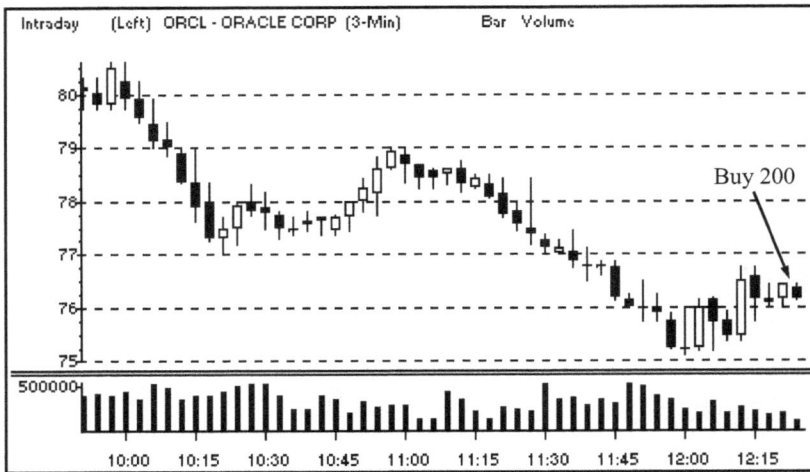

Reprinted with permission of Townsend Analytics, Ltd.

I was still watching ORCL and *MSCO* was supporting it at 76. It was a war between *SBSH* and *MSCO*. I decided to buy my position back. I bought 200 shares at 76.11. I was going to keep a very tight stop loss on this one. If the bid drops below 76, I am selling.

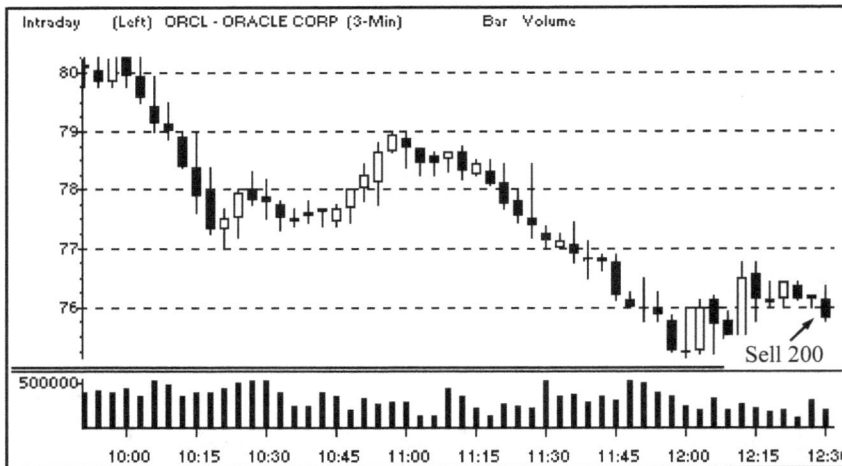

Reprinted with permission of Townsend Analytics, Ltd.

The "unthinkable" happens again. *MSCO* leaves the bid at 76, and the stock penetrates through. I sold my 200 shares at 75.88.

Source	Investment	Proceeds	COM	P&L	Return
Constant List	15,222	15,176	10.62	-56.62	-0.37%

118

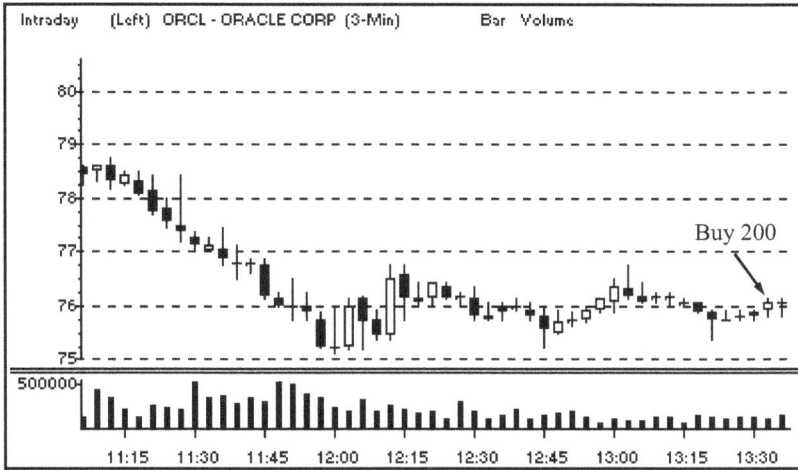

Reprinted with permission of Townsend Analytics, Ltd.

My love affair with ORCL is not over! *SBSH* left the inside offer and *MSCO* is back at the inside bid. What I liked about ORCL at this point was that the bottoms were rising, so if you didn't guess it by now, I bought 200 shares at 76.06.

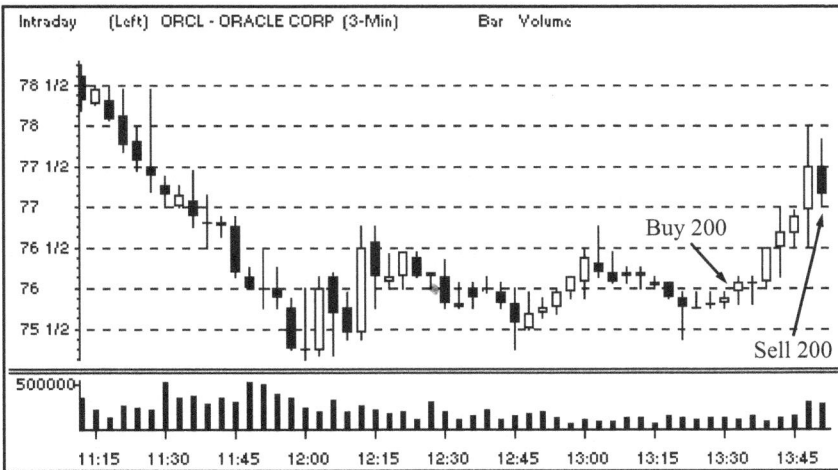

Reprinted with permission of Townsend Analytics, Ltd.

I finally had a winner. ORCL ran up sharply and I wanted to sell the stock into the buying pressure. I offered out 200 shares at 78 on ISLD. The stock hit my price, but I didn't get a fill. Then it started to pull back, and I was now chasing it down trying to get out! I finally sold 200 shares at 77.06.

Source	Investment	Proceeds	COM	P&L	Return
Constant List	15,212.50	15,412.5	10.52	189.48	1.24%

119

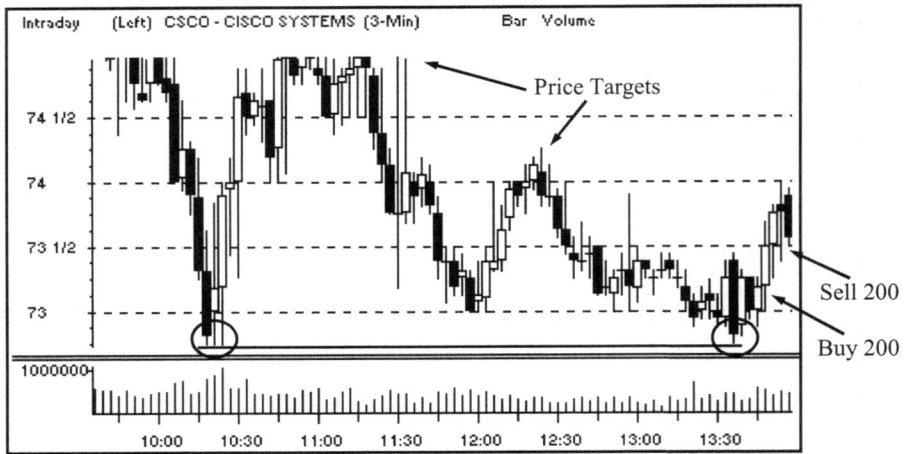

Intraday (Left) CSCO - CISCO SYSTEMS (3-Min)   Bar Volume

CSCO formed a double bottom as seen in the chart above. I bought 200 shares at 73.19 as CSCO bounced at the second bottom. I placed a stop loss at 72.94 (I felt that 73 should hold). My price target was 74.25- 74.50 (previous tops). The stock hit 74 and turned around. I sold 200 shares at 73.56.

Source	Investment	Proceeds	COM	P&L	Return
Constant List	14,637.50	14,712.50	10.50	64.50	0.44%

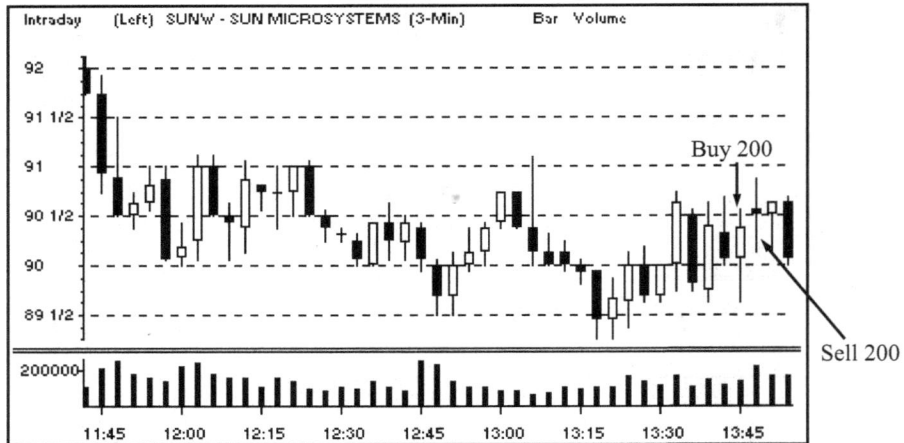

Intraday (Left) SUNW - SUN MICROSYSTEMS (3-Min)   Bar Volume

SUNW was trying to bounce. It moved back over 90. I bought 200 shares at 90.50. *MLCO* was axing the stock, lots of green prints and no price progress. The bid side had a lot of depth. Once everyone saw how serious *MLCO* was about selling SUNW, the weight shifted over and sellers came in. Having no choice, I sold 200 shares at 90.25.

Source	Investment	Proceeds	COM	P&L	Return
Constant List	18,100	18,050	10.62	-60.62	-0.33%

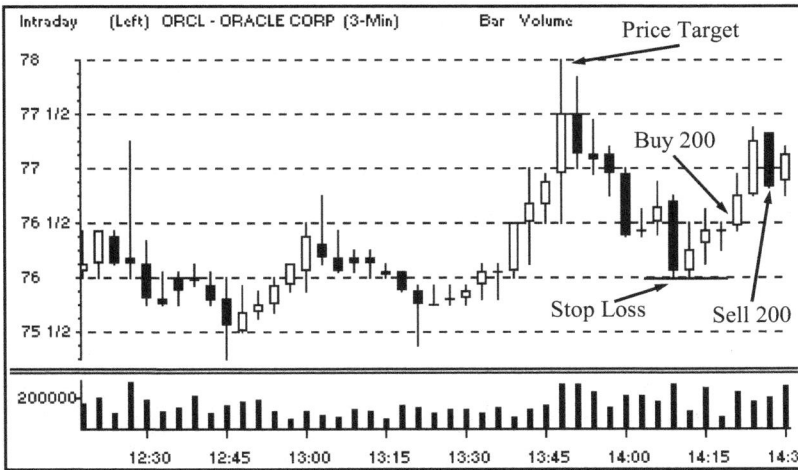

Reprinted with permission of Townsend Analytics, Ltd.

ORCL pulled back from 78 to 76. *MSCO* held it there again, and the stock was moving up. I bought 200 shares at 76.56. The stock went to 77.37, and *SBSH* showed some muscle and axed it again. I sold 200 shares at 76.88.

Source	Investment	Proceeds	COM	P&L	Return
Constant List	15,312.50	15,375	16.52	45.98	0.30%

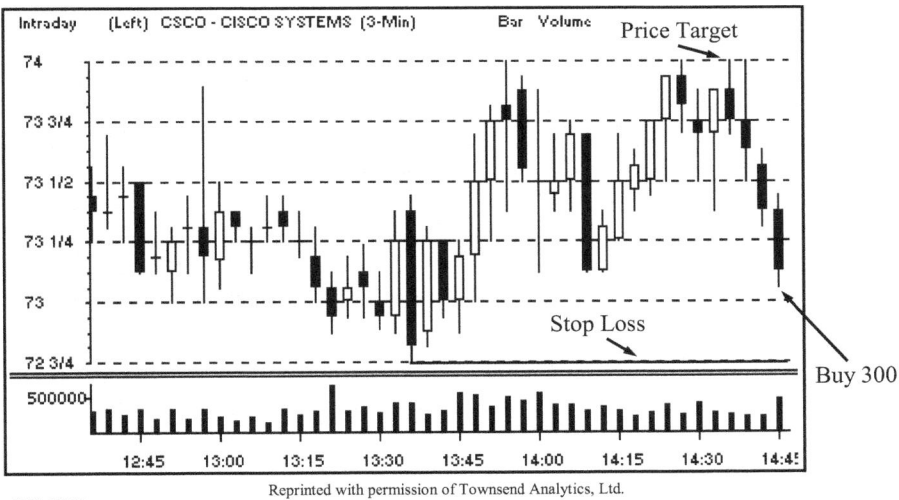

Reprinted with permission of Townsend Analytics, Ltd.

CSCO was approaching 73 again. I decided to step in front of the selling pressure and buy 300 shares at 73.12. I thought that I had two support levels in place, one at 73, and one at 72.75. I placed a stop loss at 72.69.

121

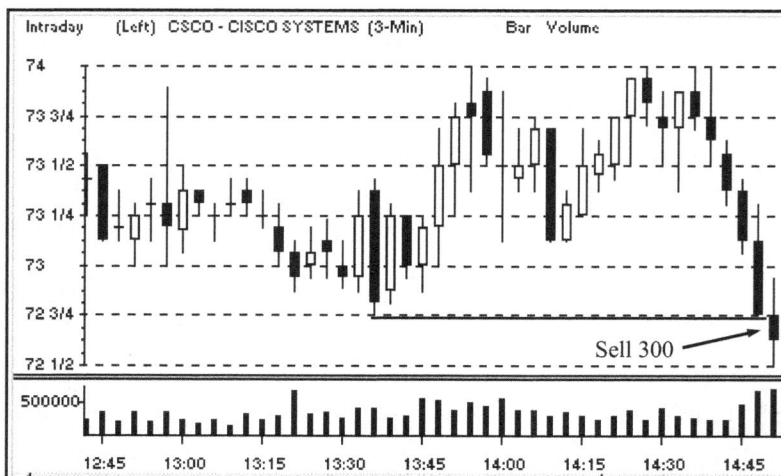

Intraday (Left) CSCO - CISCO SYSTEMS (3-Min)   Bar Volume

Sell 300

CSCO does not hold the support level this time. It takes out the 73 level and the 72.75 level. My stop loss is triggered. I sold 300 shares at 72.70. Notice the volume spikes when CSCO took out 73 and 72.75. There were many buyers there, but they still could not rebuff the selling pressure that came in.

Source	Investment	Proceeds	COM	P&L	Return
Constant List	21,937.50	21,810.93	10.72	-137.29	-0.62%

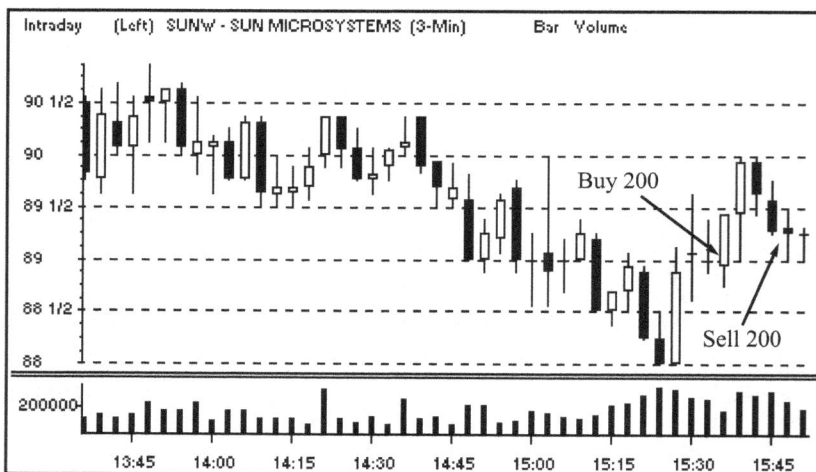

Intraday (Left) SUNW - SUN MICROSYSTEMS (3-Min)   Bar Volume

Buy 200

Sell 200

SUNW bounced at 88. I was expecting an end-of-the-day rally, and/ or a short squeeze, so I bought 200 shares at 89.12. The stock only went as high as 90 before falling back down and I sold 200 shares at 89.19.

Source	Investment	Proceeds	COM	P&L	Return
Constant List	17,824	17,838	11.32	2.68	0.01%

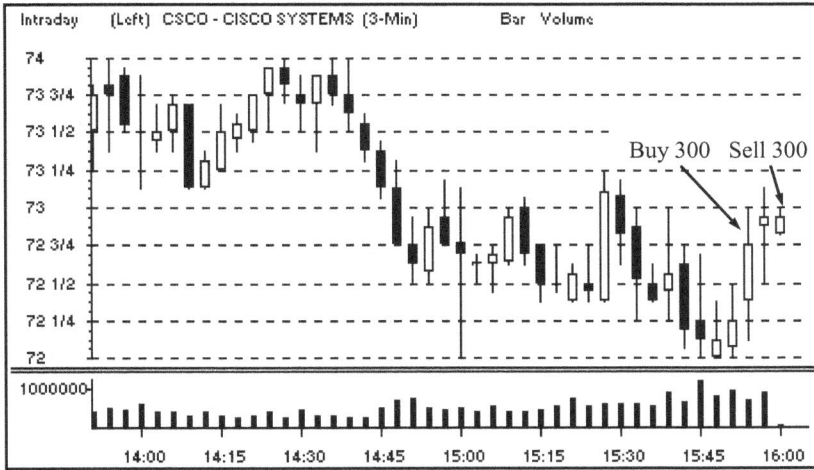

Intraday (Left) CSCO - CISCO SYSTEMS (3-Min) Bar Volume

Buy 300 Sell 300

Reprinted with permission of Townsend Analytics, Ltd.

I bought CSCO for the same reason I bought SUNW. I was looking for a rally into the close. I bought 300 shares at 72.87, and I sold them just before the close at 73. I was not going to hold any positions overnight.

Source	Investment	Proceeds	COM	P&L	Return
Constant List	21,862.5	21,900	10.73	26.77	0.12%

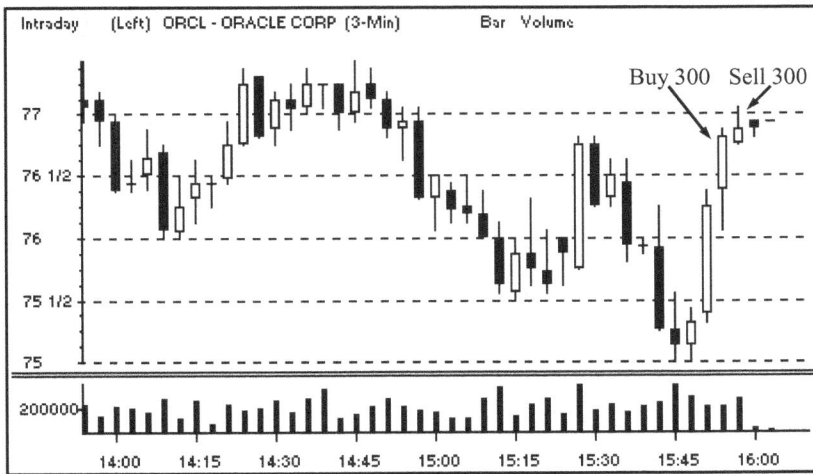

Intraday (Left) ORCL - ORACLE CORP (3-Min) Bar Volume

Buy 300 Sell 300

Reprinted with permission of Townsend Analytics, Ltd.

I also made the exact same play on ORCL. I bought 300 shares at 76.69, and I sold 300 shares at 77, just before the close.

Source	Investment	Proceeds	COM	P&L	Return
Constant List	23,006.25	23,100	10.78	82.97	0.36%

Wow! It was a record day. The final bell just rang, and the Nasdaq had just suffered its worst ever point decline. It was down 349 points for the day. The bears were waking up from their winter hibernation. The chart below shows the trading day on the Nasdaq index.

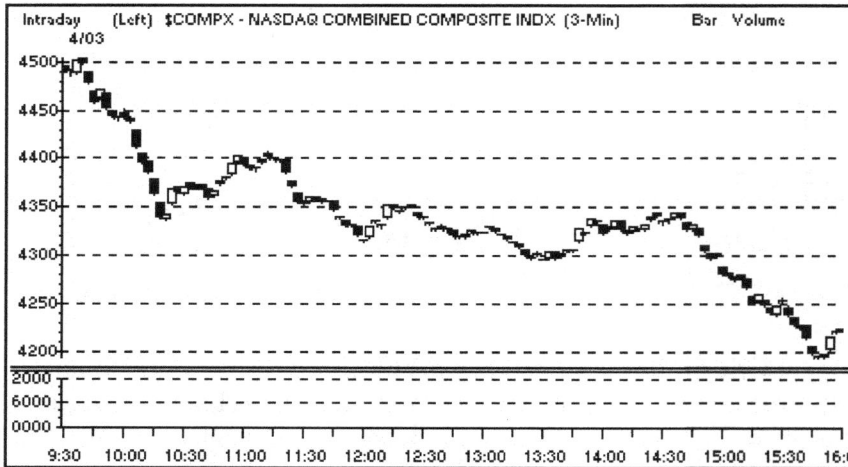

Reprinted with permission of Townsend Analytics, Ltd.

It was also a record day for the number of trades I have executed today. I kept all stop losses and trailing stops very tight. I was not letting my trades have wiggle freedom because the consequences could have been brutal. In hindsight, today's meager profits could be considered huge, because I was able to avoid losing big money trading on the long side through the worst ever, down day. It does not look good for the bulls.

Open positions: None
Total profit for 4/3/00: $47.51

Day Eleven Lessons

Do not over trade!

Keep up with major news events.

CHAPTER 15

Record Volatility

DAY TWELVE

Tuesday, April 4, 2000

The Nasdaq broke down through the support levels at 4290 yesterday, and closed at 4223, which was a very bearish sign. I didn't know what to expect today, so I had no trades planned in advance; however, I was going to be ready to buy stocks should the Nasdaq sell off hard. We have come down 16.8% over the last six trading days, so we are getting somewhat oversold.

The Nasdaq gapped up 60 points this morning. I was going to sit tight on the sidelines and not get sucked into trades the first 30 minutes of the day. I didn't want to relive yesterday all over again.

I took my sniper position, and I was waiting to take my shot. The Nasdaq, which opened up 60 points, was now in negative territory. It was selling off hard. The market had only been open 15 minutes, and the Nasdaq had already lost 121 points. It was down 61 points from yesterday's close. Suddenly, the index started to bounce and shot up almost 100 points over the next 21 minutes. It was now about 20 points off the morning high.

I wanted to jump on this rally, and buy all my favorite Nasdaq stocks; however, I was not going to do so unless I saw a clear confirmation of a reversal day. What I was looking for was for the index to take the previous top out. If it did, I would buy the pullback. I was not going to chase it early in the day.

It turned out to be a classic head fake, and within the next 27 minutes, the index took out the low of the day, and it was now free falling. It took out the 4100 level and was now trading at 4070. It was down 213 points from the open. At 10:55 AM, the Nasdaq tried to bounce, but there were just too many sellers in the street. All potential buyers were sitting on their hands, and I was doing exactly the same.

The sell off started to accelerate and panic selling was hitting the street. The Nasdaq just broke through a key psychological number, 4000. I remember when the Nasdaq finally broke out through 4000 with much fanfare, but now the breakdown came without even a pause. Within the next 15 minutes, the Nasdaq hit 3900. At 12:00 PM, the Nasdaq was down 383 points from the open. The Nasdaq bounced over the next 15 minutes, but the short-term rally only took it up to 3950 and presented an opportunity for sellers to get out.

The Nasdaq penetrated through 3900 at 12:30 PM, and traded down to 3840. It was down 443 points from the open!

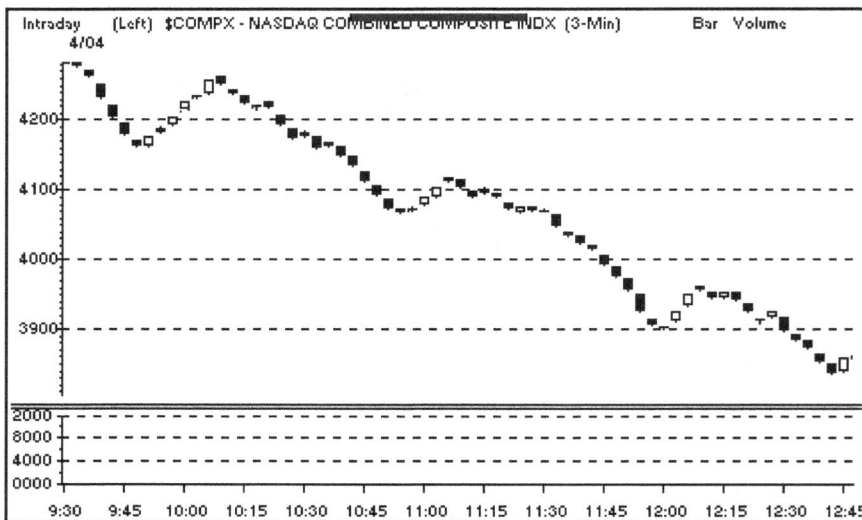

Reprinted with permission of Townsend Analytics, Ltd.

This was the biggest blood bath I have ever seen. It was very depressing to watch as billions of dollars were being evaporated. I tried to keep my focus at my post. I knew that if the bounce I was waiting for was going to take place, I would have to be very quick, or I would never get a fill on my order.

At 12:45, the index had its uptick. I had four stocks from my constant watch list in Level II montage windows. I was ready to execute an order on each one of them at a heartbeat, if I sensed a bottom. These stocks were SUNW, ORCL, CSCO and CIEN.

126

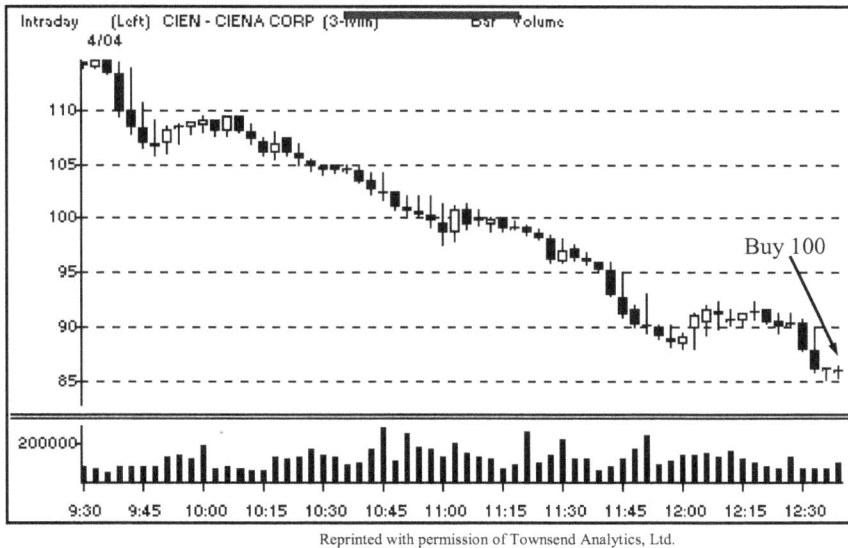

Intraday (Left) CIEN - CIENA CORP (3-Min) Bar Volume
4/04

Buy 100

Reprinted with permission of Townsend Analytics, Ltd.

As soon as I saw the uptick in the index, I bought 100 shares of CIEN at 85.31.

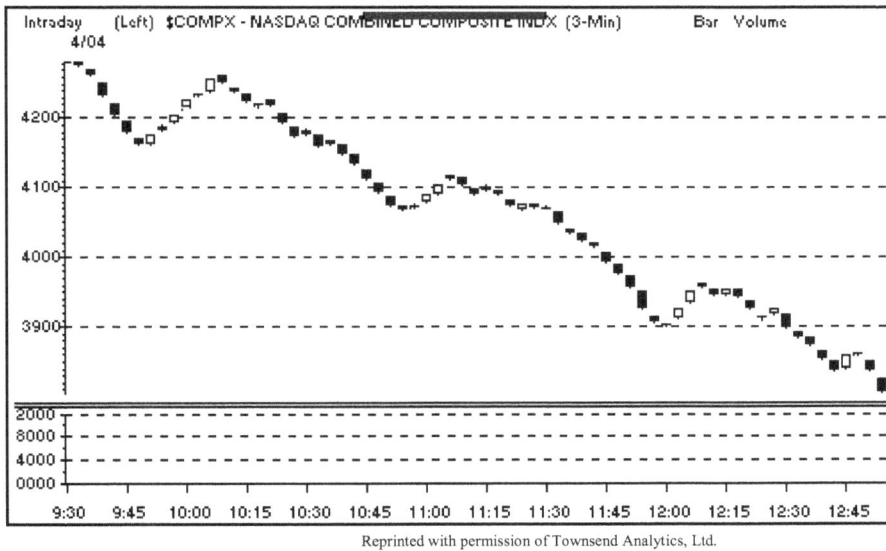

Intraday (Left) $COMPX - NASDAQ COMBINED COMPOSITE INDX (3-Min) Bar Volume
4/04

Reprinted with permission of Townsend Analytics, Ltd.

This rally did not last long at all, and the Nasdaq broke through the lows again. We were now at 3800.

Reprinted with permission of Townsend Analytics, Ltd.

As soon as the Nasdaq broke down, I sold 100 CIEN at 83.50.

Source	Investment	Proceeds	COM	P&L	Return
Constant List	8,531.25	8,350	10.28	-191.53	-2.24%

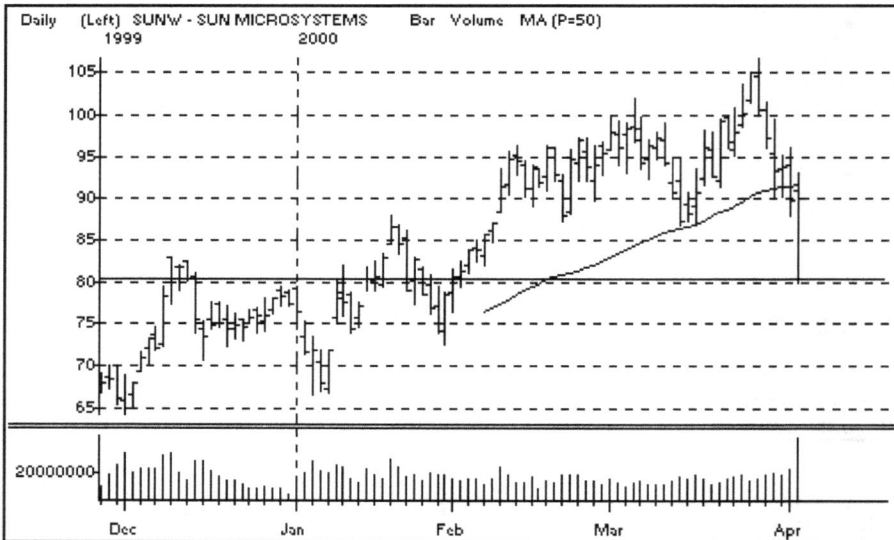

Reprinted with permission of Townsend Analytics, Ltd.

I was following SUNW very closely. It was trading around the $80 level. As you can see on the above chart, SUNW penetrated through many support levels. The bottoms it had back in the middle of March, the tops it had back in January, and the tops it had back in December of 1999. I thought it was getting to be very "cheap" at current price levels.

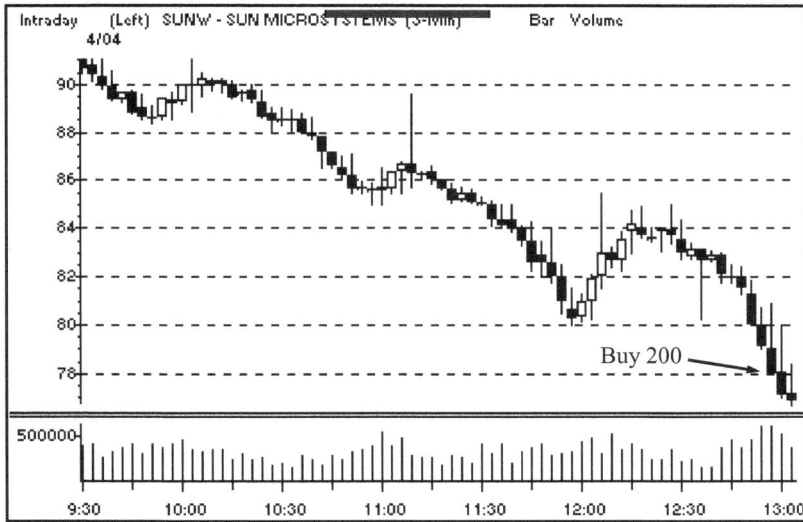

Reprinted with permission of Townsend Analytics, Ltd.

SUNW broke down through 80. It was 1:00 PM, and I decided to step in front of the crowd and catch the falling knife. I bought 100 shares at 78.37, and another 100 shares at 78.31. My strategy was to sit tight, if I caught the knife just right. Or let the knife slip through my hands with a minor cut, if SUNW was to keep falling.

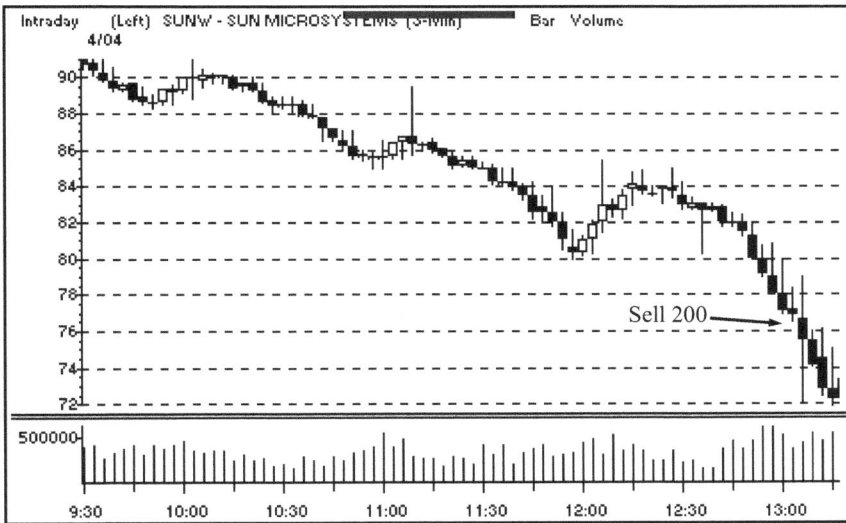

Reprinted with permission of Townsend Analytics, Ltd.

SUNW kept falling down, and I sold 200 shares at 76.67. I got away with a minor cut from the falling knife, but I didn't get killed. Now, my blood was in the street as well. It made me feel all better – Not!

Source	Investment	Proceeds	COM	P&L	Return
Constant List	15,668.75	15,334.37	18.51	-352.89	-2.25%

129

Reprinted with permission of Townsend Analytics, Ltd.

The Nasdaq kept falling down, and it was trading at 3650, well below its 200-day moving average. It broke through all support levels, and it was down a record 584 points (13.83%) from yesterday's close, and 644 points from the open! This was a crash, if I ever saw one. The New York Stock Exchange will halt trading if the Dow is down over 10% in one day. There is no such rule in effect in the Nasdaq stock market. Things were getting very scary.

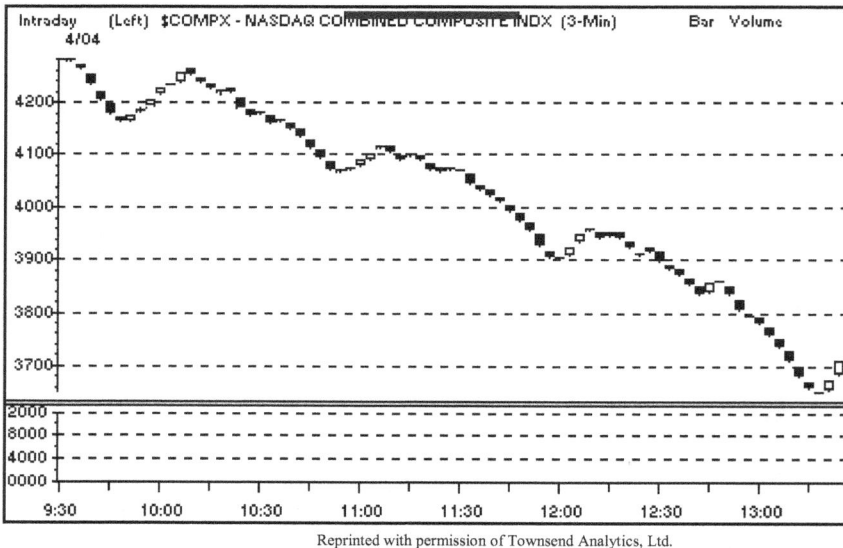

Reprinted with permission of Townsend Analytics, Ltd.

The Nasdaq hits 3649 and starts to rally. I was ready to take another shot.

130

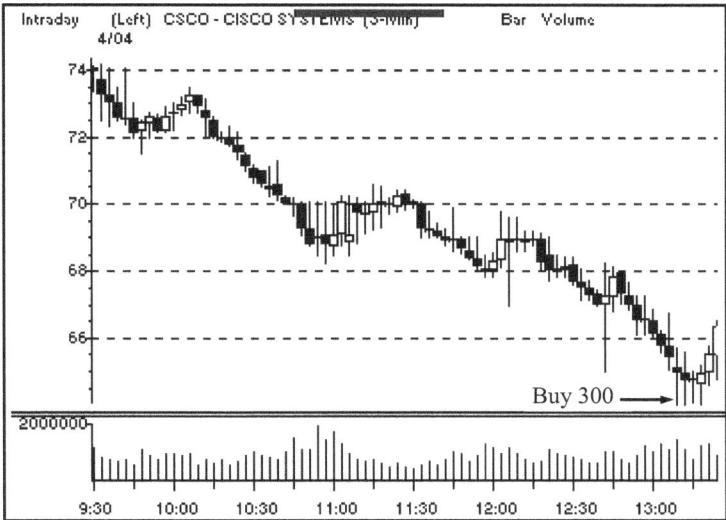

Reprinted with permission of Townsend Analytics, Ltd.

As the Nasdaq ticks up, I bought 300 CSCO at 65.24 and placed a conditional stop loss if the Nasdaq trades below 3640. My price target was 68 - 70.

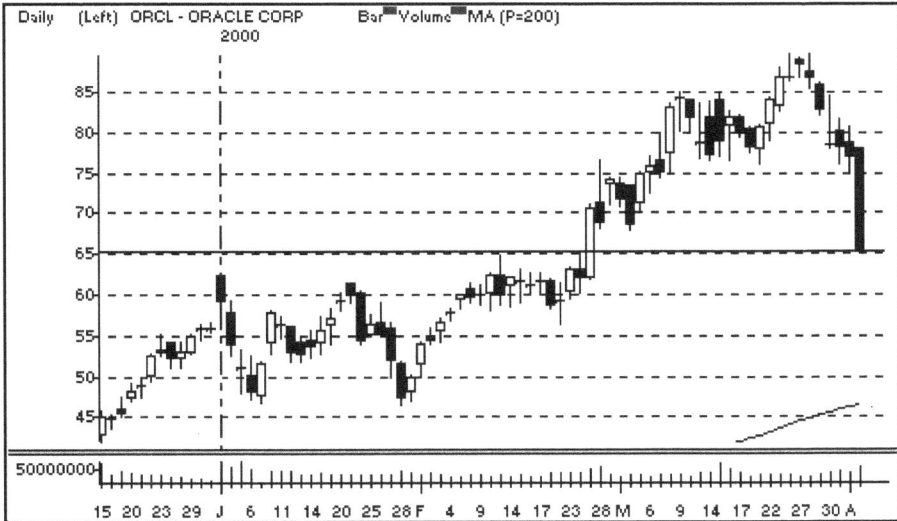

Reprinted with permission of Townsend Analytics, Ltd.

ORCL hits 65, which was the top on 2/11/00. It looked like good support, so I was looking for it to bounce at that level.

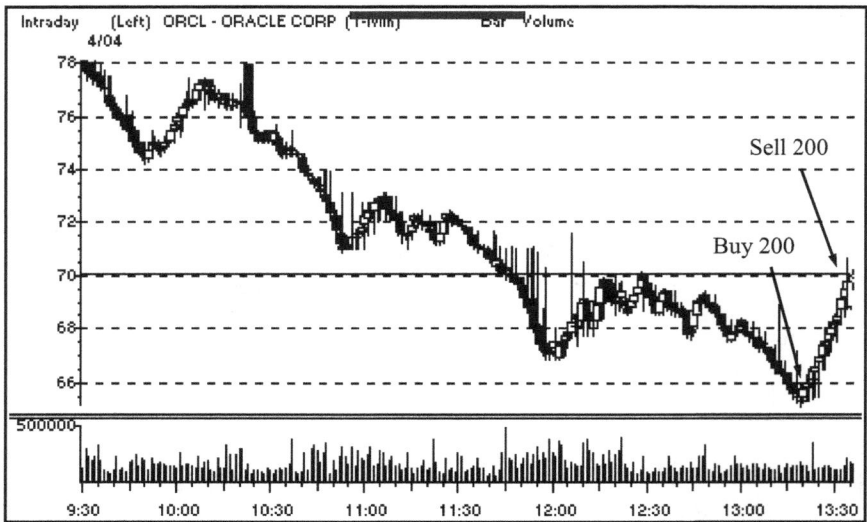

Reprinted with permission of Townsend Analytics, Ltd.

ORCL does bounce at 65. I bought 200 shares at 66.25. My price target was 70, which was resistance several times today. I placed a stop loss at 64.87 just below the low of the day. ORCL hits my price target, and I sold 200 shares at 69.88.

Source	Investment	Proceeds	COM	P&L	Return
Constant List	13,250	13,975	18.51	714.53	5.39%

Reprinted with permission of Townsend Analytics, Ltd.

CIEN was trading at 80, which was support from the tops set on 2/25/00, as shown by the horizontal line in the above chart.

132

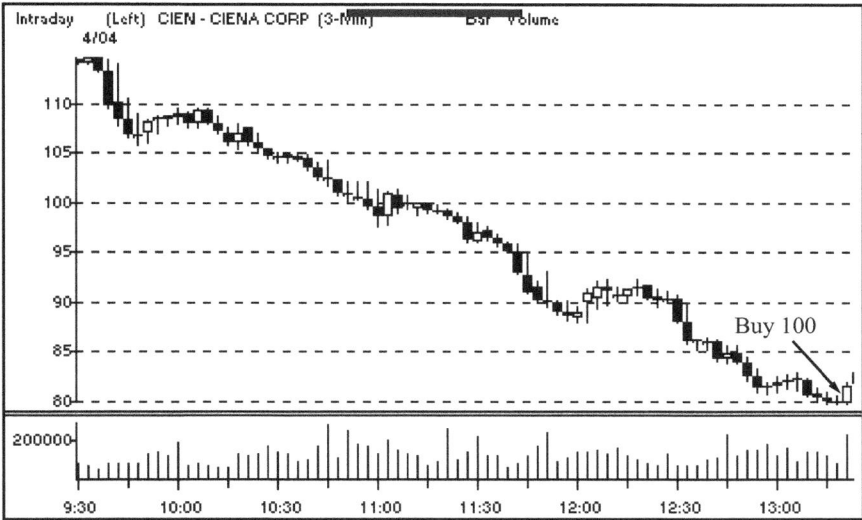

Reprinted with permission of Townsend Analytics, Ltd.

I bought 100 shares of CIEN at 81.75. My price target was 92, which was the tops at 12:15. My stop loss was at 79.75, just below today's low.

Reprinted with permission of Townsend Analytics, Ltd.

CIEN hits the bottoms it made at 12:00 around 88.50. It was showing some weakness, so I sold 100 shares at 86.44.

Source	Investment	Proceeds	COM	P&L	Return
Constant List	8,175	8,643.75	10.29	458.46	5.61%

133

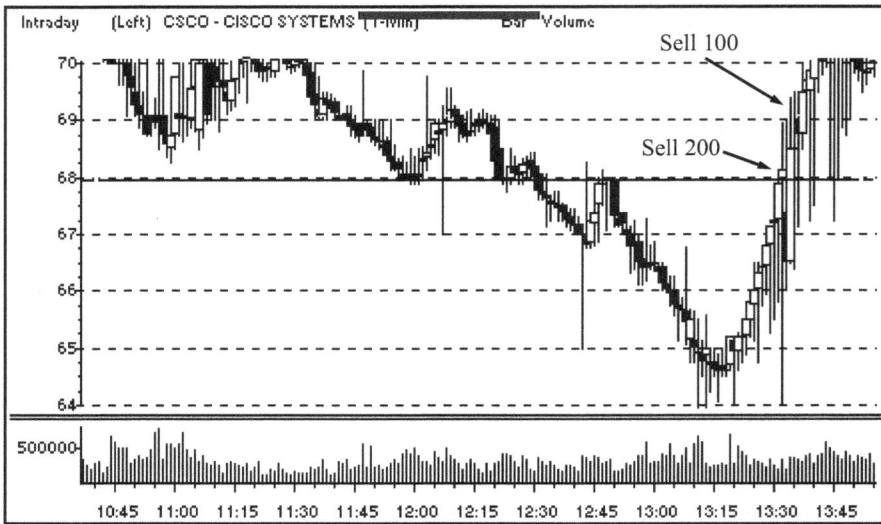

CSCO hits my price target. I sold 200 shares at 68. I sold the remaining 100 shares at 69.25 into buying strength.

Source	Investment	Proceeds	COM	P&L	Return
Constant List	19,573.83	20,525	15.70	935.47	4.78%

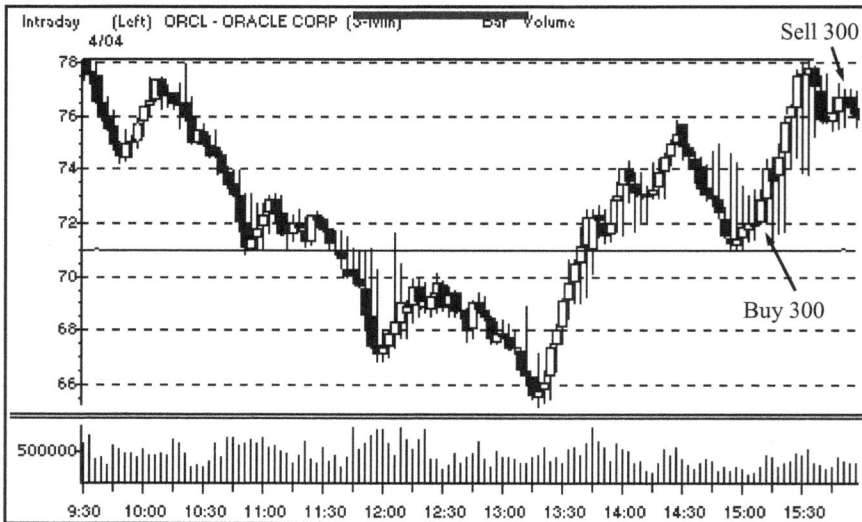

ORCL kept running up and finally pulled back. I was in my sniper position waiting to buy it again. It found support at 71.25. I bought 300 shares at 72. My price target was 78, which was the morning high. My stop loss was at 71, which was just below the last bottom made at 3:00 PM. ORCL hits my price target at 78. My sell order was not executed, and I was forced to chase the stock down before finally selling 300 shares at 76.40.

Source	Investment	Proceeds	COM	P&L	Return
Constant List	21,600	22,892.19	17.27	1,274.92	5.90%

Reprinted with permission of Townsend Analytics, Ltd.

CIEN ran up to 108, then pulled back to support levels at 92 (this was my original price target on the last trade). I bought 100 shares at 92.06. I placed a stop loss at 89.87. My price target was 105 - 115.

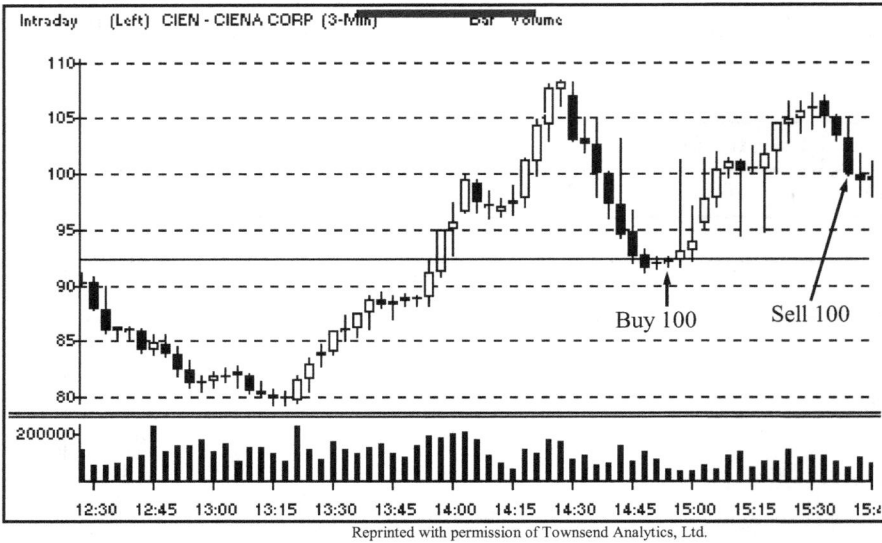

Reprinted with permission of Townsend Analytics, Ltd.

CIEN went as high as 106.50. I tried to give it a chance to move higher. I had my trailing stop placed at 103.75. The stock came back down, and my stop loss was triggered. I sold 100 shares at 100.94.

Source	Investment	Proceeds	COM	P&L	Return
Constant List	9,206.25	10,093.75	10.34	877.16	9.53%

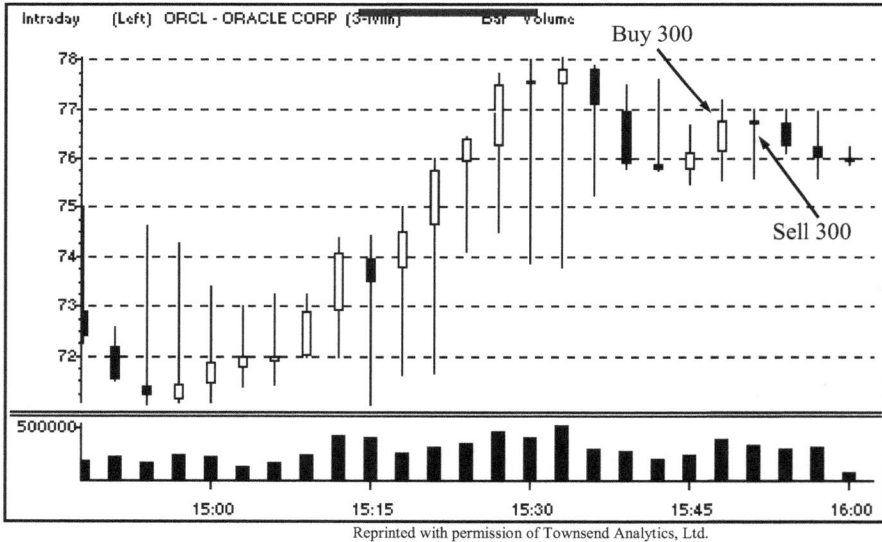

Reprinted with permission of Townsend Analytics, Ltd.

After I sold ORCL at 76.40 (once it pulled back from 78), ORCL started to move up again. I bought 300 shares at 76.94. The stock then turned back down, so I sold 300 shares at 76.50.

136

Source	Investment	Proceeds	COM	P&L	Return
Constant List	23,081.25	22,950	10.77	-142.02	-0.61%

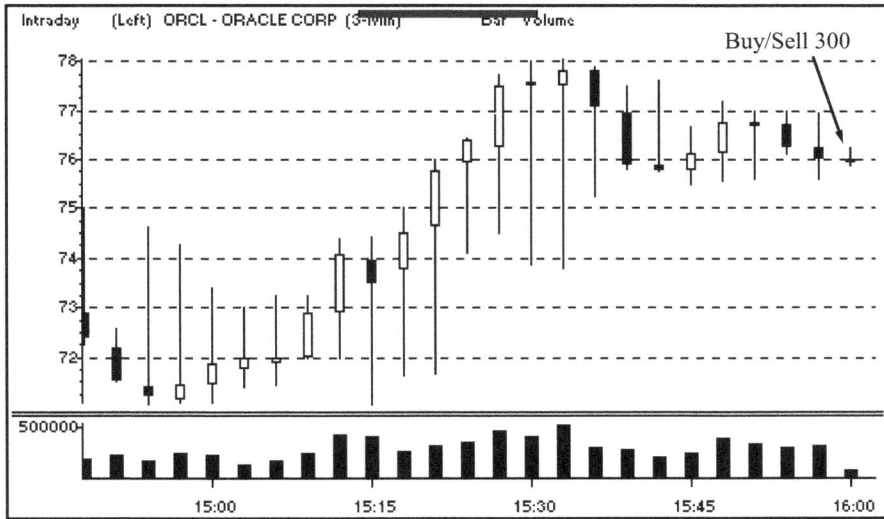

Reprinted with permission of Townsend Analytics, Ltd.

I liked the fact that the market has reversed its direction and recovered most of its loss, so I bought 300 ORCL at 76 with the intention of holding it overnight. It didn't take very long before I realized that I better turn around and sell my position and go to bed all in cash, so I sold 300 ORCL at 76.12.

Source	Investment	Proceeds	COM	P&L	Return
Constant List	22,800	22,837.50	15.27	22.23	0.10%

The reason I did not hold ORCL overnight was that I realized that most likely we will have a gap down market the next morning. Psychology moves the stock market. As it was, the Nasdaq closed the day down 75 points, and the Dow closed the day down 56 points. That was no big deal; however, what happened earlier in the day *was* a very big deal. We had a record volatility day, and the headlines would be telling that story. Newscasters are not going to focus on the closing numbers. They are going to focus on the fact that the Dow was down 504 points, and that the Nasdaq was down 584 points.

I felt that news of this kind would probably scare the public. I could see the average investor reading the headlines or watching the news and making a very simple decision. Get out of the market now, or you will never

137

get a second chance. This will create a flood of sell orders prior to the open. The Market Makers will drop the market as low as possible prior to the open, then they will buy all the stock that the public is selling, and then bring the prices back up, so they can sell the stock back to the public at a profit. It happens all the time.

This was a scary crash. The key to my success today was to wait patiently for a high percentage bounce play. I sat on the sidelines for the majority of the day. I was fooled twice! I bought CIEN and lost $191.53. I then bought SUNW and lost $352.59. I was down over $500.00, but I didn't give up. I waited for my chance. Good things happen to those who wait, according to the old saying. I was fortunate to recognize the absolute bottom, and I entered three long positions. I was able to turn the day around and finish with respectable profits.

Open positions: None
Total profit for 4/4/00: $3,596.33

Day Twelve Lessons

Be ready to buy on big down days.

If you try to catch a falling knife, make sure you get away with a minor cut - if wrong.

On extreme days be vigilant for reversals.

16

Technical Problems

DAY THIRTEEN

Wednesday, April 5, 2000

As I expected, the action in the market yesterday received major coverage from all the major networks. Newscasters were interviewing financial advisors, asking them if the worst is over. They were very careful not to use the word *crash* in any of the broadcasts; however, you could sense that nervousness was definitely present.

The futures are down sharply this morning, just as I expected. Brokerage firms were flooded with sell orders from the concerned retail investors. I didn't want to buy anything pre-market, although I expected a run-up in stock prices as soon as the opening bell rang. I was looking to buy ORCL, CSCO and RMBS.

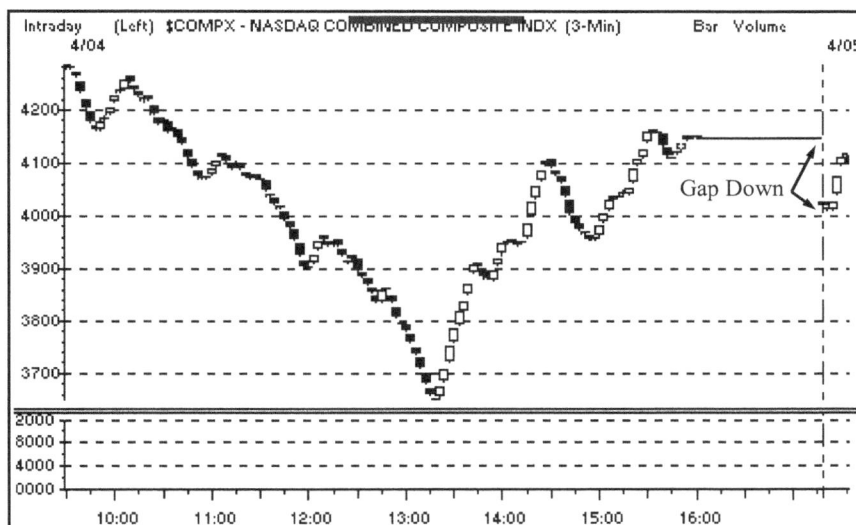

Reprinted with permission of Townsend Analytics, Ltd.

Ding! Ding! The opening bell rang and the market started trading. The Nasdaq gapped down 123 points. ORCL was trading at 73, CSCO was trading at 70.25, and RMBS was trading at 201. I sent orders out to buy 300 shares of CSCO, and 300 shares of ORCL.

The volume was very heavy this morning and SelectNet was completely down; consequently, ARCA wasn't working either. It was a buying frenzy! Stocks were running, and I could not get a fill on anything. The only way I could route an order was via ISLD or SOES. Since there was a glut of buyers, there were no offers on ISLD that I could take out in my attempt to buy CSCO or ORCL. The best ISLD offer was three points out of market. SOES was completely useless, and I got no fills using that route either. It was a frustrating morning. At first, I looked like a genius for not carrying positions overnight and selling ORCL at 76 yesterday. It was trading at 73 this morning; but now, I was not able to buy my position back, and the stock was trading at 78.

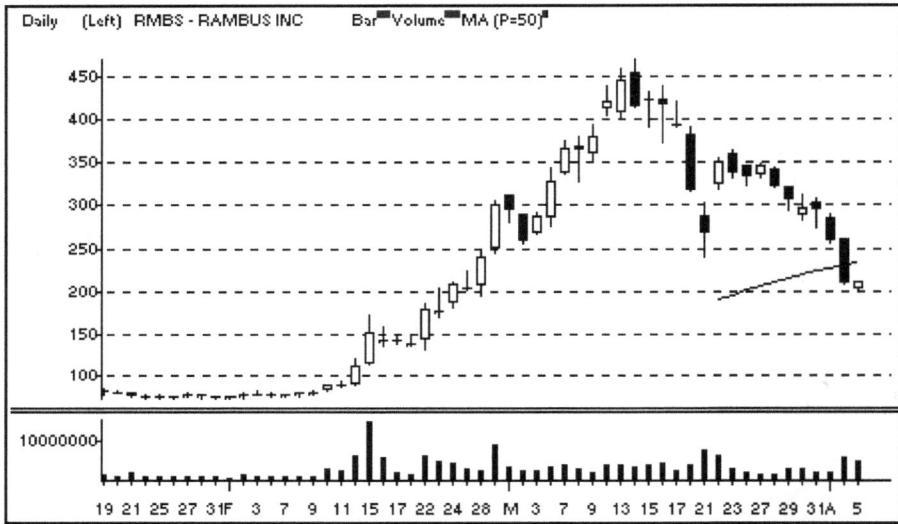

Reprinted with permission of Townsend Analytics, Ltd.

I studied the RMBS daily chart last night, and I was looking to buy it. I felt it had significantly come down in price from its high of $471 a share. I felt that a strong bounce could take it back to 270 - 300.

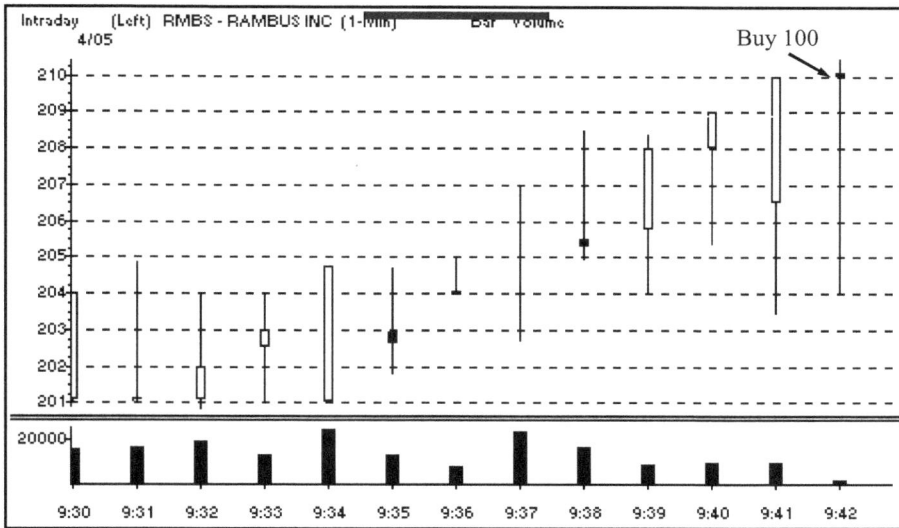

Intraday (Left) RMBS - RAMBUS INC (1-Min) Bar Volume
4/05

Buy 100

I tried to buy RMBS at the open, but SelectNet was down. I finally bought 100 shares at 210 taking an ISLD offer 5 1/2 points out of market!

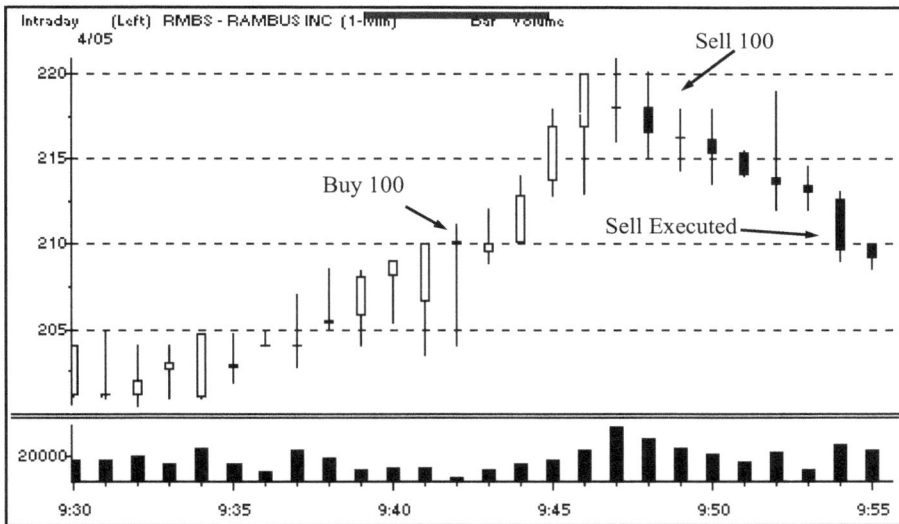

Intraday (Left) RMBS - RAMBUS INC (1-Min) Bar Volume
4/05

Sell 100

Buy 100

Sell Executed

RMBS ran up to 221. It then turned around, and started to decline. I had a stop loss on ARCA at 217.50. RMBS traded lower and my stop loss was triggered; however, SelectNet was slow (or non existent), and I was not getting a fill on my sell order. I tried to cancel the order, and it was taking a while for that as well. I was about to lose it. I finally got my order cancelled, and I entered a sell order on ISLD out of market. I sold 100 RMBS at 110.12.

Source	Investment	Proceeds	COM	P&L	Return
Watch List 1	21,000	21,012.50	10.70	1.80	0.01%

This was a sure sign I should have shut things down and gone to the beach. I watched an $1,100 profit turn to dust due to a Nasdaq malfunction. On pivotal days like today, the entire trading infrastructure was straining. The volume was so heavy, and the trading so furious, that even with direct access and DSL speed, home-based traders were at a significant disadvantage. I went downstairs and tried to regroup. I knew that it should be a great day for the bulls today. The Nasdaq has come down too much, too fast. It is due for a rally. "It was time to make money!" I told myself. I went back upstairs and waited for another opportunity.

RMBS started to move up again. The volume increased and I bought 100 shares at 210.12. My price target was 220 - 240. I placed a stop loss at 208.

Reprinted with permission of Townsend Analytics, Ltd.

I tried to give RMBS a chance. The stock went up to 215.50, and traded down. 210 looked like good support; therefore, I have not moved my stop loss up. BIG MISTAKE! The stock dropped through 208 and triggered my stop loss. I sold 100 RMBS at 206.87.

Source	Investment	Proceeds	COM	P&L	Return
Watch List 1	21,012.50	20,687.50	10.69	-314.31	-1.49%

Reprinted with permission of Townsend Analytics, Ltd.

RMBS held 203.50 again and started trading higher. I bought 100 shares at 205.56. I decided to give it some wiggle room this time, because I felt that it could go as high as 250. I placed my stop loss below the low of the day. Actually, I placed it below 200.

143

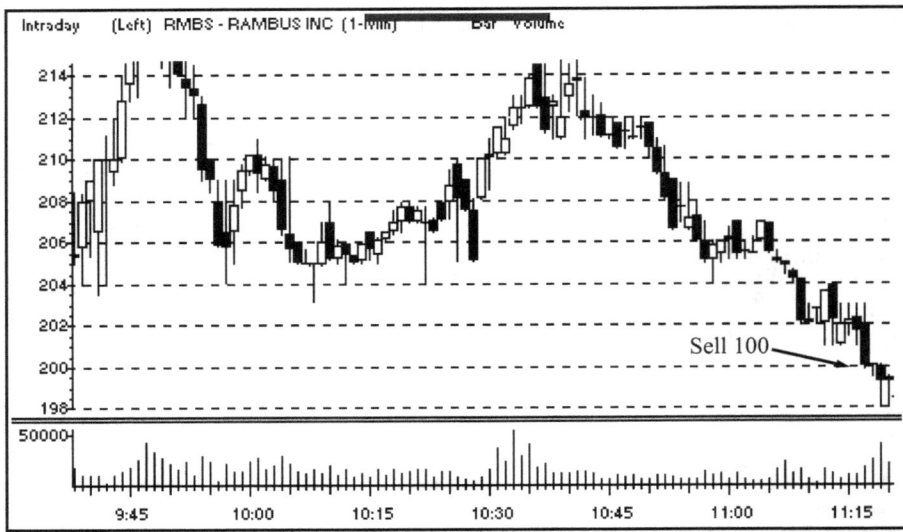

Reprinted with permission of Townsend Analytics, Ltd.

But instead, RMBS broke down through 200. I sold 100 shares at 199.94, losing a finger or two in the process.

Source	Investment	Proceeds	COM	P&L	Return
Watch List 1	20,556.25	19,993.75	10.67	-573.17	-2.79%

Back to the balcony I go. How can this be? It is a great day, and I am down almost $900.00. I felt like I should have been up $5,000.00 for the day as ORCL, CSCO, SUNW and the like were up significantly from their opening prices, and here I was, losing money. I needed to make a good trade.

Reprinted with permission of Townsend Analytics, Ltd.

MU had a very attractive pattern on the daily chart. It was up on big volume, and it just took out the highs it set two days ago.

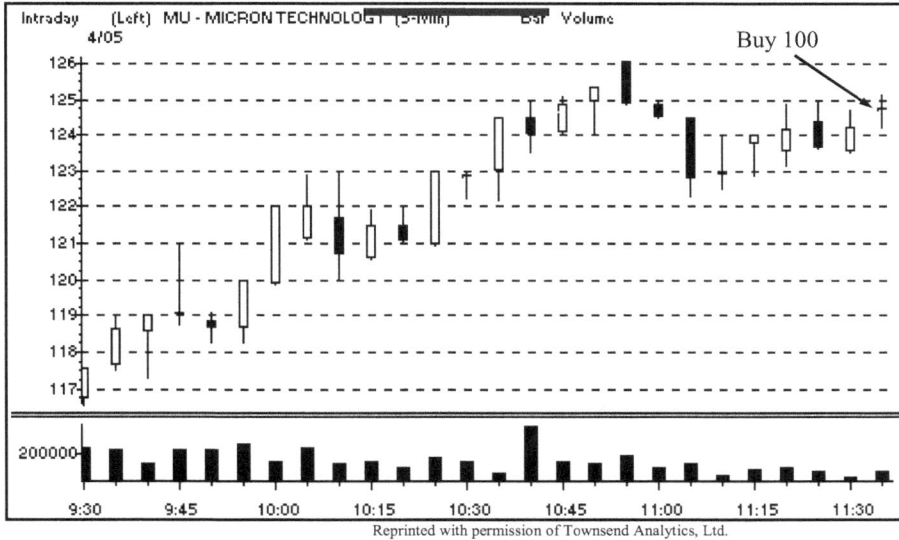

MU topped at 126, pulled back to 122.37, and was moving back up. I bought 100 shares at 124.67. I placed a stop loss at 122.12, just below the 122.37 low.

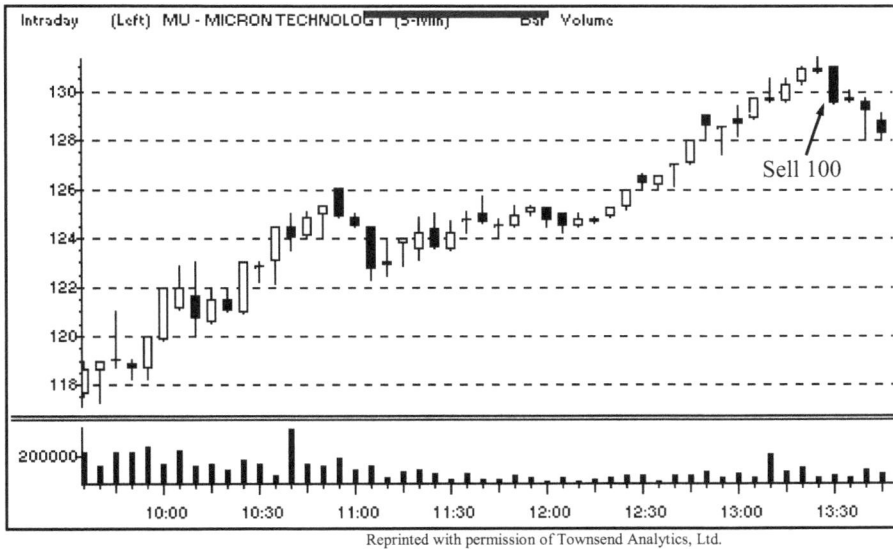

MU trades as high as 131.44. My trailing stop was placed at 129.75. The stock reversed back down through 130 and activated my stop. I sold 100 shares at 129.75. A little smile crossed my face. I needed that one.

Source	Investment	Proceeds	MBT	P&L	Return
Constant List	12468.75	12,975	10.44	495.81	3.98%

145

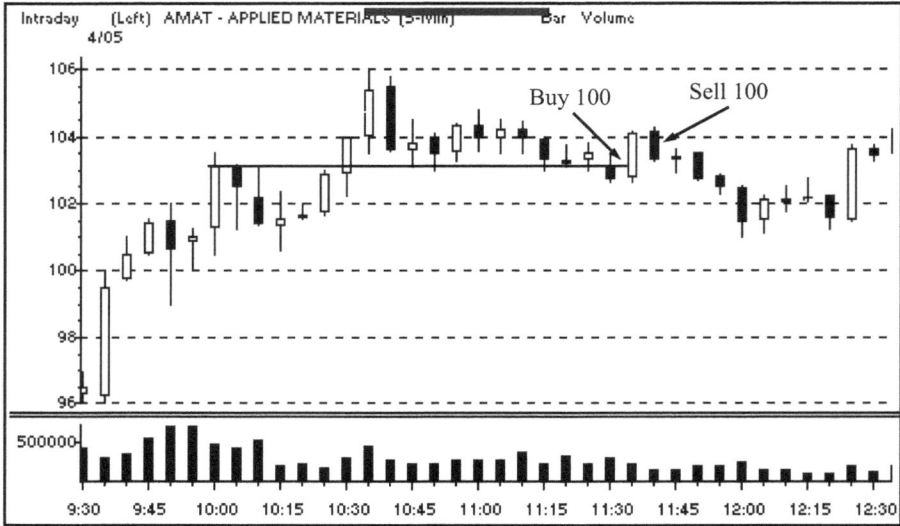

Reprinted with permission of Townsend Analytics, Ltd.

While I was in MU, I bought AMAT when it pulled back from the high at 106. I bought 100 shares at 103.37, and I sold 100 shares at 103.75. I couldn't let this one turn into a loser.

Source	Investment	Proceeds	COM	P&L	Return
Constant List	10,337.50	10,375	10.35	27.15	0.26%

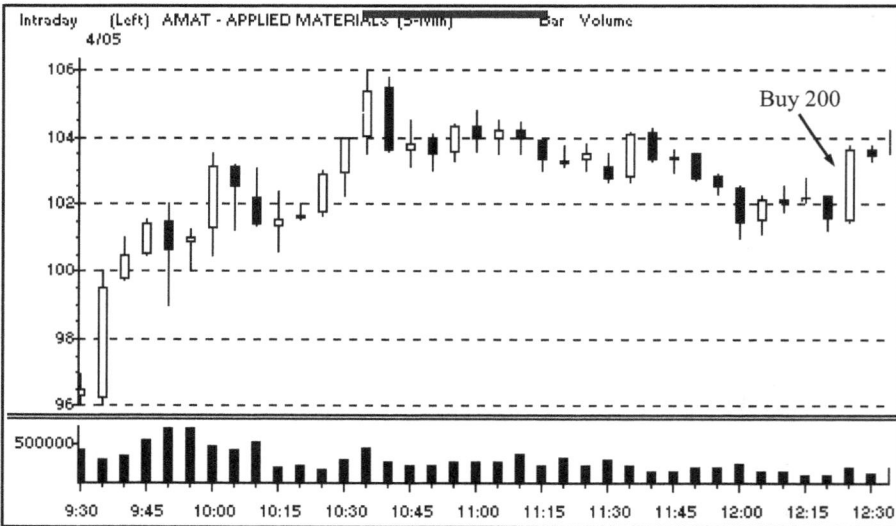

Reprinted with permission of Townsend Analytics, Ltd.

AMAT started to move back up, and I thought it could challenge the day's high at 106 and possibly the 52-week high at 110. I bought 200 shares at 103.62. My price target was 106 - 110, and I placed a stop loss a 102.62.

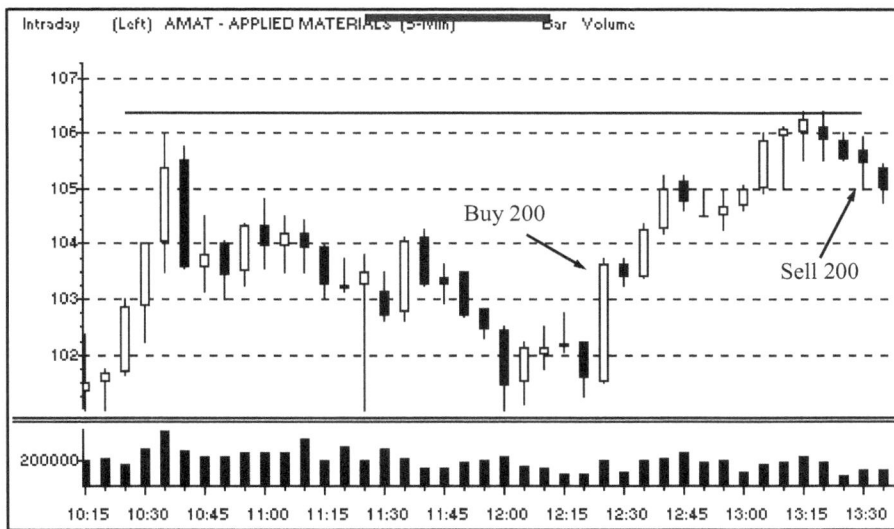

AMAT took out the top at 106, but couldn't muster a real run. It traded back down, and I sold 200 shares at 105.06.

Source	Investment	Proceeds	COM	P&L	Return
Constant List	20,725	21,012.50	10.70	276.80	1.33%

AMAT was challenging the top again. I bought 200 shares at 105.94. The stock failed to take out the top at 106.37 and started trading lower. I sold 200 shares at 105.75.

Source	Investment	Proceeds	COM	P&L	Return
Constant List	21,187.5	21,150	10.71	-48.21	-0.23%

BGEN showed up in my Pullback Scan. It has pulled back more than 50% from its 52-week high and was moving higher, on higher than average volume.

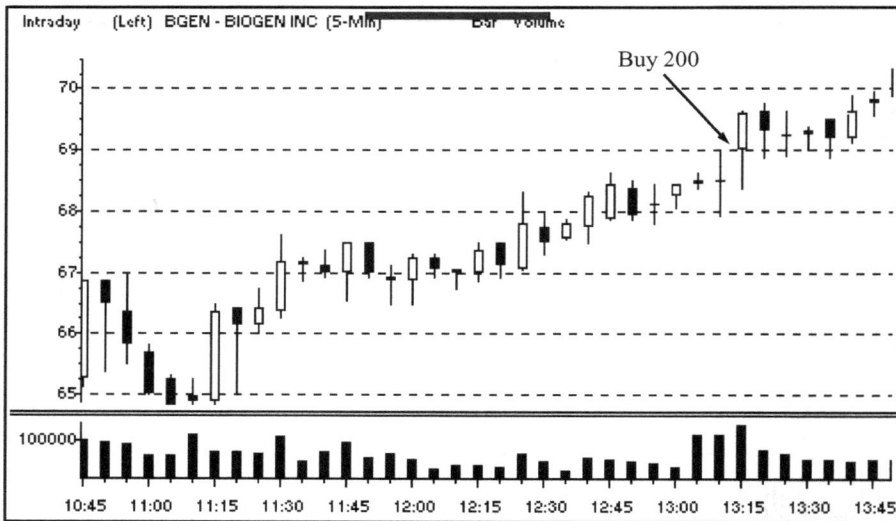

I bought 200 BGEN at 69.12 as it broke out to a new intraday high. I placed a stop loss at 68.50.

148

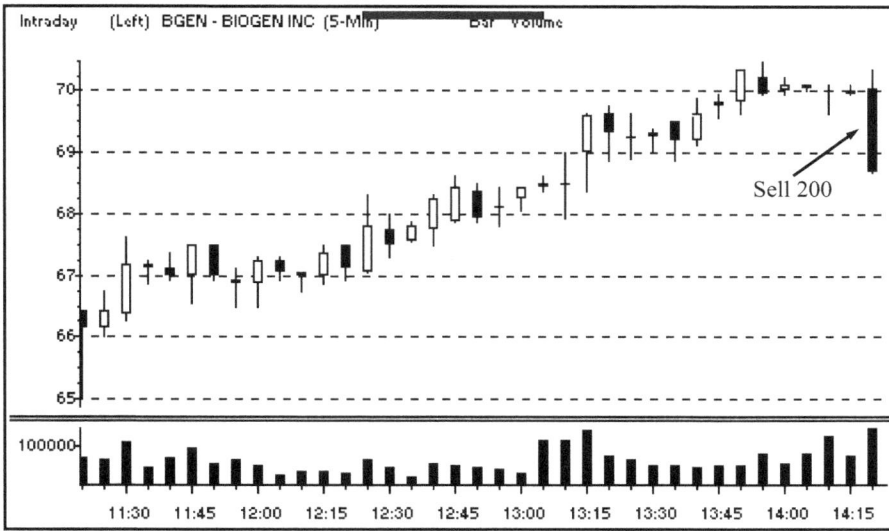

The stock went as high as 70.50. I moved my stop loss to 69.50. The stock sold off and my stop was triggered. I sold 200 shares at 69.38.

Source	Investment	Proceeds	COM	P&L	Return
Pullback Scan	13,825	13,875	10.47	39.53	0.29%

BVSN also showed up in my pullback scan. The stock has pulled back 60% from its 52-week high and was rebounding on higher than average volume.

149

Reprinted with permission of Townsend Analytics, Ltd.

I bought 200 shares at 50.14, and I added 200 more shares at 50.44 as the stock broke out to a new intraday high.

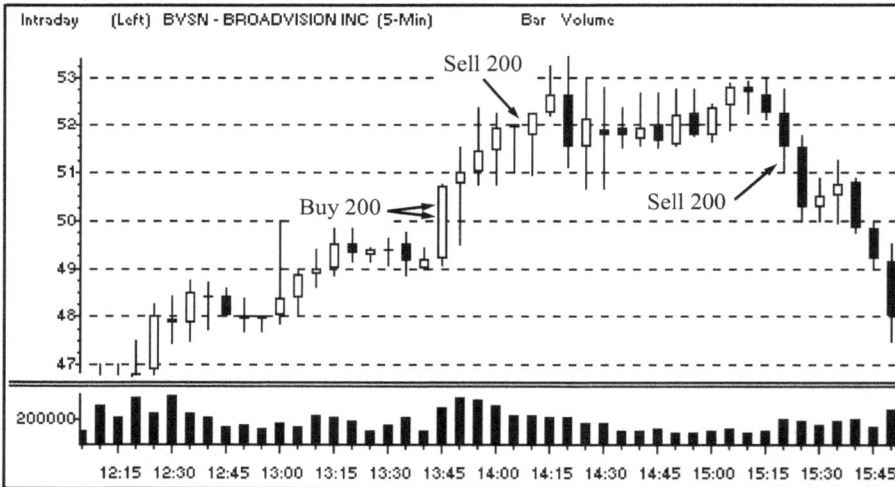

Reprinted with permission of Townsend Analytics, Ltd.

BVSN had momentum behind it. It reached 52 and hesitated for a second. I sold 200 shares at 52. The stock then went up to 53.50 and pulled back. I was giving it some wiggle room. The stock attempted to take out the 53 level again at 3:10, but failed to so. It started to sell off. I sold the remaining 200 shares at 51.12.

Source	Investment	Proceeds	COM	P&L	Return
Pullback Scan	20,115.62	20,625	23.70	485.68	0.29%

150

I was bringing up semiconductor stocks on my watch list. TXN was trying to move over its 50-day moving average.

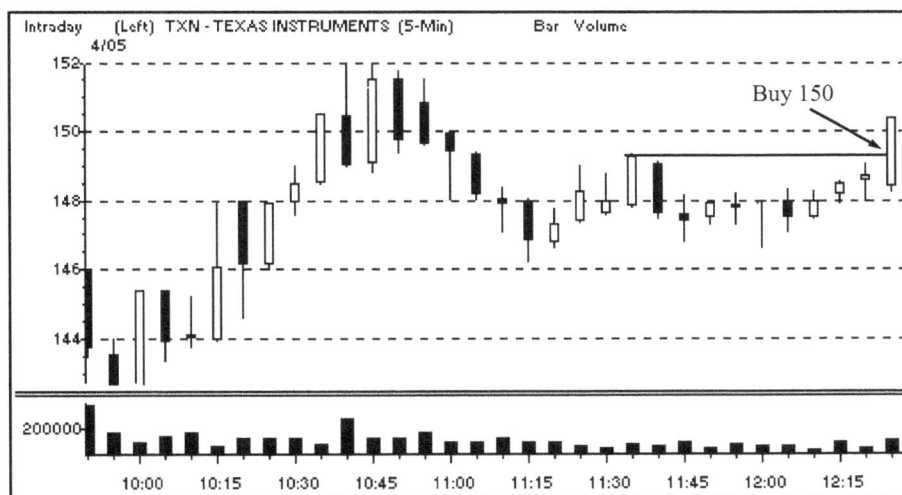

I bought 150 shares of TXN at 149.50 as the stock penetrated through the previous top at 149. I was expecting TXN to challenge the top price of 152 and possibly break out.

151

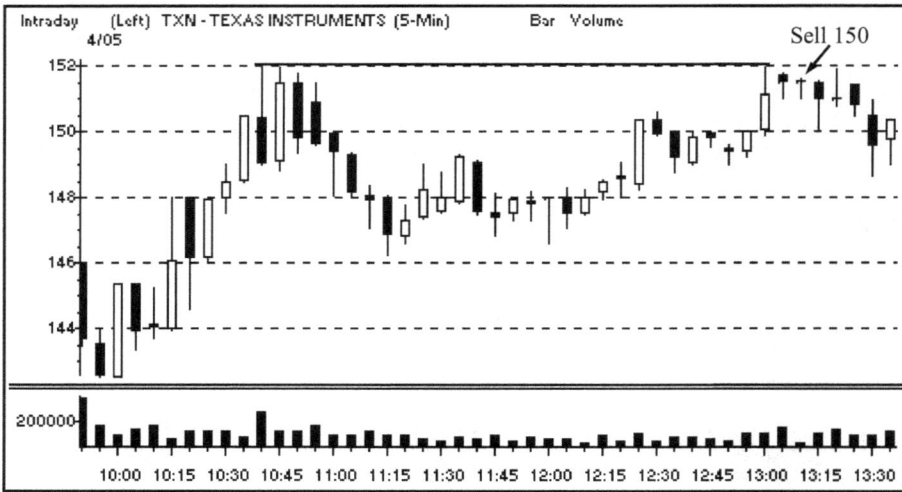

Intraday (Left) TXN - TEXAS INSTRUMENTS (5-Min)   Bar Volume

Reprinted with permission of Townsend Analytics, Ltd.

TXN went as high as 152. It was having problems at that level, and it may have formed a double top. I sold my 150 shares at 151.67.

Source	Investment	Proceeds	COM	P&L	Return
Sector Scan	22,425	22,753.12	10.75	317.37	1.41%

Basket Trading

One of the strategies I use in my trading is to find the strongest sector and buy the strongest stocks in that sector. I try to create a "basket" of stocks that will both outperform the market and the sector they belong to. For my stock selection criteria, I simply look for the most known liquid names. Here is how I manage a basket position. As the index goes up, I sell the stocks in the basket that are going down or are flat. This permits me to stay in only the stocks that are going up. When the index turns down and violates support levels, I will liquidate the entire basket. Since I hold a group of stocks in the same sector, my position window, which updates dynamically with every tick, gives me a "real-time" view of what is taking place. My open P&L tracks the changes in bid prices for the entire basket. In many cases, the trade management of a basket would also be dependent on both the number of the stocks in the basket, which can be as high as 20, and the time frame for the trade.

By this point in the day, I had turned the day around, and I was up about $700.00. That second break on the balcony really helped, and I felt as if I had the market in the palm of my hand. I was extremely bullish at this point, because the Nasdaq has come down 28% from the high on 3/24/00 to yesterday's low, and after that extreme bounce, we are continuing to trade higher.

152

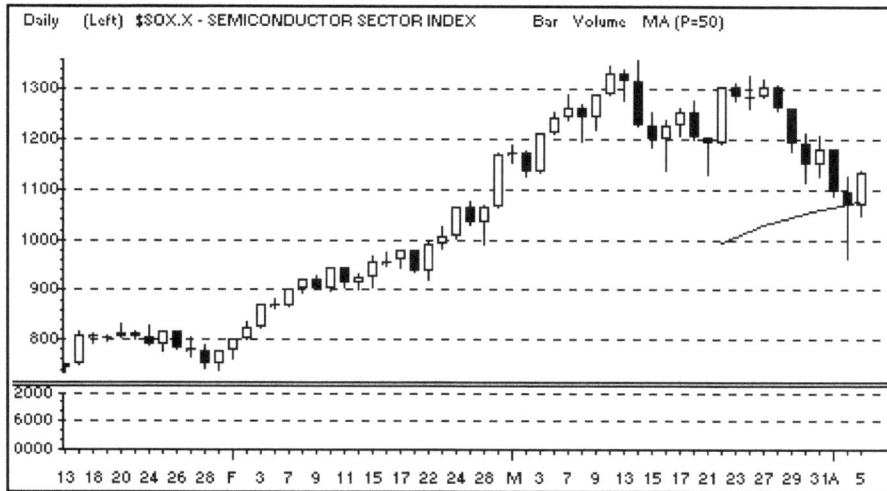

The SOX (Semiconductor Sector Index) has been outperforming the market for a while. I felt that more money was going to go into this sector as it is seen as a safe heaven for many investors. The index was at 1140, and I expected it to go to 1200 - 1250 over the next few days. This would be a 5% - 8% move.

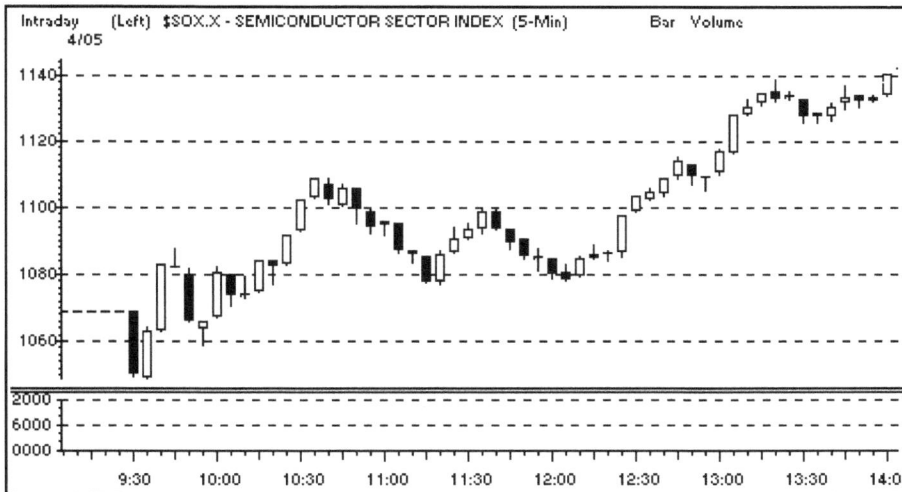

The SOX broke out to a new intraday high. At this point I was entering the following five stocks to create my basket: NVLS, LSI, MOT, PMCS, and VTSS. Keep in mind, that I will be trading these five stocks in direct relationship to the SOX.

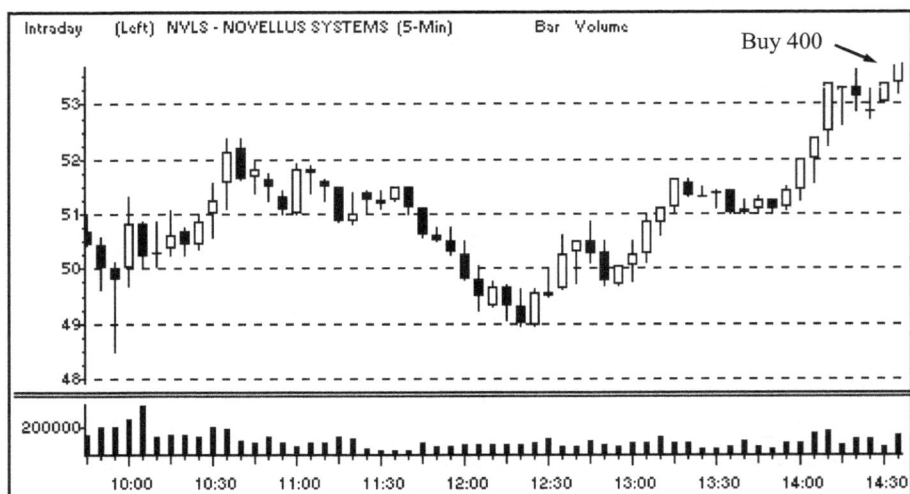

I bought 200 shares of NVLS at 53.37, and another 200 shares at 53.53.

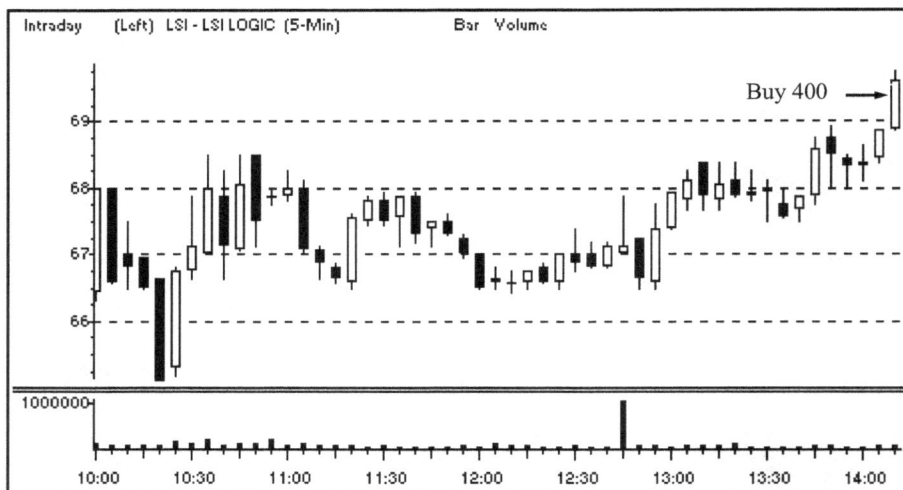

I bought 200 shares of LSI at 69.50 and another 200 shares at 69.56.

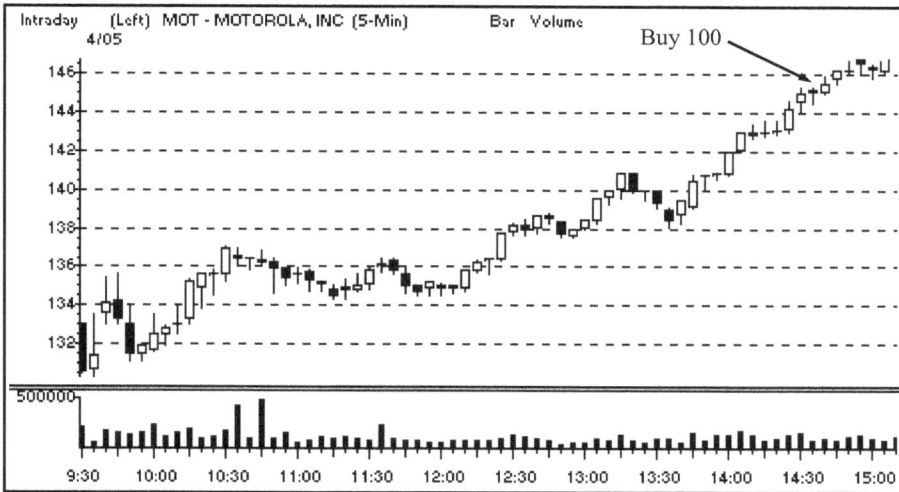

Reprinted with permission of Townsend Analytics, Ltd.

I bought 100 shares of MOT at 145.87.

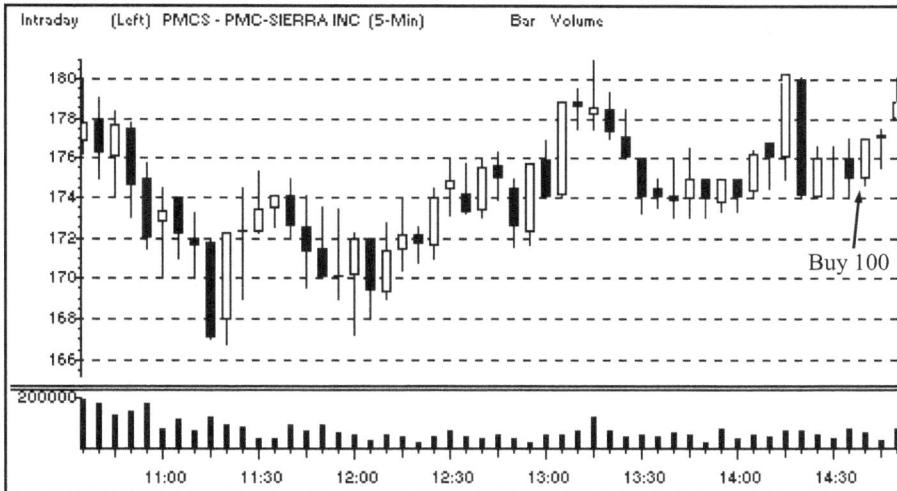

Reprinted with permission of Townsend Analytics, Ltd.

I bought 100 shares of PMCS at 174.39.

I bought 200 shares of VTSS at 90.56.

I was watching the SOX very carefully. My basket was doing well, and I was up over $1,400.00 on my various positions. My plan at this point was to sell half of my basket if the SOX hits 1215, and let the rest ride. My stop loss on the position was if the SOX broke below 1140.

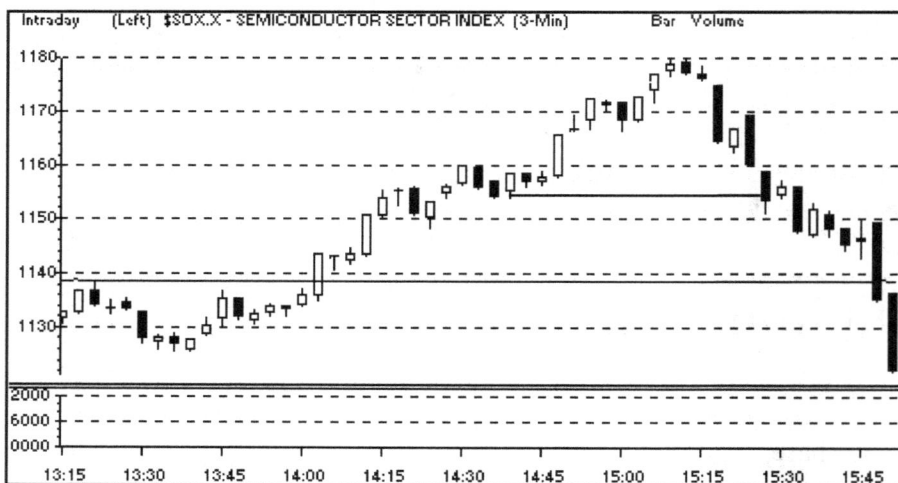

A trading system is made of rules and guidelines which you must follow religiously. There are no exceptions! The SOX peaked at 1180, and started to trade down. I have raised my stop loss to 1155 and as it broke through the support at 1155, I started to sell my positions.

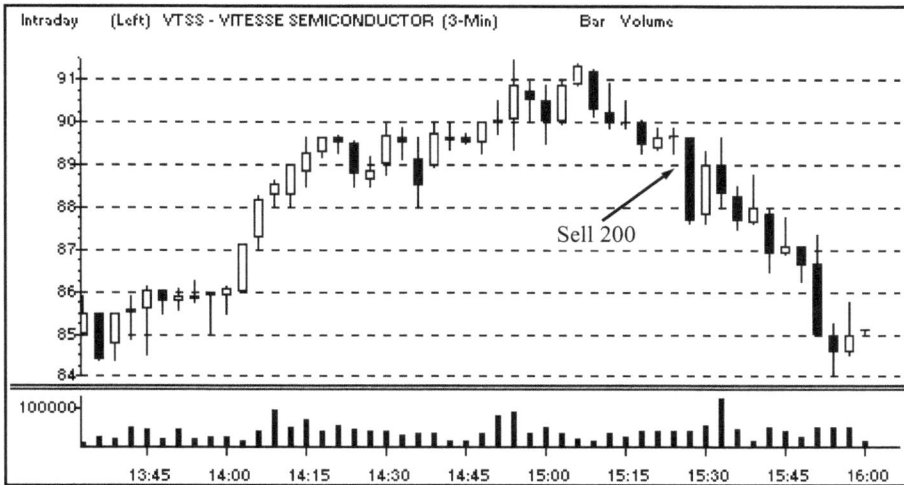

The first stock I sold was VTSS. I actually sold it before the SOX broke down, because it was under performing the basket. I sold 200 shares at 89.

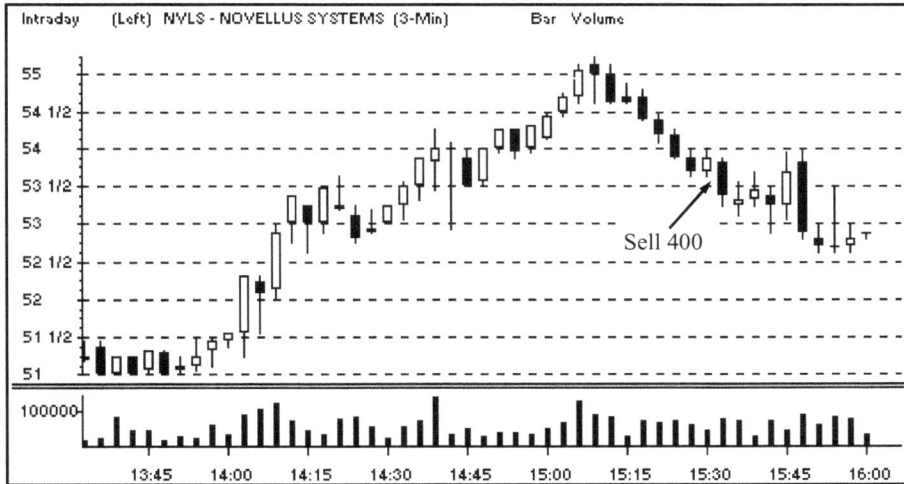

The second stock I sold was NVLS. I sold 200 shares at 53.62 and 200 shares at 53.38.

157

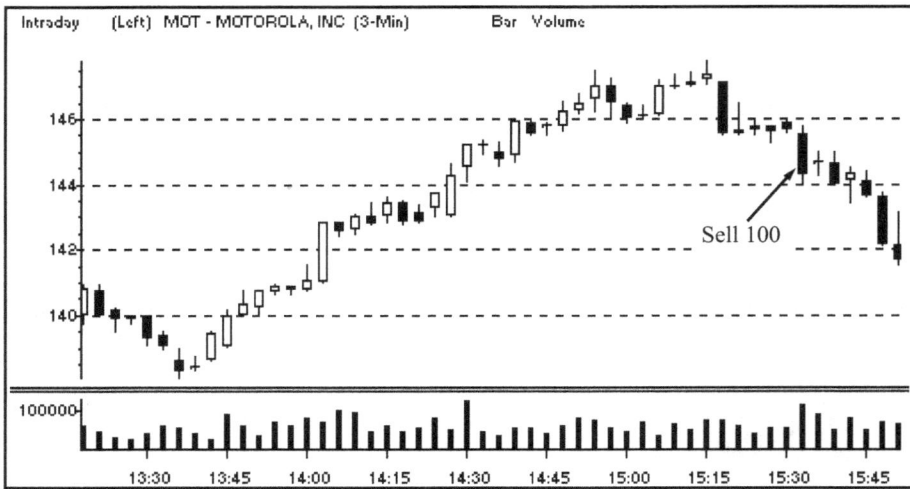

Reprinted with permission of Townsend Analytics, Ltd.

I entered a market order to sell 100 MOT. The bid was 145.25 at the time. However, the specialist saw the selling pressure coming, so he opened up the spread. I sold 100 shares at 144.25. I wasn't very happy about this one.

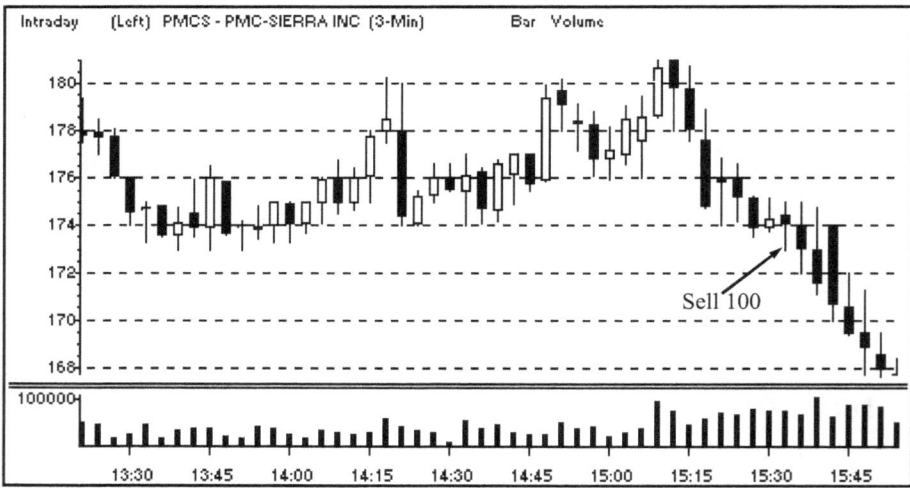

Reprinted with permission of Townsend Analytics, Ltd.

I sold 100 PMCS at 173.

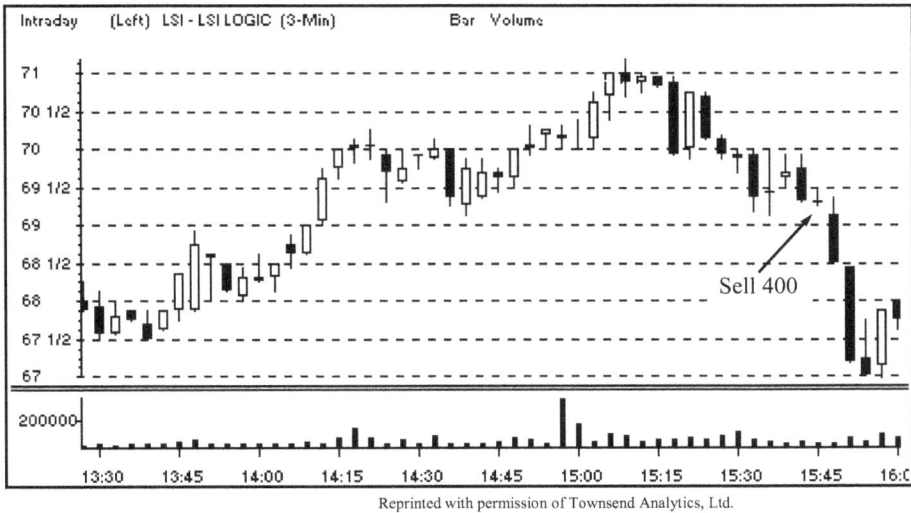

Intraday   (Left) LSI - LSI LOGIC (3-Min)   Bar Volume

Reprinted with permission of Townsend Analytics, Ltd.

I entered two orders to sell 200 shares of LSI at the market. I sold 200 shares at 69.12, and 200 shares at 69.19.

Source	Investment	Proceeds	COM	P&L	Return
Basket Trade	99,332.81	98,637.50	74.83	-770.14	-0.78%

The basket trade did not work out in this case. I was not upset that I was up $1,400 and ended up with a loss. On a percentage basis, the total wiggle of $2,100, from the high value of the basket to the sale price of the basket is completely normal. In the past, basket trades like this have yielded me great returns. The secret is that you have to be right and sit tight. The only thing that bothered me was that I still felt we were going higher over the next few days, and I just lost my position. However, risk management and money management rules must be followed, no matter what my gut feeling tells me. This is the difference between a gambler and a professional trader.

159

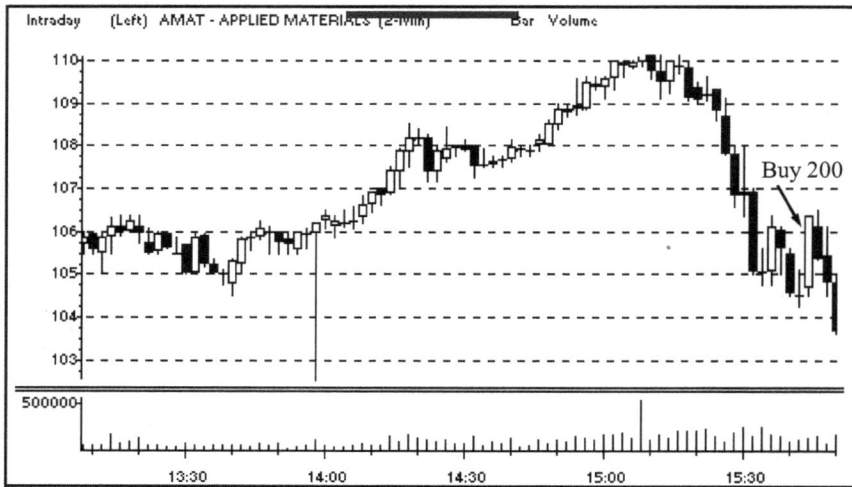

Reprinted with permission of Townsend Analytics, Ltd.

AMAT is also in the semiconductor sector. It sold off really hard from 110 to 104.50. It then bounced, and I bought 200 shares at 105.98. I placed a stop loss at 103.50. My price target was another run to the top tomorrow.

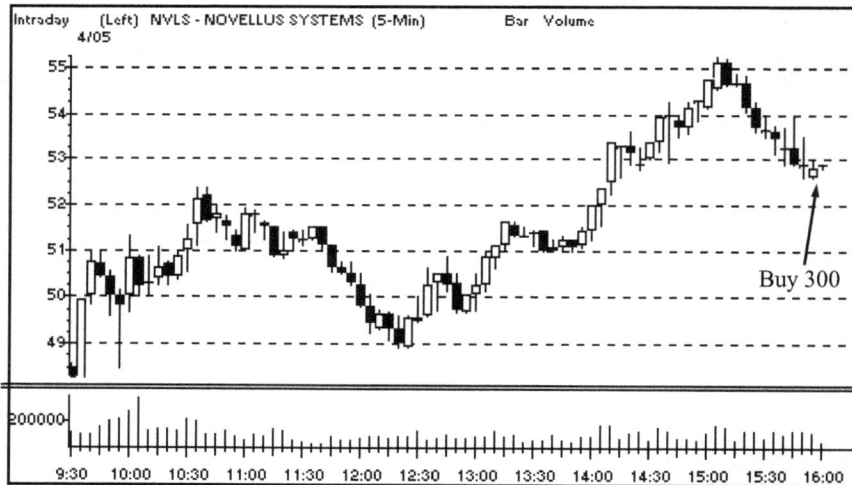

Reprinted with permission of Townsend Analytics, Ltd.

NVLS did not sell off as hard as the rest of the market. It was a sign of strength, so I bought 300 shares at 52.81.

Intraday (Left) RMBS - RAMBUS INC (5-Min) Bar Volume
4/05

Sell 100

Great traders never look back at what happened to a losing trade after they exit it. RMBS was my pick of the day. I traded it three times in the morning without any success. In fact my last exit was practically the low of the day. After the third trade on RMBS was completed, I simply took it off my trading screen, so I didn't see what took place later in the trading day.

RMBS went as high as 248.50 after I sold it at 199.94. Things like that happen all the time, and it doesn't really matter where a stock goes after I sold it, because I have to execute my trades at my exit prices regardless if I am right or wrong in my analysis. If I don't have exit prices planned in advance, including stop loss and price targets, then I am not a professional trader. If things like this drive you crazy, go back to Day Five and look at all the positions I sold that day. If I was still holding these positions right now, I would be down $17,575 from the price I sold them to the closing prices of today. I hope you are getting my point.

The reason I have included a chart of RMBS in this section is not to say, "I was right in my initial analysis and here is the proof. - RMBS went up to 248.50," but to bring up the importance of adhering to your trading system and risk management rules. The thing that drives me crazy about traders is that they always tell you about a great pick they had, and how they have left so much money behind. It is always about how much money they leave behind. I used to participate in these conversations myself, and I would share my grief about the trades that got away from me. In fact, I would even do so unintentionally while teaching a seminar. Now, every time I am about to tell a story about a trade that got away from me, I take a deep breath, and I tell myself, "No one really cares!" As they say, "Misery loves company." You might be in pain for letting a big winner go early, and you feel you have to tell the world about it. It is not going to get you anywhere. Stop feeling sorry for yourself. It is impossible to be right all the time. When you are right and

161

you have not capitalized on being right, you are simply wrong.

One of my dear friends bought XYZ stock at 70. The stock went up to 85, and he sold it. He never told me he was in the stock prior to him selling it, and after the stock has already declined back to 75. He was so proud of himself, because he bought it at 70 and sold it at 85, especially after the stock dropped back to 75; consequently, he did everything right. He then said to me, "keep an eye on it and buy it if it trades higher than 85. I have a stop buy order on it at 85 1/2 myself." I never really followed XYZ stock; however, every time I spoke with my friend he would say, "did you see XYZ stock today? It went up a couple of bucks. It is my pick of the year!" A few months go by, and XYZ stock took out the 85 level. It was now at 180. My buddy is glowing. "I told you, it is my pick of the year," he says. XYZ goes up to 240 and announces a 3 for 1 stock split. "It is my pick of the year," my buddy says. The stock ten folds, it was a great pick. My buddy was right.

No! He was wrong! Although he made a great call, he never bought XYZ back once it hit his buy target! It was his pick of the year, and he has zero dollars to show for it. Moral of the story, put your money where your mouth is. Do not use the "I should have done …" phrase. Only speak about your actions, learn from your profits and losses.

The final bell rang and the Nasdaq closed up 20 points for the day. The index gave back most of today's gains, but still managed to close up 143 points from the open. It was a very busy trading day for me. The technical problems this morning set the tone for the day. It was a roller coaster ride in which I finished the day pretty much even. I was very optimistic, trying to let profits ride; however, it proved to be very costly. I still managed all open positions according to all my risk management rules. Unfortunately, it did not yield big dividends today. I felt comfortable to hold NVLS and AMAT overnight.

Open positions: 300 NVLS, 200 AMAT.
Total profit for 4/5/00: -$83.08

Day Thirteen Lessons

Technical problems are a big part of this business.

Learn how to create and trade a basket of stocks.

17

Sitting Tight

DAY FOURTEEN

Thursday, April 6, 2000

The futures were up sharply this morning, and I watched in envy the pre-market trading of my "basket," as it was trading sharply higher. I was holding two semiconductor stocks overnight, NVLS and AMAT. Unfortunately, NVLS announced that they would offer stock for sale to raise 500 Million dollars. Consequently, it was practically flat in pre-market trading, which showed weakness, because most semiconductor stocks were trading up sharply.

I decided to sell my position in NVLS before the opening bell. I sold 300 shares at 52.94.

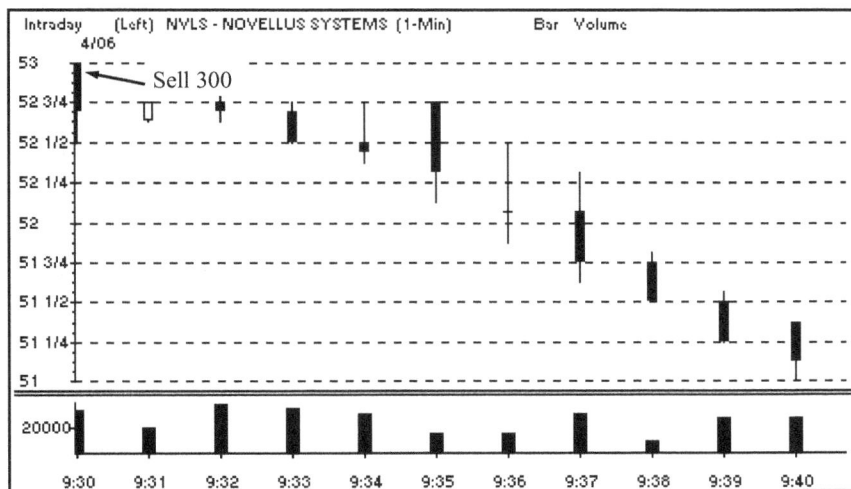

Reprinted with permission of Townsend Analytics, Ltd.

NVLS opened at 53 and fell down hard. The street was not treating NVLS the same way other stocks in the same sector were being treated today. The lack of strength pre-market was a clear signal to get out.

Source	Investment	Proceeds	COM	P&L	Return
Overnight	15,843.75	15,881.25	11.03	26.97	0.17%

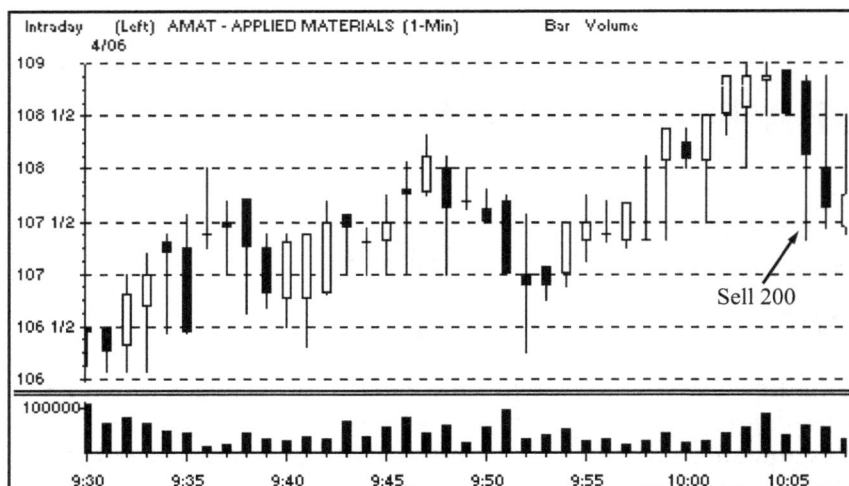

Intraday (Left) AMAT - APPLIED MATERIALS (1-Min)   Bar Volume
4/06

Sell 200

Reprinted with permission of Townsend Analytics, Ltd. Courtesy of MB Trading

Unlike NVLS, AMAT gapped up and ran from the open. I was sitting tight in this trade. I wanted to give AMAT a chance to breakout to a 52-week high. Once AMAT hit 109, I moved my stop loss to 107.75. I felt that the 108 level should hold, but it didn't. AMAT traded down and triggered my stop loss. I sold 200 shares at 107.50.

Source	Investment	Proceeds	MBT	P&L	Return
Overnight	21,191.81	21,500	10.72	297.47	1.40%

Daily (Left) XRX - XEROX CORP   Bar Volume MA (P=50)

Reprinted with permission of Townsend Analytics, Ltd. Courtesy of MB Trading

I have had XRX on my Constant watch list for a while. Today, I noticed that XRX seem to have bottomed two days ago and is now trading up.

164

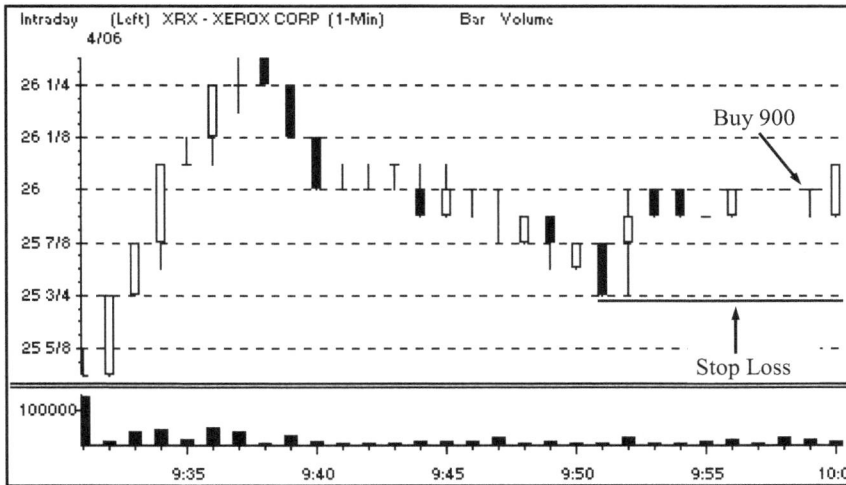

Reprinted with permission of Townsend Analytics, Ltd. Courtesy of MB Trading

XRX ran from the open. It topped at 26.31, then it went down to 25.75 where it found support. It bounced back up to 26, which presented some resistance for the stock. As soon as the offer on the stock went up to 26.06, I entered three limit orders to buy 300 shares. One was priced at 26.06, one was priced at 26.12, and one was priced at 26.18. To my great surprise, I had all three orders filled at 26, so I bought 900 shares of XRX at 26.00. My price target was 28 - 29, and I placed a stop loss at 25.69.

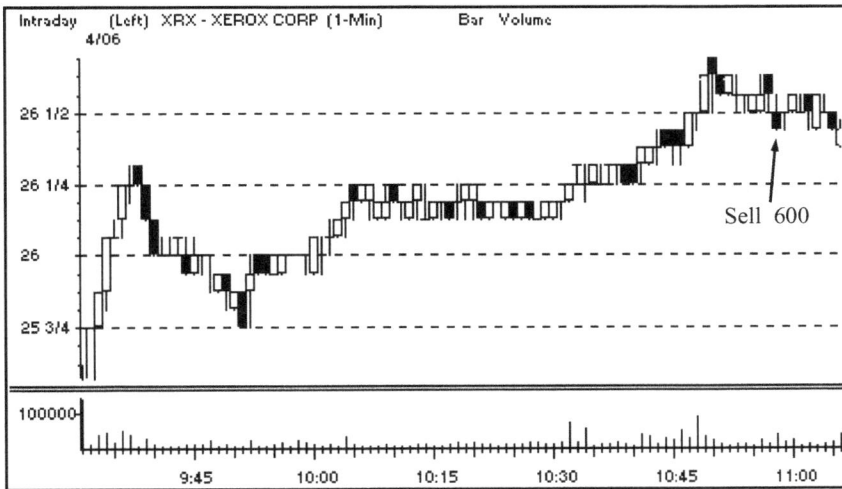

Reprinted with permission of Townsend Analytics, Ltd. Courtesy of MB Trading

XRX topped at 26.75. I remembered how fast things turned around yesterday, so I moved my stop loss for 600 shares to 26.44. XRX traded lower and activated my stop. I sold 600 shares at 26.44.

165

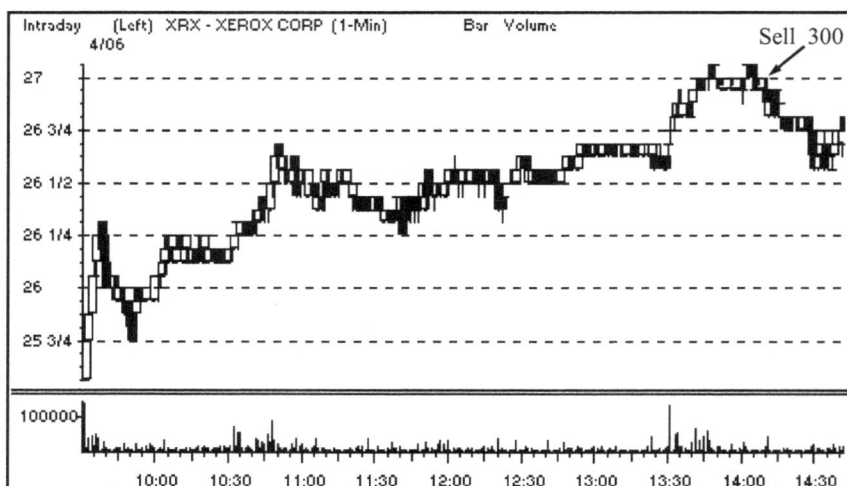

Reprinted with permission of Townsend Analytics, Ltd.

After I sold 2/3 of my XRX position, it traded as low as 26.25. It then moved back up and went as high 27.06. There was a lot of resistance there. The stock tried to take that price level out again, but was failing to do so. I didn't like the signs of weakness, so I sold my last 300 shares at 27.

Source	Investment	Proceeds	COM	P&L	Return
Watch List 1	23,400	23,987.50	25.81	561.69	2.40%

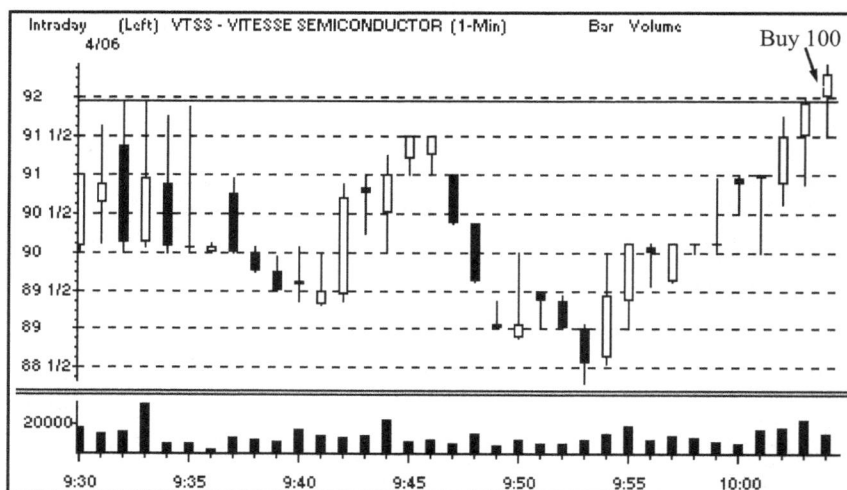

Reprinted with permission of Townsend Analytics, Ltd.

VTSS broke out to a new intraday high. I bought 100 shares at 92.31. This was a pure reaction trade on my part, to a stock that was running. Normally this is a BIG mistake. But the excitement of getting in on a nice run got the best of me and I jumped in without thinking.

166

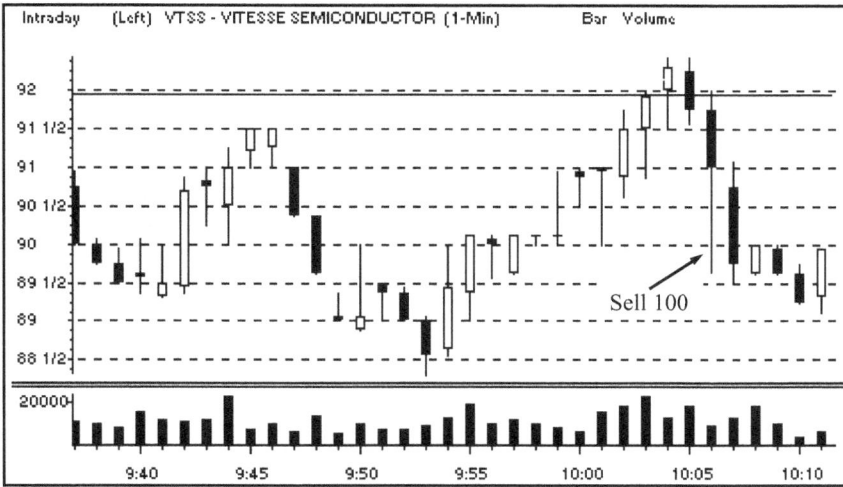

Indeed, it was a mistake. I had to give the trade a lot more wiggle room, than I would give a trade that was entered on a pullback. As VTSS pulled back and traded under 90, I sold 100 shares at 89.94.

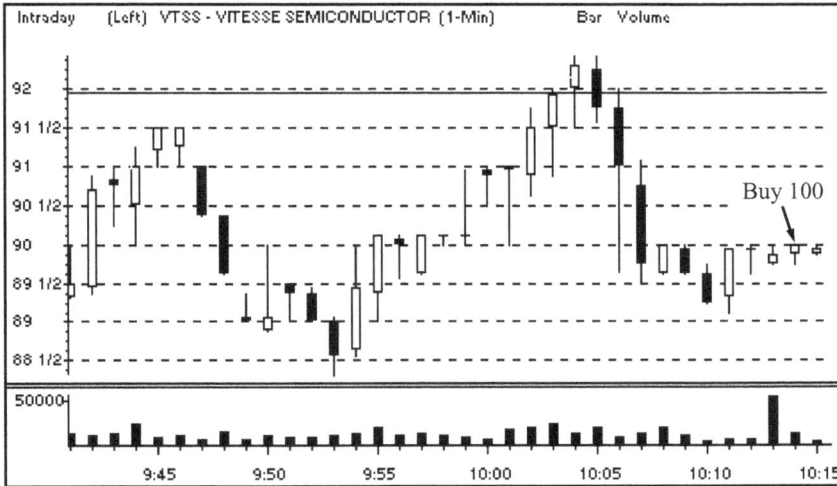

Once VTSS bounced back up from 89.37, I bought 100 shares at 90. My price target was 92 - 95, and I placed my stop loss at 89.25.

167

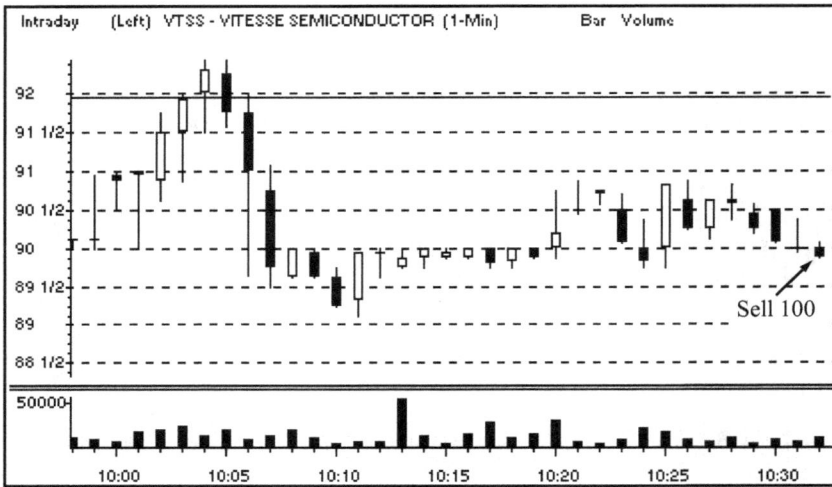

Reprinted with permission of Townsend Analytics, Ltd.

VTSS traded up to 90.75. It was in a trading channel between 89.75 to 90.75. *RSSF* was the Ax on the stock. He was at the inside offer the entire time. Another interesting thing was that *BTRD*, which is an ECN, was constantly at the inside offer as well. It is normal to have an ECN at the inside market; however, *BTRD* would be the only one at the inside showing 100 shares for sale. What caught my attention was that thousands of shares would trade at that price, and *BTRD* was still showing 100 shares. How can it be?

Actually, it happens all the time. There is a fascinating way to deceive traders who use Level II quotes. Let's say I wanted to sell 10,000 shares of XYZ stock. I can place a *RESERVE* (Iceberg/Hidden) order on ARCA to sell 10,000 XYZ stock at 33, showing only 100 shares at a time. My order is hidden. If anyone looked at the Level II montage, they will see 100 shares are available on the offer at 33 on the ARCA ECN. These 100 shares, can trade over 100 times. 100 x 100 = 10,000.

Since I noticed that there was an obvious seller on *BTRD* using reserve orders to hide his hand, I decided to get out of the trade. I sold 100 shares at 89.82.

Source	Investment	Proceeds	COM	P&L	Return
Watch List 1	18,233.35	17,975	22.10	-258.35	-1.42%

168

Reprinted with permission of Townsend Analytics, Ltd

CHKP is on my Constant watch list. It has been moving back up after a 55% pull back in price. It was trading at the high of the day, and I felt that the stock could go back up to the high 190's.

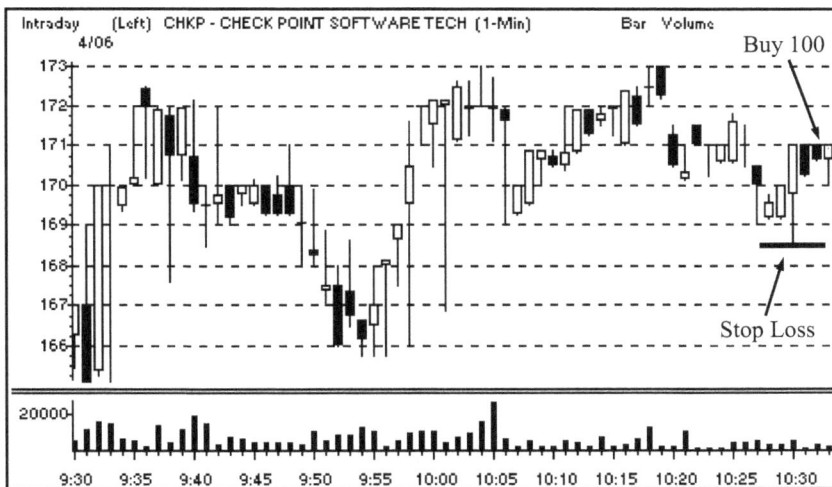

Reprinted with permission of Townsend Analytics, Ltd.

CHKP bounced at the 169 level, which looked to be a decent support level for the stock. I bought 100 shares at 170.87. My price target was 180 - 195. I placed a stop loss at 168.50.

169

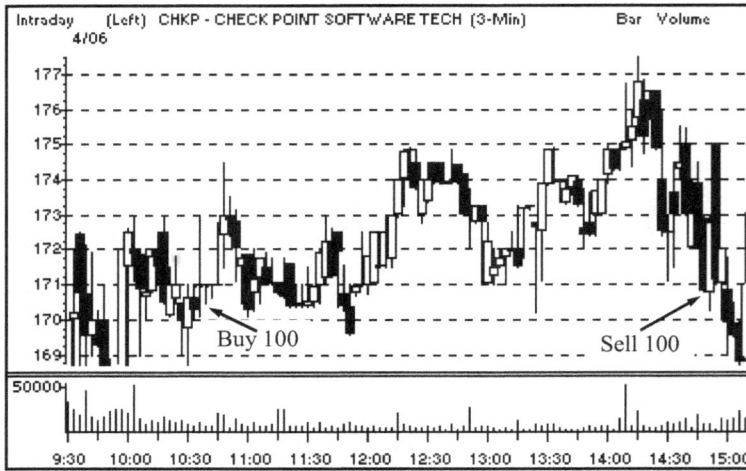

Intraday (Left) CHKP - CHECK POINT SOFTWARE TECH (3-Min)   Bar Volume
4/06

Buy 100   Sell 100

Reprinted with permission of Townsend Analytics, Ltd.

The stock traded up all the way to 177.50. I raised my stop loss to 171. I was going to give this trade the wiggle room it needed as I was a believer that CHKP could easily reach 200 and possibly 220. Was greed clouding my better judgment? Yes! CHKP pulled back down and activated my stop loss. I sold 100 shares at 170.47 I wasn't upset at all. I wanted to give a volatile stock a chance to make me big money, and I ended up sacrificing a few hundred dollars of paper profit for that potential reward.

Source	Investment	Proceeds	COM	P&L	Return
Constant List	17,087.5	17,047.5	10.57	-50.57	-0.30%

Daily (Left) PHCM - PHONE.COM INC   Bar Volume MA (P=50)

Reprinted with permission of Townsend Analytics, Ltd.

PHCM showed up on my Pullback Scan. It has pulled back over 55% from the highs set 3/10/00. I thought the stock could bounce back up to 140 - 160.

170

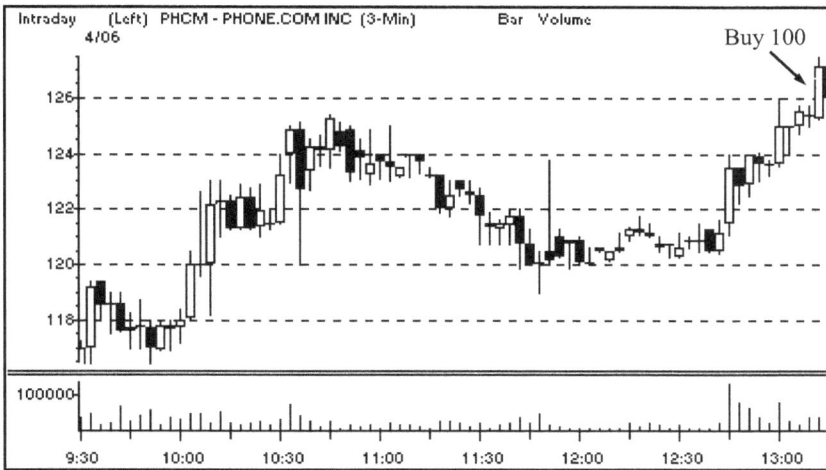

PHCM broke out to a new intraday high. I bought 100 shares at
127.25. My price target was 160. I placed a stop loss below today's low at
116.50. I was going to give PHCM some real wiggle room. I felt I was right
and I should sit tight.

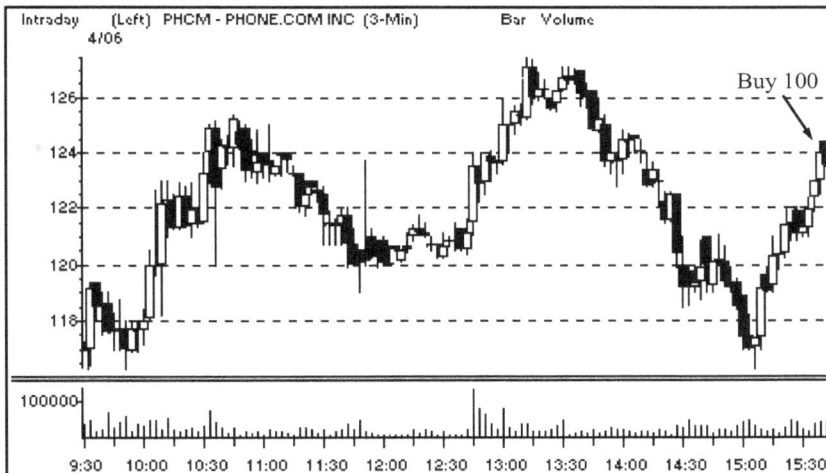

There were a lot of buyers in the stock and one very serious seller.
HMQT was a very active Ax. He sold the stock so hard that it almost took
the low of the day out. Lucky for me, it didn't. The stock bounced up, and I
bought another 100 shares at 12412. The market was in strong rally mode
into the close. However, *HMQT* was selling PHCM hard. He did not let the
stock run with the market. He had to sell today. I have seen many of these
incidents happen, but I was not going to let *HMQT* shake me out of my position, no way! PHCM closed at 118 and was trading at 122 - 125 in after-
hours action. I wasn't worried. I had my money where my mouth was.

The bulls won the battle today as the Nasdaq closed in the green two days in a row. When the final bell rang, the index was up 98 points from yesterday's close. Let's see if we can make it three days in a row, bouncing off the extreme intraday low we hit on Tuesday. I am sitting tight in my PHCM position.

Total profit for 4/6/00: $577.00
Open positions: 200 PHCM

Day Fourteen Lessons

Sitting tight on conviction has its rewards, but only if you keep your stops.

If a stock shows weakness in pre-market trading relative to its sector, consider exiting the trade.

It is important to identify the Ax and to stay out of his way when you day trade; however, if you are entering a longer term swing trade, don't let the Ax shake you out of your position.

CHAPTER 18

Thank God It's Friday

DAY FIFTEEN

Friday, April 7, 2000

I felt very tired this morning. It has been a long week, and I was looking forward to the weekend. The sentiment in the street was very bullish. The market gapped up open and my overnight position looked promising. I was somewhat concerned about next week, which will be the official kickoff of the earnings season. I wrote in my notes for today not to carry any positions over the weekend.

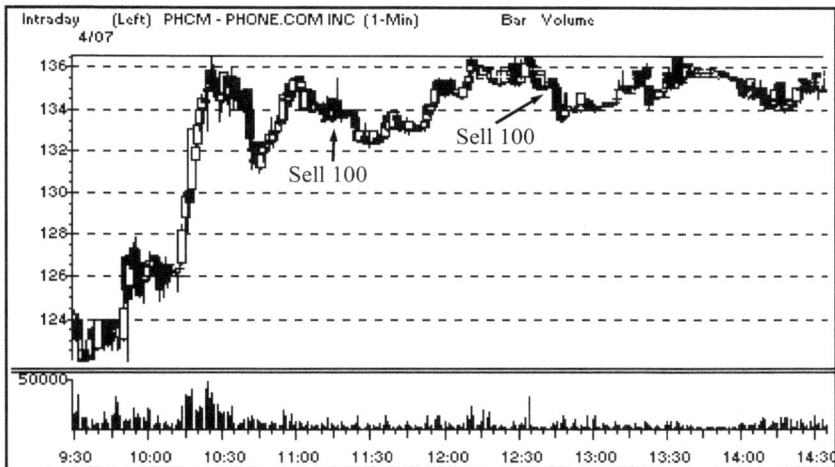

Reprinted with permission of Townsend Analytics, Ltd.

PHCM had a nice run from 122 to 136.50. It pulled back to 131. I was sitting tight. The stock made another run from 131 to 135. I didn't like the fact that the stock could not reach the top, so as it pulled back from 135, I sold 1/2 of my position, 100 shares at 133.62. At 12:15 PM, PHCM went up to 136.50 again and couldn't make a higher high. At 12:35 PM, it hit 136.50 for the third time today and couldn't penetrate through. *HMQT* was back at the inside offer. Since 136.50 was a major resistance level for the stock, I sold 100 shares at 134.75. I didn't like the downside risk at this point.

Source	Investment	Proceeds	COM	P&L	Return
Pullback Scan	25,127.50	26,837.50	20.90	1,689.10	6.72%

173

Once I closed my PHCM position, I decided to call it a day and end the week. I was very happy with my results for the week. I did not see any setup that I wanted to trade, and I wasn't going to risk having a bad trade ru- in my weekend. I wanted to start next week on a strong note, taking off the profits made on my last trade and the entire week.

Open positions: None
Total profit for 4/7/00: $1,689.10

Ding! Ding! The weekend is here signaled the closing bell. The bulls won again, and the Nasdaq was up 178 points from yesterday's close. The Third week of the challenge was over. It was a great week in which I was able to capitalize on some great opportunities. On Monday, I started the week trigger happy, and I ended up basically flat. The Nasdaq was down 349 points that day, so I was very happy that I didn't lose a lot of money. Tues- day was a record volatility day. After I had two losers in SUNW and CIEN, I was finally able to have a good entry on ORCL, CIEN and CSCO. I ended the day with big profits. On Wednesday, I had technical difficulties and frus- trations, which were costly. I was able to turn the day around, but I gave it all back on my basket trade. Thursday was an average day with the regular win- ners and losers. On Friday, I closed my overnight PHCM position and closed the week with a big winner.

My total profits for week three were $5,826.86. I faxed my broker a request for a check in the amount of $6,000.00. After all, Friday is payday!

Southwest Securities 1201 Elm St. Suite 3500. Dallas, TX 75270	SIPC	88-88 1113 214354
	DATE	AMOUNT
PAY ********6,000DOLLARS 00CENTS Pay To	4/ 7/00	$*****6,000.00
TONY OZ LAGUNA HILLS, CA 92654		

Day Fifteen Lesson

Don't risk ending a good week with a bad trade.

174

CHAPTER 19

After-Hours Trading

DAY SIXTEEN

Monday, April 10, 2000

I had a very interesting weekend with my family. My sixteen-year-old brother came to visit me. He is a junior in high school, and he is trying to make the football team for his senior year. The T-shirt he was wearing caught my eye. It said, "Play to win or get off the field."

We were talking about his experiences in training camp, and I was admiring the will power and discipline my brother has been demonstrating. He is determined to make the team this year, but above all, he has faith that he will. I was amazed to hear about the physical and emotional pain his peers have to go through as they are trying to fulfill their dream of dressing up on Friday night and having their number called to get on the field for the next play.

I felt it was pure. There was no money on the line to motivate these young souls; however, there is nothing they want more than to be on the team and play to win. They will give their heart and soul in their effort to be the best they can be. I learned a great lesson this weekend watching the evident pain on my brother's face. What was amazing though, he didn't complain about it even once. On the contrary, I saw pride in his eyes. He is proud of his accomplishments, and above all, he is doing something he truly loves and enjoys.

Although my motivation is not as pure as my brother's, since there is a lot of money on the line in my profession, I still felt that I had something in common with him. We both love, and are proud of, what we do. I truly love trading stocks, and I consider myself very fortunate to be able to do it full-time. If you ever wanted to take on this profession, I think it is very important that you understand that the most important aspect of trading stocks for a living is having fun with it. Do you look forward to the open of the market everyday? Does the market still interest you? You must have a passion for the market and truly enjoy what you are doing. It is no secret that most people can only excel at something they truly enjoy doing.

I did an extensive research this weekend, and I came to the conclusion that the market might be weak over the next few days. The reason I came to this conclusion was simply because the Nasdaq has bounced 800 points from the low it set on Tuesday to the closing number on Friday. This was quite a run, and it may be time for a rest.

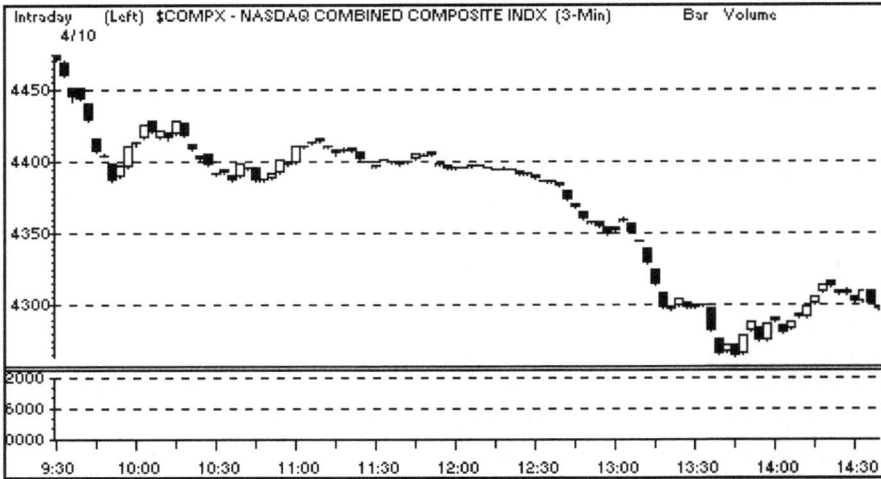

Reprinted with permission of Townsend Analytics, Ltd.

The Nasdaq gapped up and sold off sharply. The classic morning bounce, which took place at 9:50, was weak. The index then flat-lined and traded in a tight channel for two hours. At 12:45, it started to sell off sharply. It found some support around 4270 and started bouncing back up around 1:45.

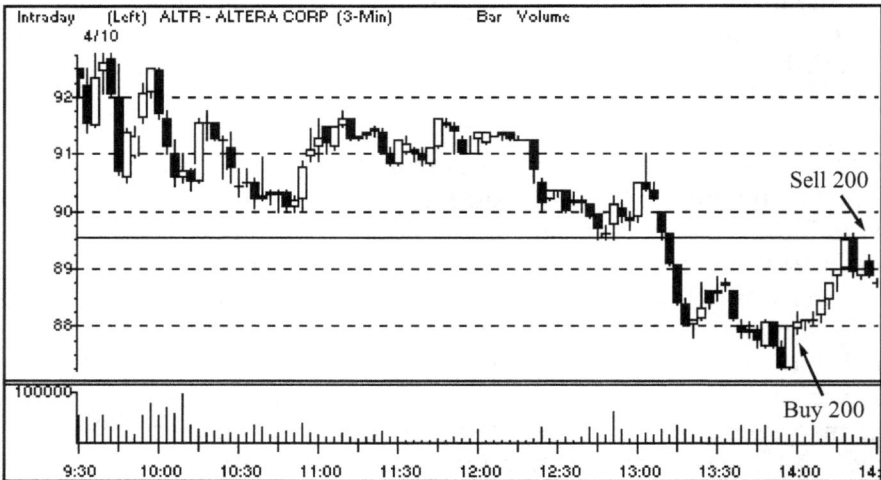

Reprinted with permission of Townsend Analytics, Ltd.

As the index bounced, I bought 200 shares of ALTR at 87.87. I placed my stop loss at 87.12, which was below today's low. My price target

176

was 90 - 92. ALTR traded up to 89.50, which was the previous support level at 12:45 PM. This support level was penetrated and now was acting as resistance. Once I saw ALTR could not break through the resistance level, I sold 200 shares at 89.06.

Source	Investment	Proceeds	COM	P&L	Return
Constant List	17,575	17,812.50	12.10	225.40	1.29%

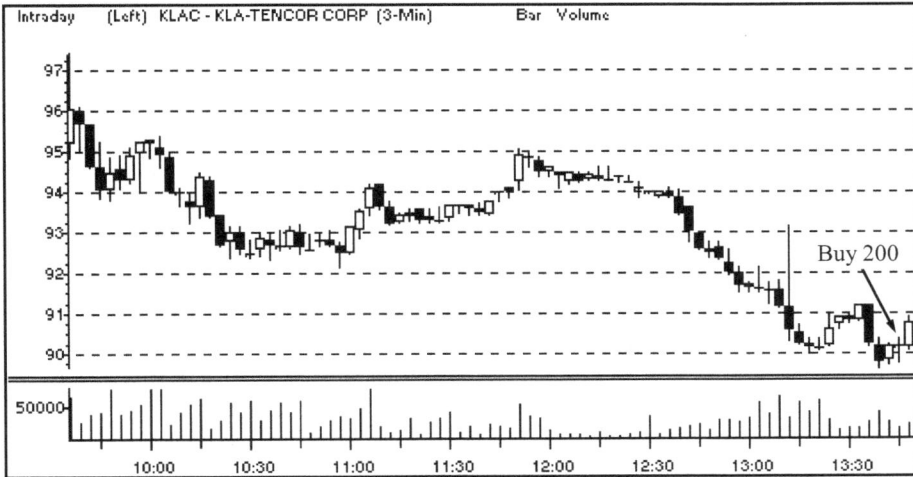

At the same time I was in ALTR, I also bought 200 KLAC at 90.25. My price target was 94. I placed a stop loss at 89.68, which was below today's low.

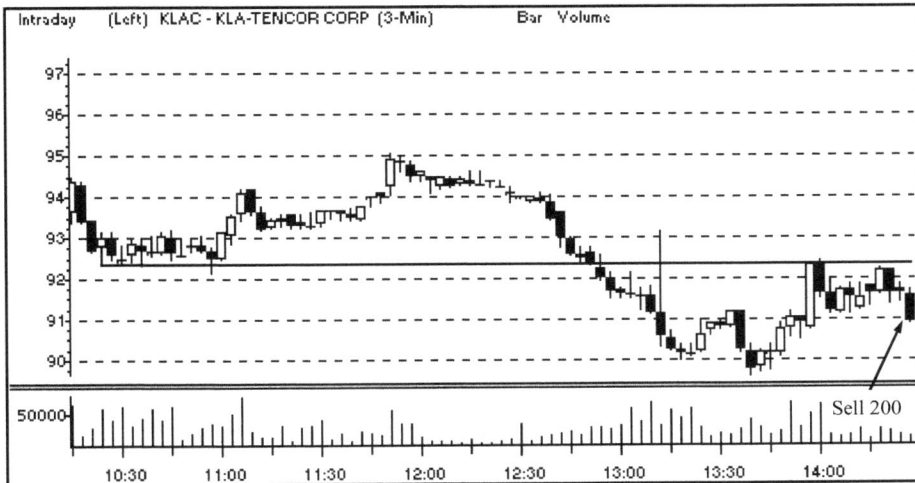

KLAC had a very quick bounce. It went as high as 92.50, which was the price level of the morning lows. It pulled back a little, then tried to make it to that price level again at 2:18, but failed to do so. It turned back down, so I sold 200 shares at 91.12.

Source	Investment	Proceeds	COM	P&L	Return
Constant List	18,050	18,225	10.62	164.38	0.91%

Reprinted with permission of Townsend Analytics, Ltd.

While I was in both ALTR and KLAC, I also bought 200 shares of AAPL at 127.06. My price target was 130 - 131. I placed a stop loss at 125.94, just below today's low.

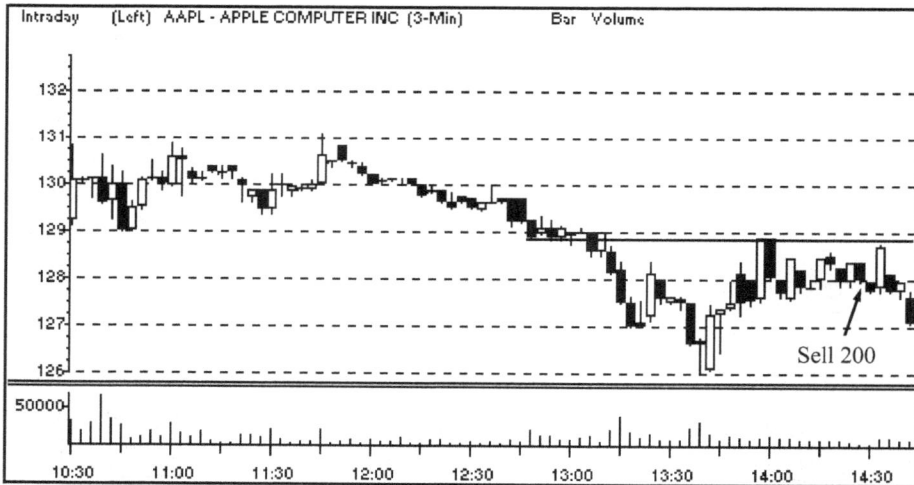

Reprinted with permission of Townsend Analytics, Ltd.

If you watched any of these three examples carefully, support and resistance were classic. AAPL topped at 128.87, which was the bottom of the bear flag it set from 12:45 - 1:10 prior to breaking down. I was hoping to get a little bit more out of each one of these positions than the very next resistance level, so I did not have sell orders ready at those levels. I wanted to give each one of my trades a chance, therefore, I didn't capture the maximum hindsight profits. Once I saw AAPL was struggling, I sold 200 shares at 128.

Source	Investment	Proceeds	COM	P&L	Return
Constant List	25,412.50	25,600	10.86	176.64	0.69%

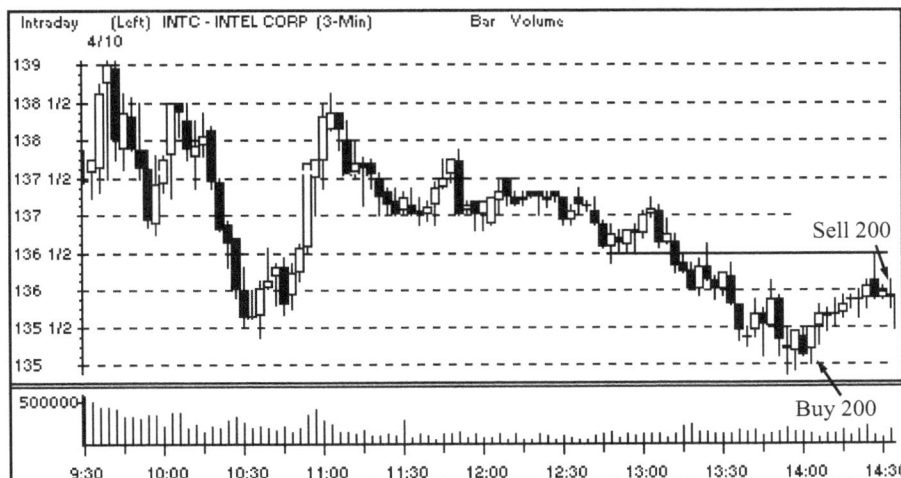

Reprinted with permission of Townsend Analytics, Ltd.

While I was in KLAC, ALTR and AAPL, I also bought 200 shares of INTC at 135.12, also playing a bounce off the bottom. My price target was 136.50, and I had a stop loss placed at 134.75, which was just below today's low. I had been managing four open positions at the same time. INTC ran up to 136.50. I did have a sell order for 200 shares at that price, but, I didn't get picked up. The stock then reversed and traded lower. I cancelled my limit order to sell for 136.50 and sold 200 shares at 135.94.

Source	Investment	Proceeds	COM	P&L	Return
Constant List	27,025	27,187.50	13.92	148.58	0.55%

I closed all four positions, and I made a total profit of $715.00. It was no home run, but it felt good to start the final week of the challenge with four winners. As the challenge was entering its last week, I was feeling more and more relaxed. I would be lying to you if I said there was no added pressure to perform well during these four weeks; however, I felt that I was just doing my usual thing – trying to take money out of the market.

179

When I was planning for this last week of trading, one of my goals was to trade smarter than I did in the previous three weeks. When I log into my trading software every morning, I have to enter my password. I feel that I should tell you what my password is (which means I will have to change it once this book is published). My password is "Trade Smart." This has been a good reminder every morning before I execute my first trade that my first goal in trading is to trade smart.

From the time in which I closed my positions to the closing bell, the market went straight down and closed at the low of the day. The Nasdaq was down 287 points from the open and closed down 258 points from Friday's close. The bears were once more in the driving seat. For obvious reasons, I did not carry any long positions overnight. I managed to have a positive day in a big down market and that was a great feeling. I felt that I traded smart today.

Do You Believe in Free Money?

This is going to make a very interesting lesson; however, I must disclose that I might never again be able to do what I am about to tell you right now, anytime in the future, nor that I was able to do it in the past.

The following is a chart of KLAC. It was the second stock I traded today, and it is a stock I watch on a daily basis. It is on my Constant watch list. I bought KLAC earlier today at 90.25, and I sold it at 91.12 around 2:20. As you can see the stock sold off hard and closed the day at 83.81.

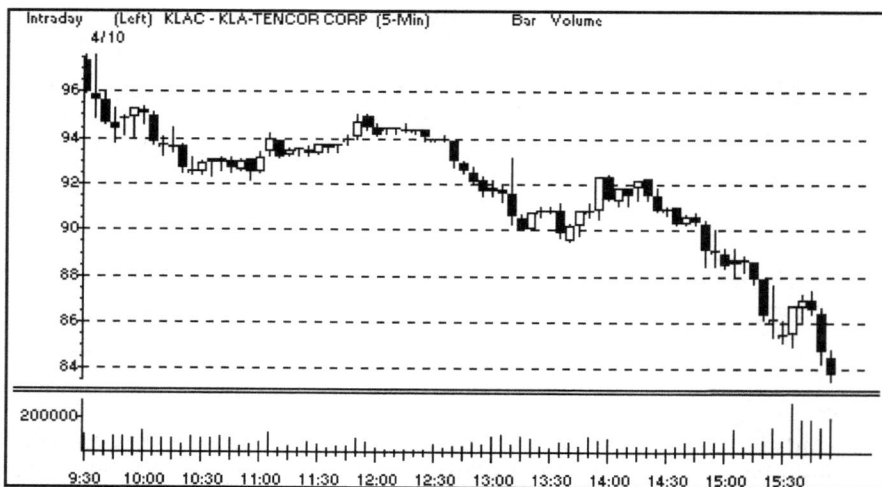

Reprinted with permission of Townsend Analytics, Ltd.

180

After the bell, I was entering my executed trades into my journal. I was watching the after-hours action on the four stocks I traded earlier. KLAC Level II montage looked like this:

KLAC t		V 5,159,300	H 97.62	
POS		**83.81**	L 83.50	
NEWS 4/10/00		-13.62	O -13.50	

Name	Bid	Size	Name	Ask	Size
REDI	81	100	ISLD	84.87	100
ISLD	80	200	REDI	85	600
INCA	80	300	INCA	85	700

The spread opens up after-hours, because the market is not very liquid. The best bid for KLAC as shown on the Level II montage is at 81 for 100 shares on the REDI ECN. The second best bid is for 200 shares on ISLD ECN at 80, and for 300 shares on INCA ECN. The best offer is at 84.87 for 100 shares on ISLD ECN. The second best offer is at 85. There are 600 shares offered at that price on REDI ECN, and 700 shares offered at that price on INCA ECN.

Something very interesting happened next. There was someone who really wanted to buy KLAC, and there was someone who really wanted to sell KLAC. They both entered orders almost simultaneously. This is what the Level II montage looked like.

KLAC t		V 5,159,300	H 97.62	
POS		**83.81**	L 83.50	
NEWS 4/10/00		-13.62	O -13.50	

Name	Bid	Size	Name	Ask	Size
INCA	84	2000	ISLD	81.12	800
REDI	81	100	REDI	85	600
ISLD	80	200	INCA	85	700

I couldn't believe my eyes. Before you could say "click," I already clicked on the offer, and bought 300 shares at 81.12 on ISLD. I immediately clicked on the bid and sold 300 shares at 84 using ARCA.

Source	Investment	Proceeds	COM	P&L	Return
Constant List	24,337.50	25,200	15.34	847.16	3.48%

The Level II montage looked like this for another fraction of a second or so:

KLAC t	V 5,159,300	H 97.62
POS	**83.81**	L 83.50
NEWS 4/10/00	-13.62	O -13.50

Name	Bid	Size	Name	Ask	Size
INCA	84	1700	ISLD	81.12	500
REDI	81	100	REDI	85	600
ISLD	80	200	INCA	85	700

I did it again, buy 300 at 81.12 on ISLD, sell 300 at 84 on ARCA. After these orders were executed, the Level II montage looked like this:

Source	Investment	Proceeds	COM	P&L	Return
Constant List	24.335.50	25,200	15.34	847.16	3.48%

KLAC t	V 5,159,300	H 97.62
POS	**83.81**	L 83.50
NEWS 4/10/00	-13.62	O -13.50

Name	Bid	Size	Name	Ask	Size
INCA	84	1400	ISLD	81.12	200
REDI	81	100	REDI	85	600
ISLD	80	200	INCA	85	700

Three time is a charm. Buy 300 at 81.12, I only got 200 shares filled, because that was all that was left on ISLD. Sell 200 shares at 84 on ARCA.

Source	Investment	Proceeds	COM	P&L	Return
Constant List	16,225	16,800	13.56	561.44	3.46%

After the last order was executed, the Level II montage looked like this:

KLAC t		V 5,159,300	H 97.62		
POS		**83.81**	L 83.50		
NEWS 4/10/00		-13.62	O -13.50		
Name	**Bid**	**Size**	**Name**	**Ask**	**Size**
INCA	84	1200	ISLD	84.87	100
ISLD	81.12	(100)	REDI	85	600
REDI	81	100	INCA	85	700

The 100 shares circled on the Bid on ISLD were the left over of my last order to buy 300 shares on ISLD. I cancelled the order for the remaining shares.

That was a lot of fun wasn't it? I realize that many of you are confused and don't understand exactly what took place. To simplify things, think of it as two different exchanges. I bought KLAC from one exchange, and I sold it on another exchange for a higher price, because the buyers there were willing to pay more. You probably noticed that my orders were entered in multiple of 300 shares. The reason is that my default was set that way. I was not going to try and change the number of shares in my default, that would have taken a few precious seconds and would have possibly taken the opportunity away. I had to be fast.

I agree this is not exactly free money, but it wasn't my birthday, so it felt like it was. I felt that this is going to be a great week. I'm sure that I would be talking about this last trade for a long time. It would be very challenging to try and explain it to my wife tonight.

Open positions: None
Total profit for 4/10/00: $2,970.76

183

Day Sixteen Lessons

Your number one goal is to trade smart.

The after-hours market is inefficient, so be careful when you place orders after-hours.

20

Nasdaq Looking for Support

DAY SEVENTEEN

Tuesday, April 11, 2000

The sell off yesterday indicated that caution must be taken today. The Nasdaq closed at the low of the day, which indicated that there was an 80% chance of making a lower low today. Anytime an index closes at the bottom 10% of its day's trading range, there is an 80% chance of making a lower low the following day. If an index closes at the top 10% of its day's trading range, there is an 80% chance it will make a higher high the following day. The higher high or the lower low can take place anytime during the day, so these stats do not necessarily imply that the index will actually gap open to that higher high or a lower low.

The futures were down sharply this morning and tech stocks were trading lower in pre-market trading. When the opening bell rang, the Nasdaq opened down 94 points. I was in my sniper position watching my Constant list of stocks for a buy-the-dip opportunity.

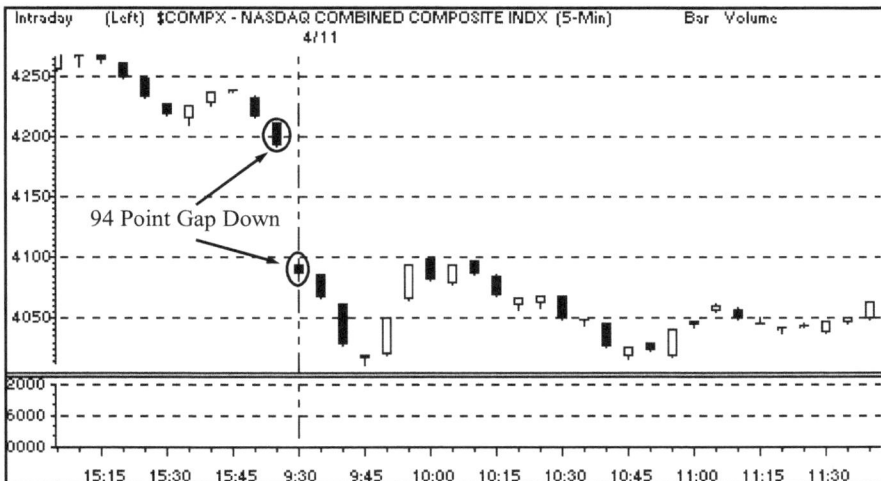

Reprinted with permission of Townsend Analytics, Ltd.

Following its 94 point gap down, the Nasdaq sold off another 85 points within the first 15 minutes, and was down 179 points from yesterday's close. The Index found support at 4015, and turned back up. 4100 was about where it opened, and served as resistance around 10:00. The index turned back down, again, to the 4020 level. We were now in a defined channel between 4015 which is the support level and 4100 which is the resistance level.

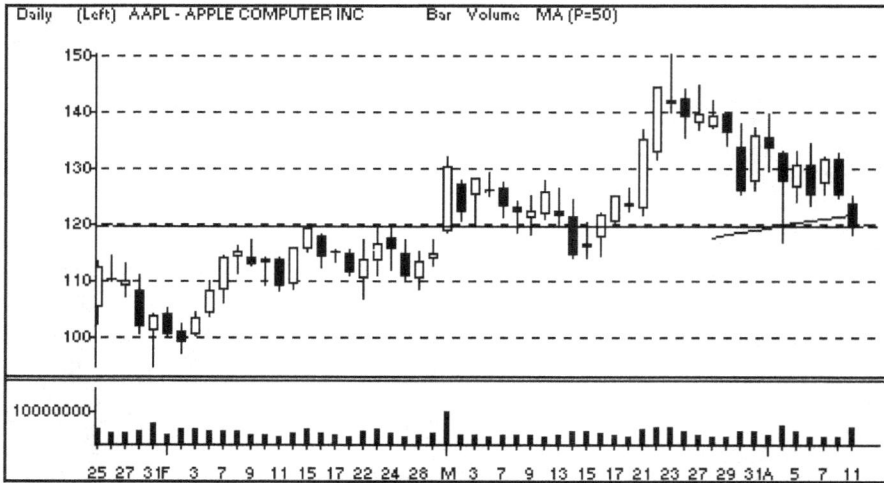

Reprinted with permission of Townsend Analytics, Ltd.

AAPL was trading around 120. It just broke under its 50-day moving average, and I felt that the 120 level should be good support for the stock. If that level is to hold, I felt that AAPL should go back to the 132 level, which was the top area during the previous four days and in the beginning of March.

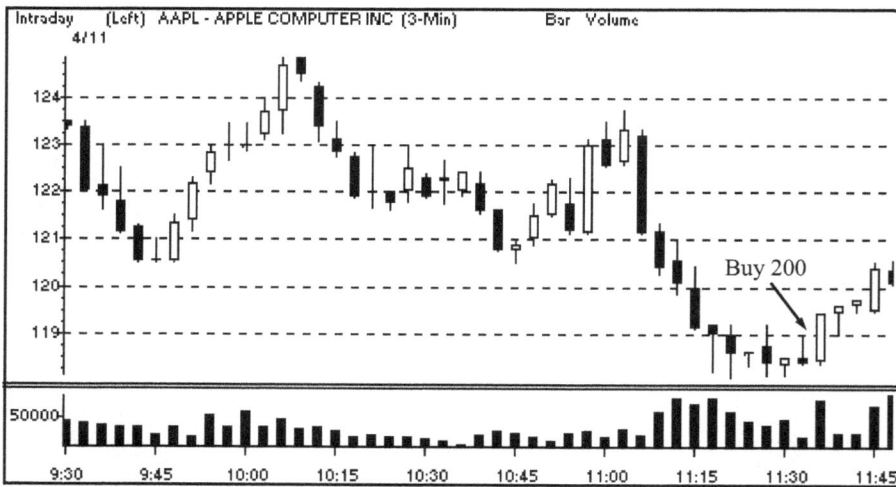

Reprinted with permission of Townsend Analytics, Ltd.

The Nasdaq held the 4020 level and started to move back up. AAPL seemed to have found a bottom as well. Note how the volume was drying up from 11:15 - 11:35. The volume increased and AAPL penetrated through 119. I bought 200 shares at 119.06. My price target was 122 - 130. I placed a stop loss at 118.12, which was below today's low.

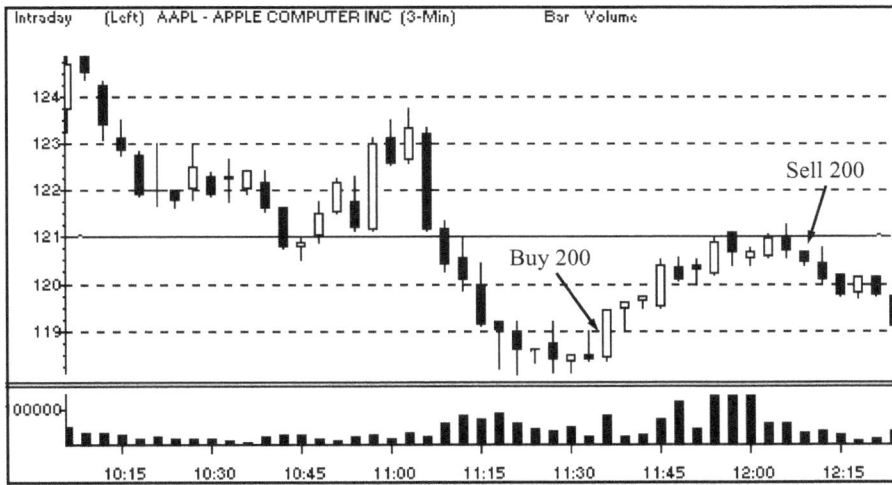

Reprinted with permission of Townsend Analytics, Ltd.

AAPL hits the first level of resistance at 121.12 at 11:57 and turns back down slightly. I am giving it a little bit of wiggle room at this point. The stock makes another attempt to take out the resistance level at 12:06 but is only able to trade 0.06 higher than the high at 11:57. This was a sign of weakness, so I sold 200 shares at 120.57.

Source	Investment	Proceeds	COM	P&L	Return
Constant List	23,812.50	24,112.50	10.81	289.20	1.21%

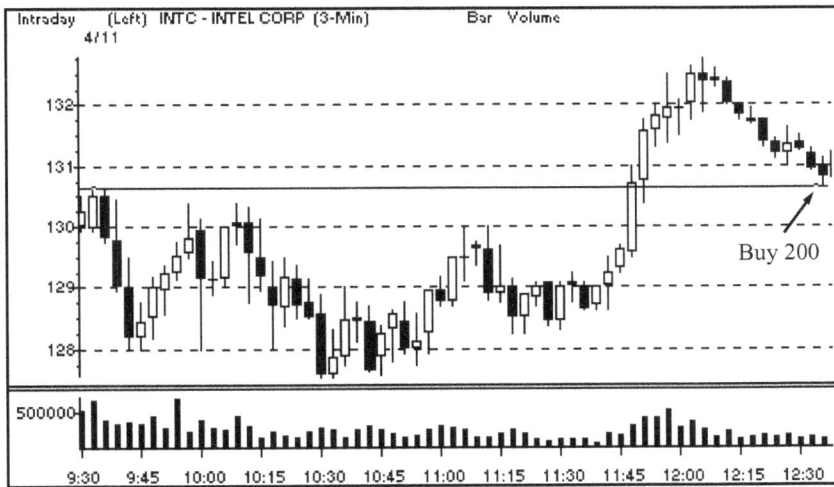

Reprinted with permission of Townsend Analytics, Ltd.

INTC had a strong showing. Once the Nasdaq bounced, INTC out-performed it and broke out to a new intraday high at 11:55. I was waiting for INTC to pull back. I had a buy limit order in at 130.81, which was 0.12 high-er than the morning top (9:30). INTC pulled back and I got a fill. I bought 200 shares at 130.81. I placed a stop loss at 129.94.

187

Reprinted with permission of Townsend Analytics, Ltd.

INTC bounced at the support level of 130.75. It was gaining momentum, and it penetrated through 132. The action on the Level II screen suggested that INTC had lost momentum. I moved my trailing stop up to 131.94. INTC went under 132, and I sold 200 shares at 131.94.

Source	Investment	Proceeds	COM	P&L	Return
Constant List	26,162.50	26,387.50	10.88	214.12	0.82%

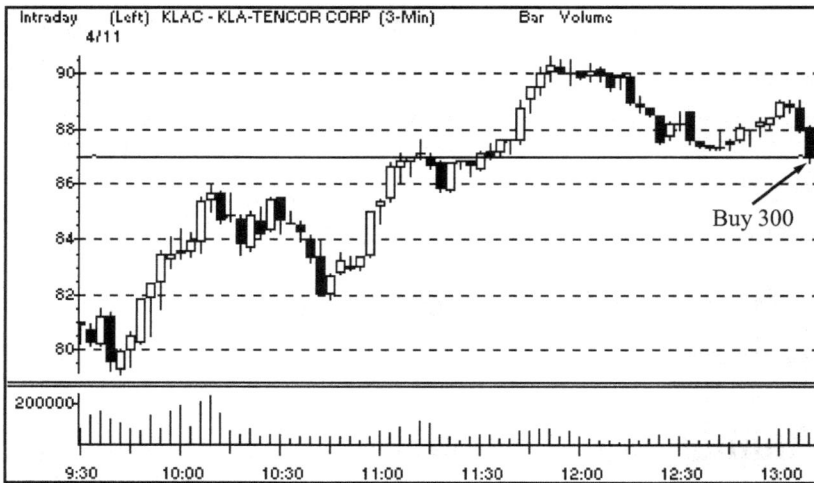

Reprinted with permission of Townsend Analytics, Ltd.

KLAC pulled back from the day high of 90, and was trying to bounce at the support level created by the tops it had between 11:00 - 11:45. I bought 300 shares at 87.62. I placed a stop loss at 85.94, which was just below the high the stock made at 10:06. My price target was 92.50, which was resistance when I traded it the previous day.

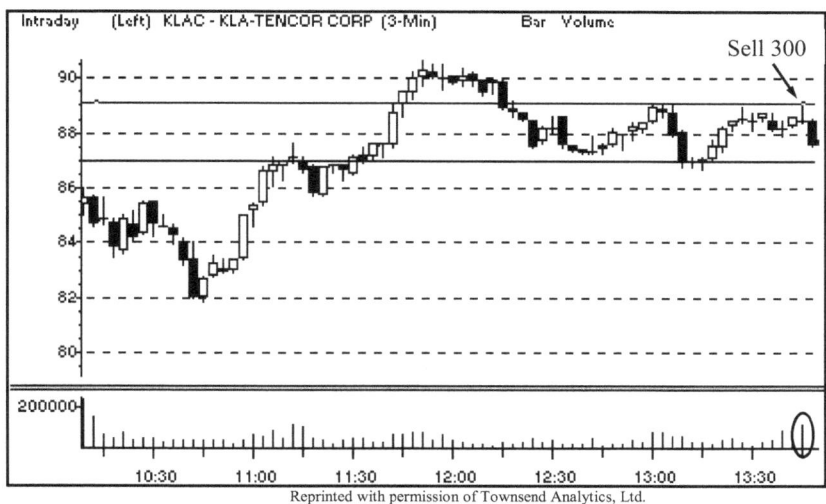

Intraday (Left) KLAC - KLA-TENCOR CORP (3-Min)   Bar Volume

Sell 300

Reprinted with permission of Townsend Analytics, Ltd.

KLAC bounced at support, but it hit resistance at 88.87 around 1:30. Fifteen minutes later, the stock traded through 88.87, but could not go through 89. *MSCO* was axing the stock at 89. He was the only one at the inside offer. Note the volume spike when KLAC was trying to take out the resistance. Once I saw that *MSCO* was not likely to leave his inside offer position, the stock started to tick down, and I sold 300 shares at 88.62.

Source	Investment	Proceeds	COM	P&L	Return
Constant List	26,287.50	26,587.50	10.90	289.10	1.10%

I have just completed my third trade of the day, and I was up almost $800.00. It was a great feeling. My confidence level was very high as I have completed ten trades this week without a loser. I wanted to enjoy the moment, so I went down to my balcony for some fresh air. Prior to me leaving the trading desk, the market started to sell off.

As I was watching the kids playing in the school yard down the mountain, I was recapping everything that has been taking place during this challenge. I was trying to analyze my performance so far and compare it to my expectation levels prior to entering this challenge. Although the dollars and cents do make all the difference in the world, the two most important things I wanted to accomplish were not to break any rules, and to trade smart. I really believed the rest would take care of itself.

At the end of every trading day, I asked myself if I had broken any of the rules and if I was trading smart. And, with three and a half days left in the challenge, I was asking myself whether the rest actually did take care of itself. I then remembered that it is not over until the fat lady sings, and I had better walk upstairs and see if I can find high probability setups. I felt really good as I was making my way to my trading desk.

189

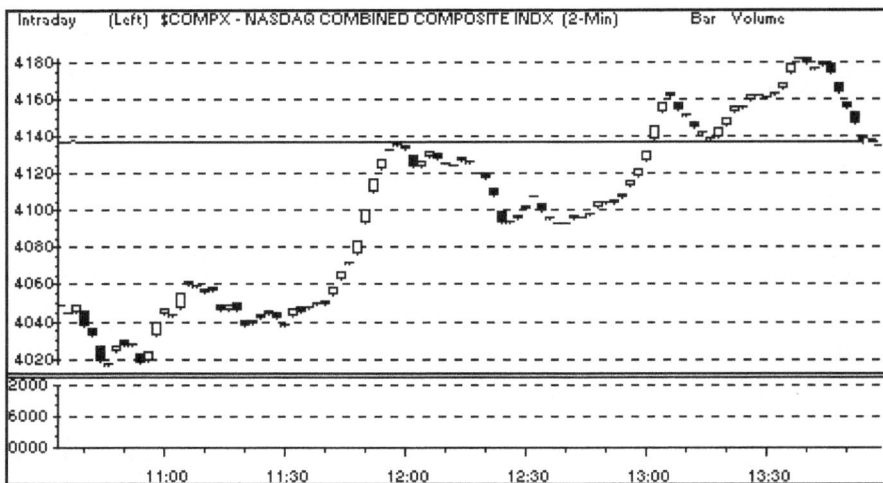

While I was downstairs for the last 10 minutes, the Nasdaq pulled
back from its high. It was hitting intraday support levels, which I felt should
hold.

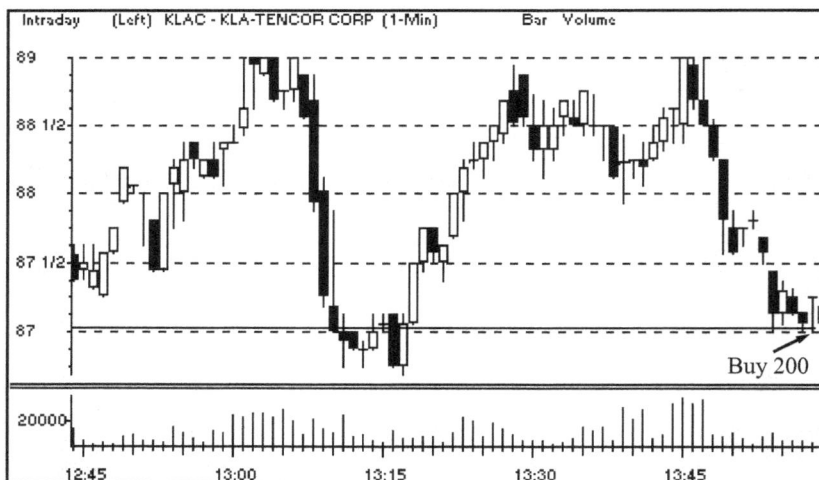

I still had KLAC on my primary order entry Level II screen, and as
the Nasdaq was hitting the support level at 4138, KLAC was trying to
bounce at 87 or so. I bought 200 shares of KLAC at 87.06. Note that KLAC
was also trading in a channel between 87 to 89. If KLAC bounces with the
Nasdaq, I can expect it to go to 89 again. My conditional stop loss was
placed at Nasdaq 4132.

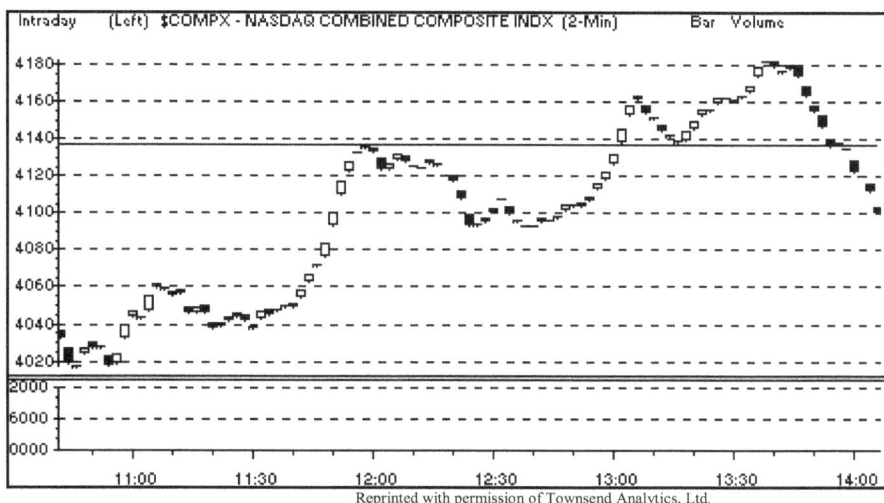

Reprinted with permission of Townsend Analytics, Ltd.

The Nasdaq broke down through the support level.

Sell 200

Reprinted with permission of Townsend Analytics, Ltd.

As the index took out the 4132 level, my stop loss was activated. I sold 200 shares at 86.78.

Source	Investment	Proceeds	COM	P&L	Return
Constant List	17,412.50	17,356.25	10.29	-66.83	-0.38%

My perfect week was now over. I have taken my first loss of the week. But I did not feel bad about it at all, because I executed according to the rules and guidelines of my trading plan. The trade answered the criteria prior to entering it, so it wasn't a loss caused by breaking the rules.

191

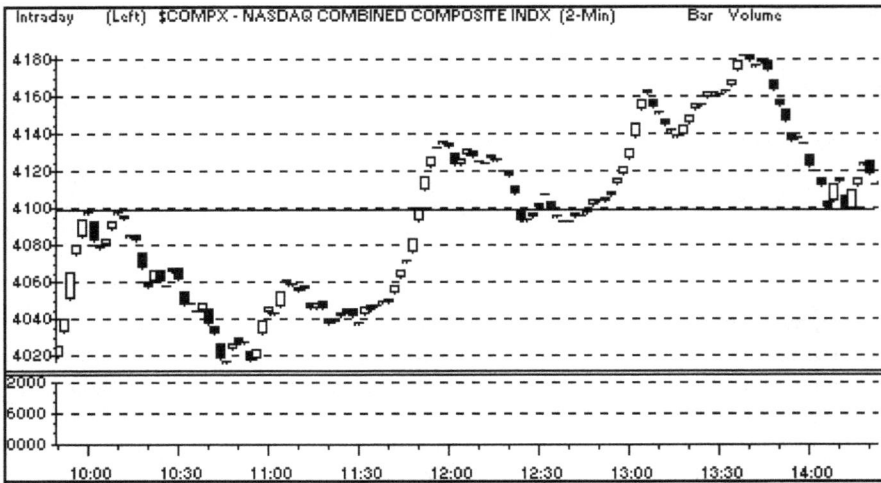

Reprinted with permission of Townsend Analytics, Ltd.

The Nasdaq found support at the morning highs - 4100. I bought 200 shares of INTC at 132.25 when I saw that the 4100 level was holding. INTC went as high as 133, then started to pull back. I sold 200 shares at 132.56. Unfortunately, we only captured the Nasdaq chart at the time. However, it was the Nasdaq chart that prompted both the entry and exit of this trade as shown above.

Source	Investment	Proceeds	COM	P&L	Return
Constant List	26,450	26,512.50	10.89	51.61	0.19%

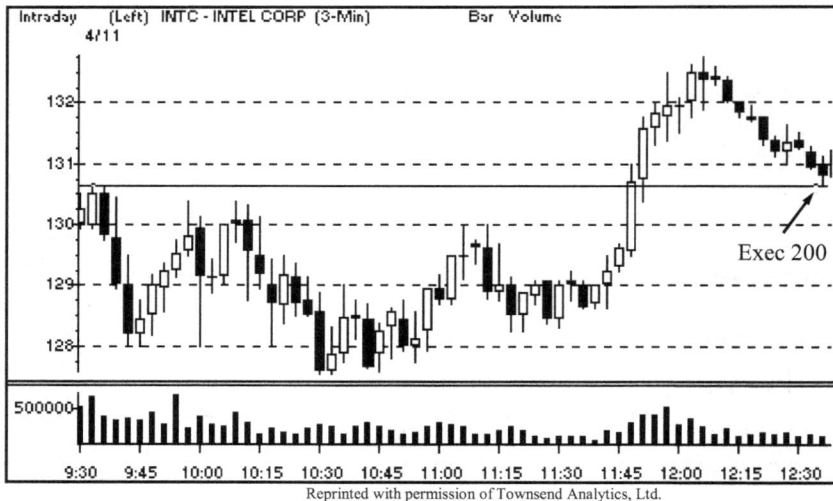

Reprinted with permission of Townsend Analytics, Ltd.

Do you remember my second trade of the day, in which I bought INTC at 130.81, which was just above support? I will be trying to make the exact trade again. Note the 130.50 morning high is the support level I was playing off earlier.

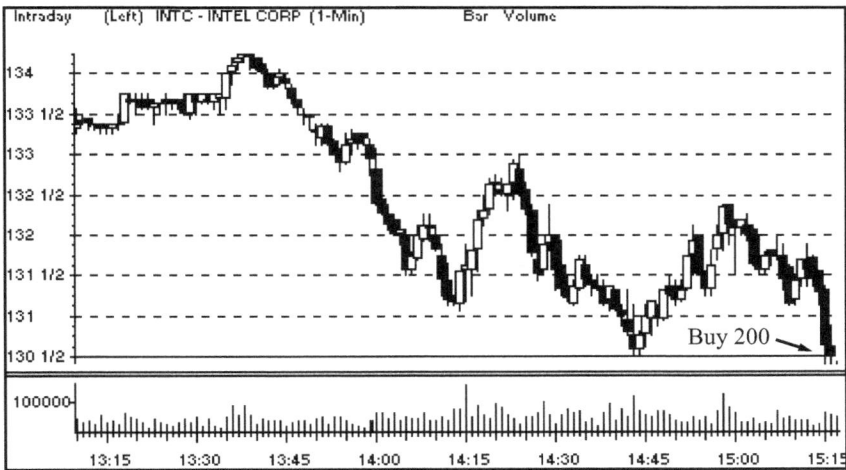

Reprinted with permission of Townsend Analytics, Ltd.

INTC traded back down to support. I bought 200 shares at 130.62. I placed a stop loss at 129.50. My price target was 133 - 134.

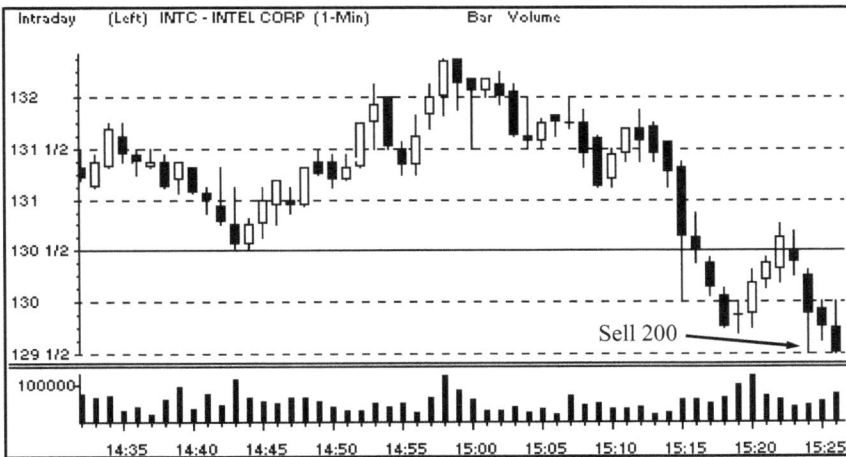

Reprinted with permission of Townsend Analytics, Ltd.

The trading Gods were not answering my prayers this time. INTC bid hits 129.50, and I was stopped out of my position. There was so much size at 129.50, that it was painful to see my stop loss order go live and sell me out of the trade. In fact, all the ECNs were lined up to buy INTC at 129.50, and I got a price improvement of 0.03 on my order. I sold 200 INTC at 129.53, only to watch it begin racing back up to 133.50 over the next 25 minutes. My stop loss got me out at the absolute low! Can you feel my pain?

Source	Investment	Proceeds	COM	P&L	Return
Constant List	26,125	25,906.25	13.87	-232.62	-0.89%

193

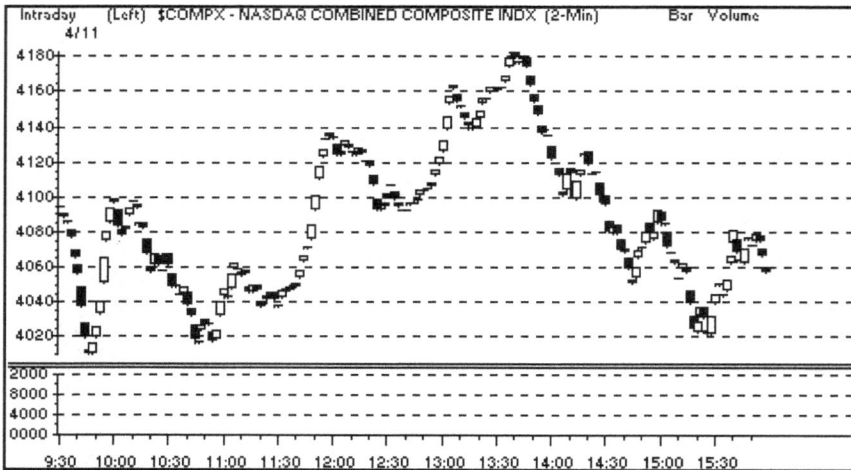

Reprinted with permission of Townsend Analytics, Ltd.

I really liked the fact that the Nasdaq held the 4015 - 4020 level. I felt that it might have found support, and I was willing to put my money where my mouth was. I was going to carry a long position overnight. My stop loss on the position will be if the Nasdaq breaks below 4000.

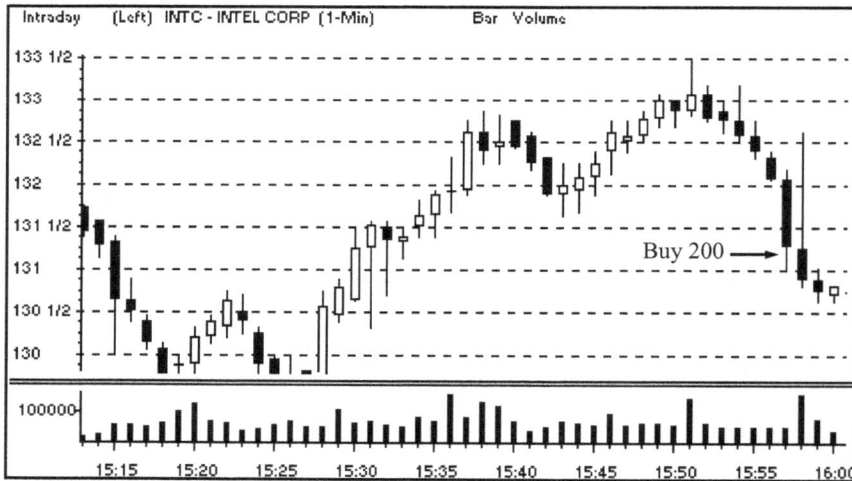

Reprinted with permission of Townsend Analytics, Ltd.

I chose to buy INTC, because it showed strength all day. In case you didn't feel my pain when I sold INTC at 129.50 at 3:25, please look at the above chart and see for yourself how every uptick was pulling another hair out of my balding head.

I bought 200 INTC at 131.20 and took it to bed. I felt really good about Nasdaq's ability to hold 4000. I am going to make a killing on this trade tomorrow, which will more than make up for the last loss I took on it.

194

The bears are still in the driver's seat as the Nasdaq lost 132 points from yesterday's close. In this down market, I felt that I was trading very well, yet I wasn't making oodles of money. I think I was still riding high from Monday's after-hours trading. In any case, I did have five winners and two losers today. The last trade I made was a close call as the stock bottomed exactly where my stop loss was placed. However, I managed risk according to my plan, so I couldn't be upset about it even though INTC hit my initial price target. It is very painful when it happens, but tomorrow is a new day.

Open positions: 200 INTC
Total profit for 4/11/00: $577.00

Day Seventeen Lessons

Never get over confident.

You will at times sprint (sell) the absolute low.

CHAPTER 21

Sweet Dream or a Nightmare

DAY EIGHTEEN

Wednesday, April 12, 2000

There were times in my career when I slept in and woke up ten minutes before or even after the opening bell. It is not a major problem if I am not holding a position overnight, but if I am, I am in big trouble. I will find myself running upstairs to my office, start my trading program, and react to the first tick I see. I will lose all the strategy I originally had for the trade for the simple reason that I was not AWAKE yet. These scenarios, although rare, are comparable to trading stocks in your sleep, and more often than not, it is a nightmare. To avoid this common mistake, give yourself enough time in the morning, so you are alert when the market opens.

I had a very interesting dream last night in which I was trading very actively. I was buying and selling stocks at lightning speed and my P&L was showing great profits. At some point, I noticed that XYZ stock, which I have sold earlier in the day, was up 60 points from the price I thought I sold it at; however, instead of actually selling the stock, I bought more, and I was now holding 2000 shares. My open P&L was reading +$120,000.

As soon as I realized that I still owned the stock, I was trying to sell it. But the stock was falling down fast now, and I couldn't get out. It was down 80 points since I tried to sell it, and I am now down $40,000 on my position. The stock now turns around and races up. I am trying frantically to cancel my order. I can't get it to cancel! The stock is up 100 points, it is flying. I finally got a confirmation that my order was cancelled. The stock is up 150 points, but I don't see it in my position window. I look at the confirmation screen, and it says that I sold it for $150,000 loss. How can this be? There is something wrong. I saw a confirmation that my order was cancelled, what is going on? Can someone help me?! Please help me! I can't afford to lose this much.

Suddenly, I wake up. I am very nervous. It was just a dream, "Relax," I tell myself. I take a deep breath. But something looked very odd. The sun was up and it was very bright. I turned my head around and glanced at the alarm clock. "Oh my God!" I screamed. It is 6:48 AM. I slept in. The market is open, and I held INTC overnight!!! I jumped out of bed as if I was bitten by a rattle snake. I raced up the stairs on my way to my trading desk. "How could I have done this?" I was thinking to myself. How am I going to explain to everyone that I slept in? I broke the rules. The challenge is over. All the hard work is flushed down the toilet. It took me about three and a half hours to start my trading software, at least it seemed that long. INTC was down to 129. I didn't even try to analyze what was going on. I entered an order to sell 200 shares at the market on ARCA.

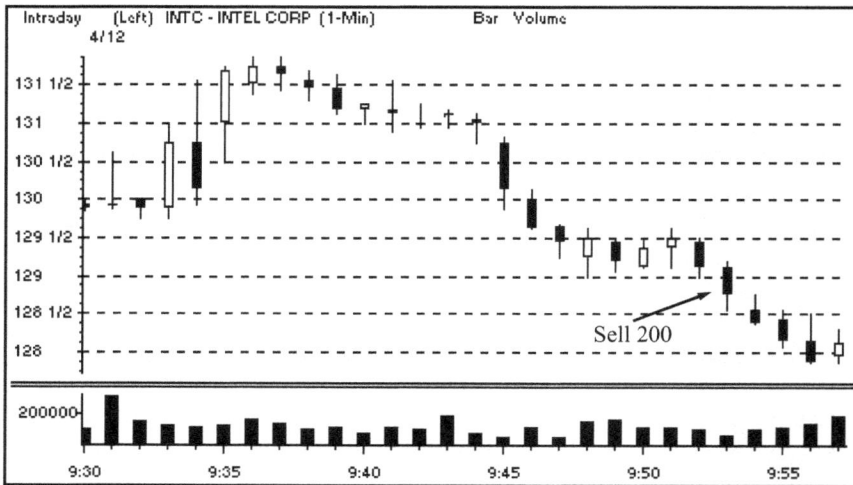

Reprinted with permission of Townsend Analytics, Ltd.

I sold 200 shares at 128.34, and at first, I didn't know if I was awake or if I was sleeping, but I knew one thing for sure. It was a nightmare.

Source	Investment	Proceeds	COM	P&L	Return
Constant List	26,240.62	25,668.75	13.86	-585.62	-2.23%

I was certainly wide awake now! All I had to do was look at my P&L for the day then glance at the INTC chart and see that I would have been in-the-green on this trade had I not slept in. Staring at this harsh reality was like splashing ice-cold-water in my face.

I decided to quit for the day. I was not in the right mental state of mind to continue trading, so I went back downstairs and spent some time with my two-year-old son before he had to go to school. About 45 minutes went by, and my wife took my son and left the house.

I went back upstairs and sat at my computer. The Nasdaq was down 200 points from yesterday's close. It penetrated through support at 4000 and was trading at 3855. I felt that I should have an opportunity to make some of my losses back. All I wanted was to wipe out the loss I suffered on INTC. I wanted to break even, so I could forgive myself for making a human error and sleeping in this morning. Obviously, I was very frustrated with myself, and I knew I just need one chance to turn the day around. "C'mon, give me a good setup," I yelled at my computer.

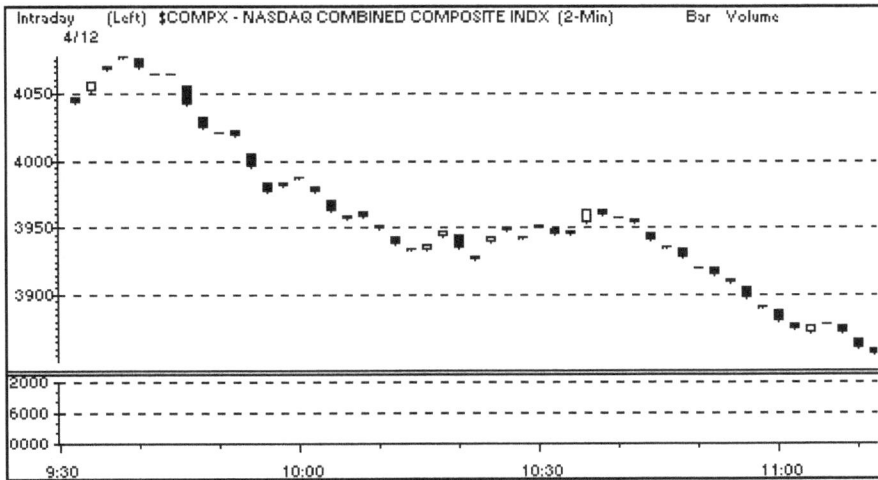

Reprinted with permission of Townsend Analytics, Ltd.

The above chart shows the activity on the Nasdaq from the open to the point when I went back upstairs. It is amazing how humans' defense mechanism works when they screw-up. And that was exactly what I did, and I was trying to make all the excuses, but deep inside I knew that I was at fault.

Taking the Blame

If you have been in the business long enough and have talked to day traders, you must have heard horror stories of big losses a day trader suffered because something that was outside of his control took place. I couldn't tell you how many times I have heard these type of stories told by numerous day traders over the years. At one of the Day traders of Orange County meetings, a day trader was telling one of these stories. He told us that he took a short position in EGRP, and the next day the stock went to the moon. He wanted to cover his position, but his browser-based brokerage firm was down all day, and he could not get them on the phone; consequently, he lost his entire account. I felt really bad for this day trader who caught a really bad break and lost all his money. However, a fellow trader who stood next to me, said, "I don't feel sorry for you, it is all your fault!" At first, I was surprised to hear what this guy said as it wasn't very compassionate at all, but then he said, "Tony, I am fed up with these idiots who come here and tell us how they lost all their money and it wasn't their fault." I was listening really carefully as this guy turned to the day trader who told us the story and said, "You want to know why it was your fault? Well, first, you put twice the

199

equity you had in your account into ONE stock - that is very stupid. Next, you chose to trade with a browser based broker, obviously you did not do enough research to see what happens if your broker goes down. Finally, judging from your personality, you wouldn't have taken the loss and cut your position, because you were already down so much money in the position. You had no plan that you were trading with, i.e. no price target or stop loss. Frankly, I think you were in denial the entire time and as a result, blew out your account."

The day trader who just got the "speech" from the guy who stood next to me, cursed at him and walked away. Then, this guy looked me in the eye and said, "I betcha I nailed it right on the head." I didn't say a word, but I knew that he did nail it right on the head.

The moral of this story is very simple, you can't afford to make the mistake of going into denial and blaming your losses on something that was "out of your control." A professional day trader takes the blame for all consequences of his trading. By taking the blame, a day trader can recognize his mistakes and learn from them. If he doesn't take the blame and confess to being wrong, there is no way that he can learn the lesson.

In my case, the something that was "out of my control" was my alarm clock, which was not setup properly to go off at 4:45 AM. I later learned that my son played with the buttons and things were changed. However, it is my responsibility to check it before I go to sleep every night.

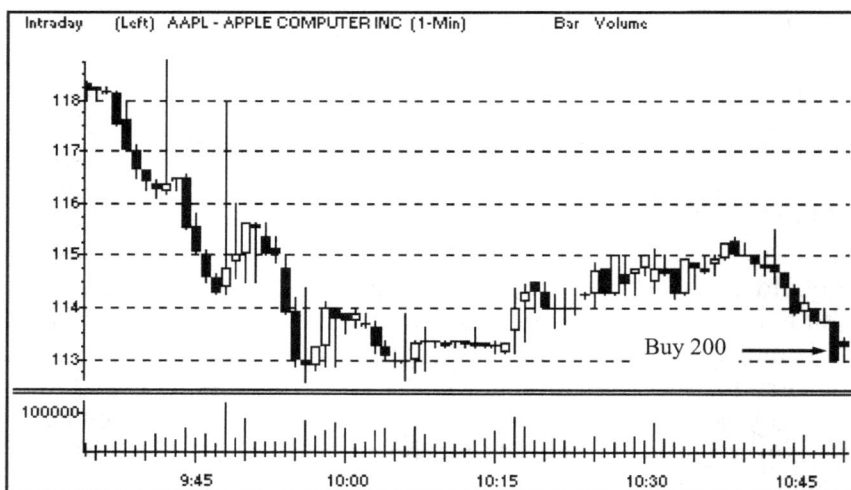

Intraday   (Left) AAPL - APPLE COMPUTER INC (1-Min)   Bar Volume

Reprinted with permission of Townsend Analytics, Ltd.

As I was screaming at my computer to give me a setup that I could trade, AAPL was reaching the support levels it set earlier in the day. I said

200

"thank you," and I bought 200 shares at 113.31. I felt that the support at 112.75 should hold, so I placed a stop loss at 112.62 , knowing that it would probably never trigger. My price target was the tops at 115.25. I would, however, give AAPL a chance to go higher, and if I am able to sell it at 116.50, I will be up for the day. "It shouldn't be a problem," I told myself.

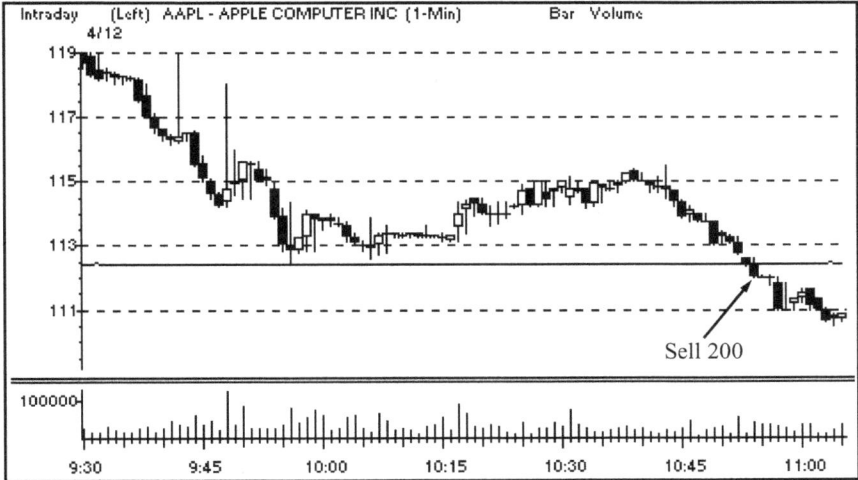

Reprinted with permission of Townsend Analytics, Ltd.

I was wrong! 112.75 was not strong support and AAPL broke through it. My stop was activated and I sold 200 AAPL at 112.37.

Source	Investment	Proceeds	COM	P&L	Return
Constant List	22,662.5	22,475	10.75	-198.25	-0.87%

I actually had no problem with this trade. It was managed and executed properly. But I was now down almost $800, so I still needed a winning trade; however, when you are running cold you should quit trading. Even though I knew this rule, I wasn't going to give in. And I was going to pay the price to learn this lesson all over again.

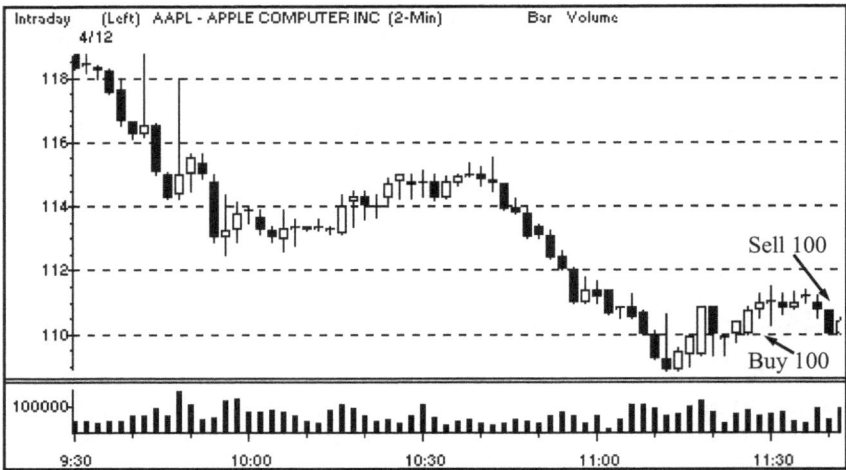

AAPL bounced at 109.25. I bought 100 shares at 110.12. My price target was 115. My stop loss was placed at 108.87, which was just below today's low. AAPL went up to 111.50. *FBCO* was axing the stock, and it pulled back. I sold 100 shares at 110.75.

Source	Investment	Proceeds	COM	P&L	Return
Constant List	11,012.5	11,075	11.87	50.63	-0.46%

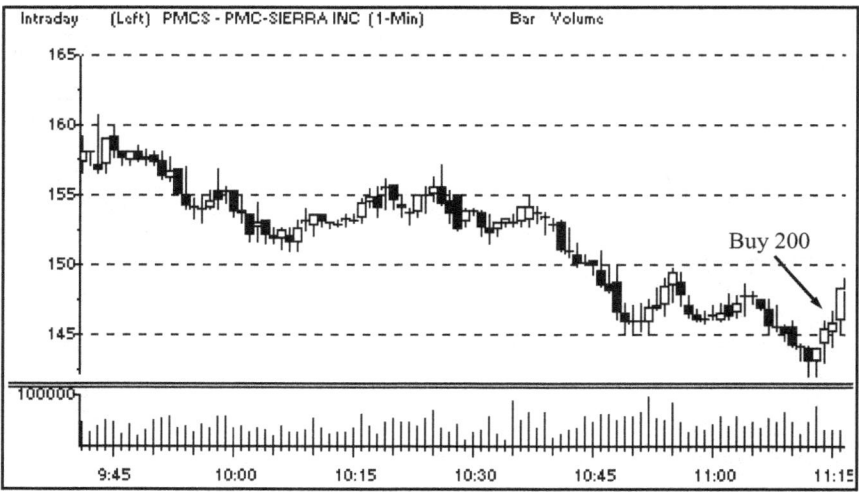

PMCS found support at 143 and bounced. It penetrated through resistance at 145. I bought 200 shares at 147.56. My price target was 155. I placed a stop loss at 144.75.

Intraday   (Left) PMCS - PMC-SIERRA INC (1-Min)   Bar   Volume

Sell 100

Reprinted with permission of Townsend Analytics, Ltd.

PMCS peaked at 153.50. I was sitting tight in the trade. I was up $1,163.00 when the bid hit 153.37. I could have sold my position right there and turned around my entire day. However, I thought that the market had bottomed, and that it would be going straight up from here, and I didn't want to lose my position. I placed a trailing stop for 100 shares at 149.94. I placed a stop for the remaining 100 shares at 147.50. I then raised my price target to 178 - 185. PMCS broke down through 150, and my first stop loss was activated. I sold 100 shares at 149.81.

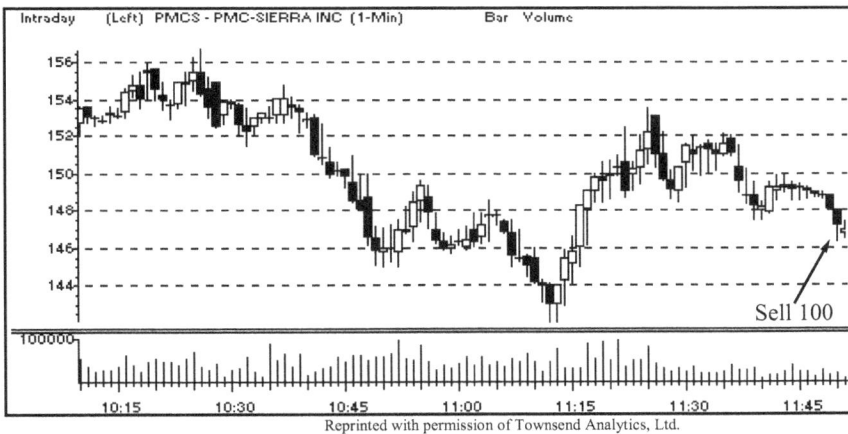

Intraday   (Left) PMCS - PMC-SIERRA INC (1-Min)   Bar   Volume

Sell 100

Reprinted with permission of Townsend Analytics, Ltd.

PMCS broke down through 147.50. My stop loss was activated. I sold the remaining 100 shares at 146.50. It may seem to many of you that the trailing stop should have been at a much higher price; however, you must understand that PMCS is a very volatile stock. It can move 20 points faster than another stock will move 0.50. Last Tuesday, the trading range on PMCS was more than 62 points. Therefore, five points is not that much for this stock.

Source	Investment	Proceeds	COM	P&L	Return
Constant List	29,512.50	29,631.25	20.99	97.96	0.33%

203

Reprinted with permission of Townsend Analytics, Ltd.

While I was in PMCS, I also bought 100 shares of QCOM at 134.62. I felt that the market had bottomed and QCOM should make it back to the previous highs at 139 and possibly go as high as 145. I placed a stop loss at 132.62, which was below today's low.

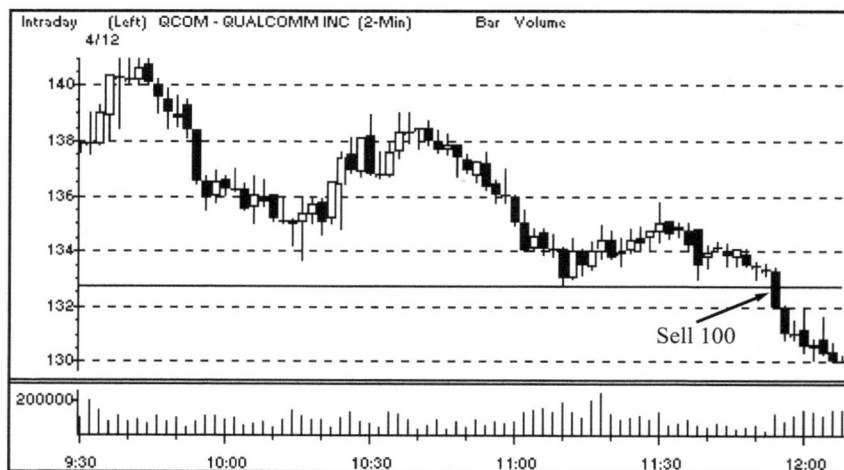

Reprinted with permission of Townsend Analytics, Ltd.

QCOM breaks through the low of the day. My stop is activated. I sold 100 shares at 130.87. It was a much bigger slippage than I anticipated. My order was activated once the bid hit 132.62 but it was 1.75 below that before it was executed.

Source	Investment	Proceeds	COM	P&L	Return
Constant List	13,462.50	13087.5	10.44	-385.44	-2.86%

204

I was having a bad day. I couldn't believe the lousy fill I got on my stop loss order. My loss was almost double what I was willing to lose on the trade. However, that is a part of the business. In fast moving markets, a stock can fall down a lot further than where my stop loss is activated prior to my order getting executed.

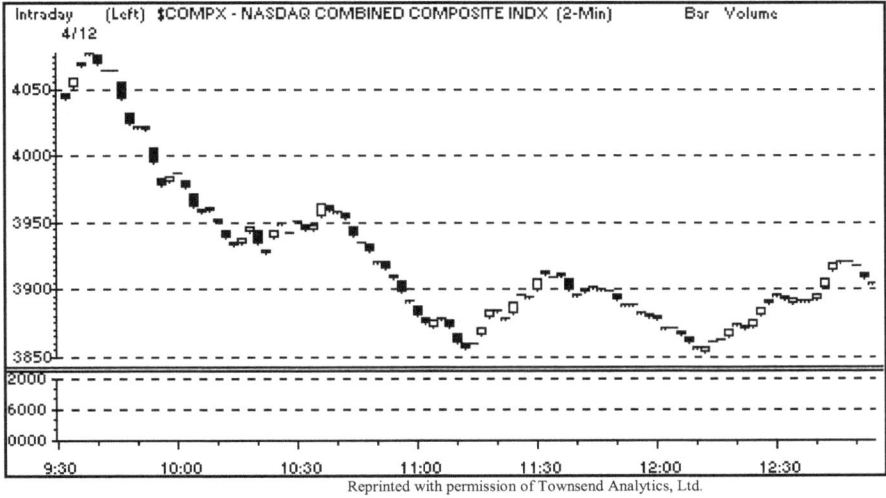

Reprinted with permission of Townsend Analytics, Ltd.

Here is another look at the Nasdaq chart. As you can see, when QCOM broke down to a new intraday low at 11:50, the Nasdaq was well off its low of the day. QCOM under performed the market. The Nasdaq was approaching its 3850 support level at 12:15. It managed to hold that level and trade back up.

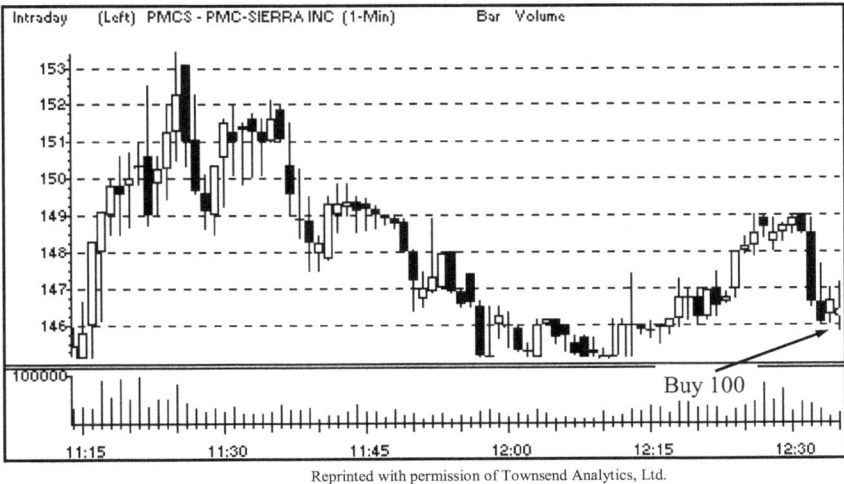

Reprinted with permission of Townsend Analytics, Ltd.

As the Nasdaq moved up, PMCS found support at 146. I bought 100 shares at 146. I placed a stop loss at 144.75. My price target was 153.

205

PMCS went up to 151. I wasn't going to let it fall through me this time. I sold 100 shares at 150.12 when I saw the first sign of weakness.

Source	Investment	Proceeds	COM	P&L	Return
Constant List	14,600	15,012.5	10.5	402.00	2.75%

What a great feeling. I just made up for the QCOM loss. I was studying the market very closely. It was bleeding heavily. I was looking at stocks, which I had previously traded at prices three times this high, a mere six weeks ago, now falling down even further. I was feeling the pain of the bulls. My blood was in the streets right along with theirs.

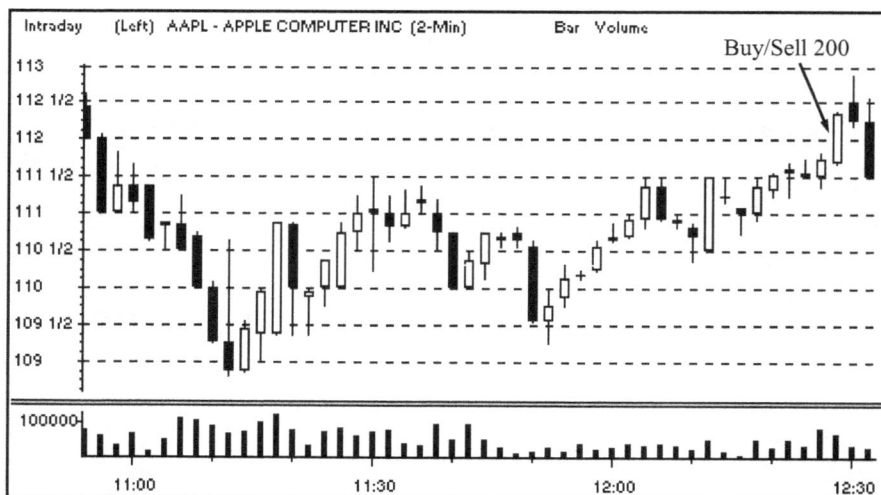

AAPL was gaining some strength. I bought 200 shares at 112.06. I thought it could go as high as 115, but the stock did not look too strong as *FBCO* was axing it again, so I sold 200 shares at 112.

Source	Investment	Proceeds	COM	P&L	Return
Constant List	22,212.5	22,200	15.75	-28.24	-0.12%

One of my rules is: When things don't look right, get out quickly. This is exactly what I did on this last AAPL trade.

Reprinted with permission of Townsend Analytics, Ltd.

After I sold PMCS at 150.12 around 12:50, it traded back down to 146 and change. It then started to gain steam and was about to challenge the 151 high. I reacted to the quick run the stock had and I bought 100 shares at 150.44 and 100 shares at 150.75. I thought PMCS was going to breakout and go to 156. I placed a stop loss at 149.50. This is a very tight play for a volatile stock like PMCS.

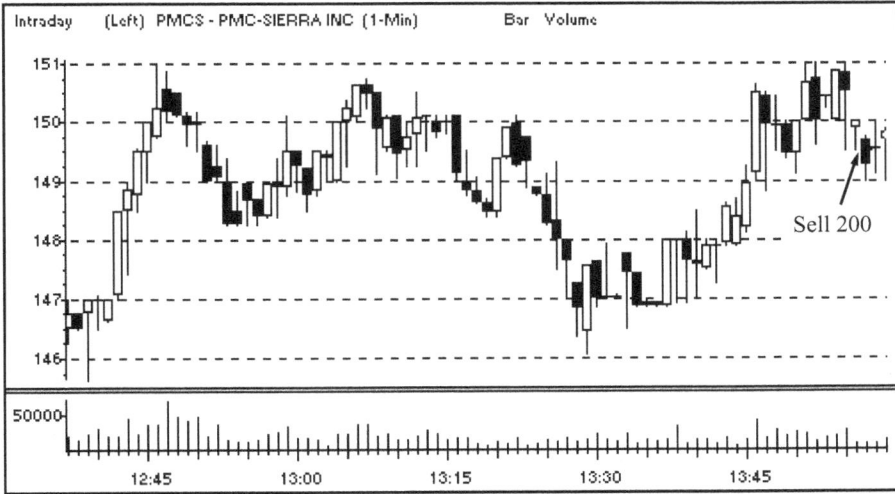

Reprinted with permission of Townsend Analytics, Ltd.

PMCS did not take out the highs at 151. It started to pull back, and it activated my stop loss. I sold 200 shares at 149.25.

I jumped the gun on this trade fearing that if PMCS was to breakout, I would not be able to get into the trade. I didn't have a great entry, so I had to cut the stock at the first sign of weakness. I was really struggling, because I was arguing with the tape. I felt that today should be the low, and that we would bounce strong from here. I was looking for a swing trade setup for with multi-point gain potential.

Source	Investment	Proceeds	COM	P&L	Return
Constant List	30,118.75	29,850	16.00	-284.75	-0.94%

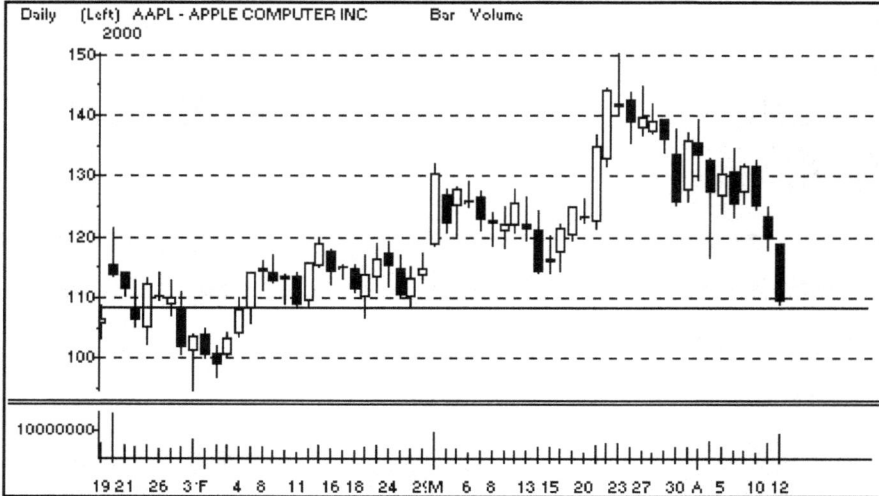

Reprinted with permission of Townsend Analytics, Ltd.

AAPL was a perfect candidate. It has pulled back in price sharply. It was right at what I thought should be decent support levels, and I thought that with the slightest bounce in the market, AAPL should be back to 125 - 132. I felt this trade had a 75% chance to be a winner.

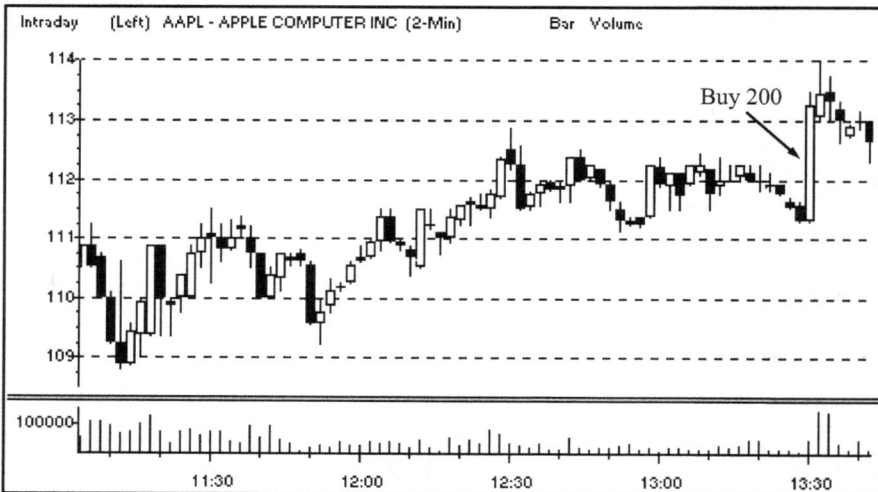

Reprinted with permission of Townsend Analytics, Ltd.

208

As the volume increased, I bought 200 shares of AAPL at 112.50. My price target was 125 - 132. I placed a stop loss at 109.87. I felt that I should give the trade some wiggle room, but if the stock goes under 110, I will have to cut it.

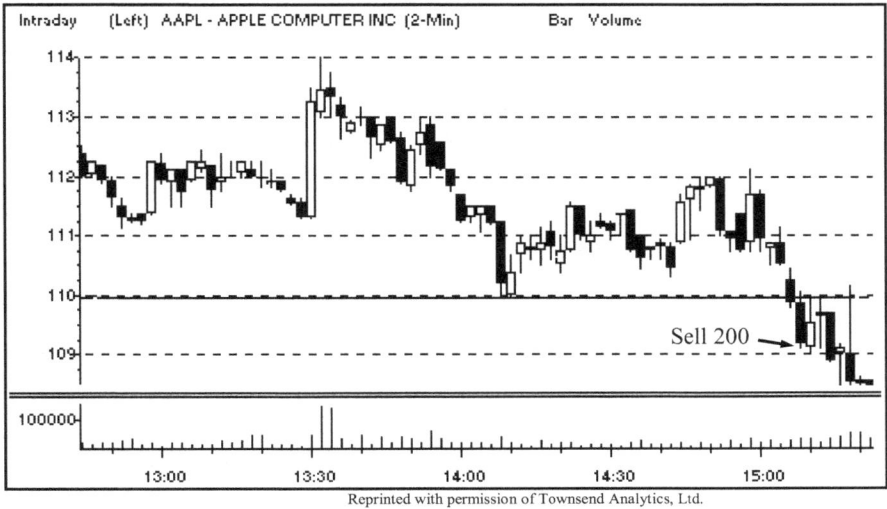

Reprinted with permission of Townsend Analytics, Ltd.

AAPL went as high as 114. It then sold off sharply with the market. It hit 110 right on the nose (around 2:05PM) and bounced. I survived the sell off and my stop loss was not activated. AAPL bounced back up to 112. The weight of the market finally broke it down, though. AAPL penetrated through 110 at 15:10 PM, and my stop loss was activated. I sold 200 shares at 109.

Source	Investment	Proceeds	COM	P&L	Return
Constant List	22,500	21,800	12.24	-712.24	-3.16%

If you haven't figured it out by now, I was having a "wonderful" day at the market. I had taken my biggest loss on a single stock in the challenge early this morning on INTC, and now, I have a new name which answers to the biggest loss taken on a single stock in the challenge. I want you to understand, though, that I was not trying too hard or was taking unnecessary risks. This is how I really trade, day in and day out. Losing is a part of the job, and I am glad you are getting to see all aspects of it.

After this last loss on AAPL, I realized that I had to keep things a little bit tighter. I was down $1,587.45 for the day. That is $1,000 more than I was down after the INTC disaster this morning. I knew I should have quit trading for the day, but, emotionally, I just couldn't. At this point, I wanted to make small profitable trades to build momentum and confidence going into the last two days of the challenge.

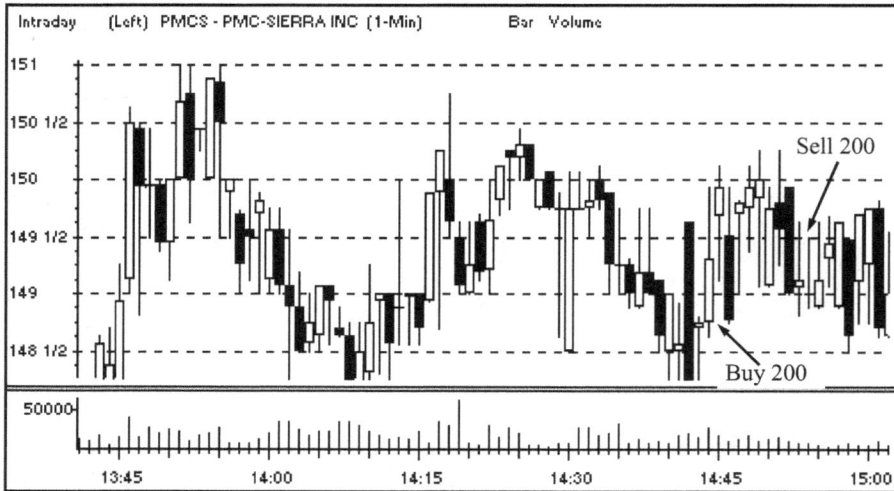

I was playing the channel on PMCS. I bought 200 shares at 148.81. The stock peaked at 150.25, and pulled back. I sold 200 shares at 149.37.

Source	Investment	Proceeds	COM	P&L	Return
Constant List	29,762.50	29,875	11	101.50	0.34%

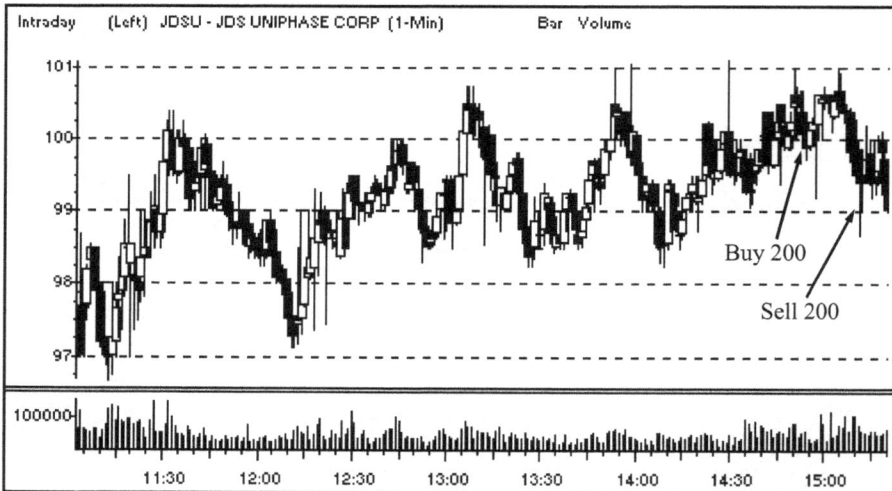

I bought 200 JDSU at 99.96. Stock peaked at 101. It then sold off sharply. I sold 200 shares at 99.12.

Source	Investment	Proceeds	COM	P&L	Return
Constant List	19,993.75	19,825	10.66	-179.42	0.90%

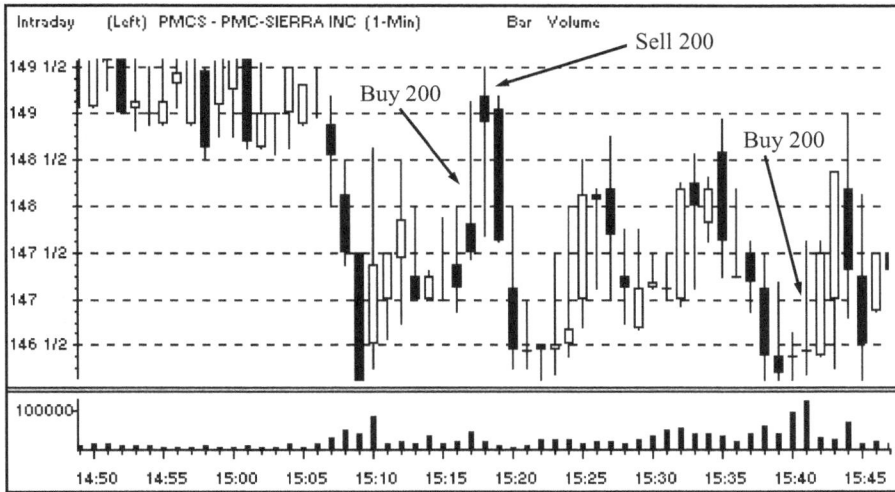

Reprinted with permission of Townsend Analytics, Ltd.

I bought PMCS again at 148.15, as it bounced up from 145.50. I sold it into strength at 149.12. I bought 200 shares at 147 and held into the close. The stock closed at 147.81.

Source	Investment	Proceeds	COM	P&L	Return
Constant List	29,637.50	29,824.22	11	175.72	0.59%

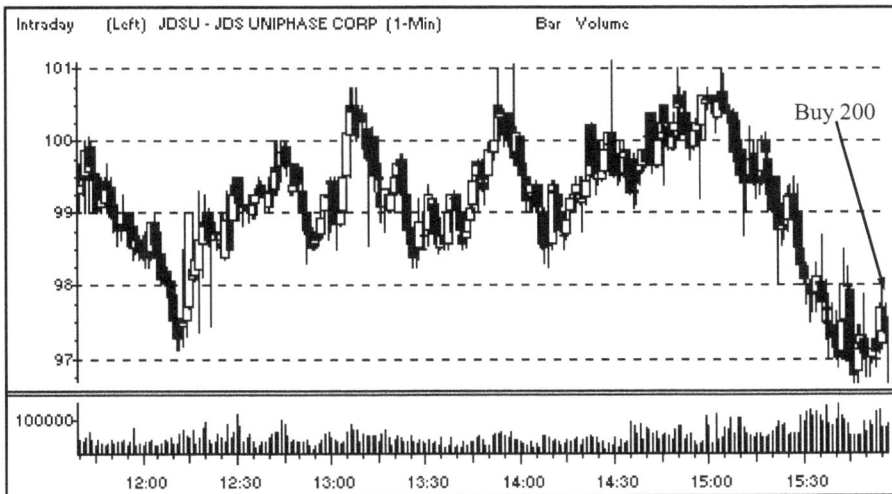

Reprinted with permission of Townsend Analytics, Ltd.

I also bought 200 shares of JDSU at 98.06 just before the close.

211

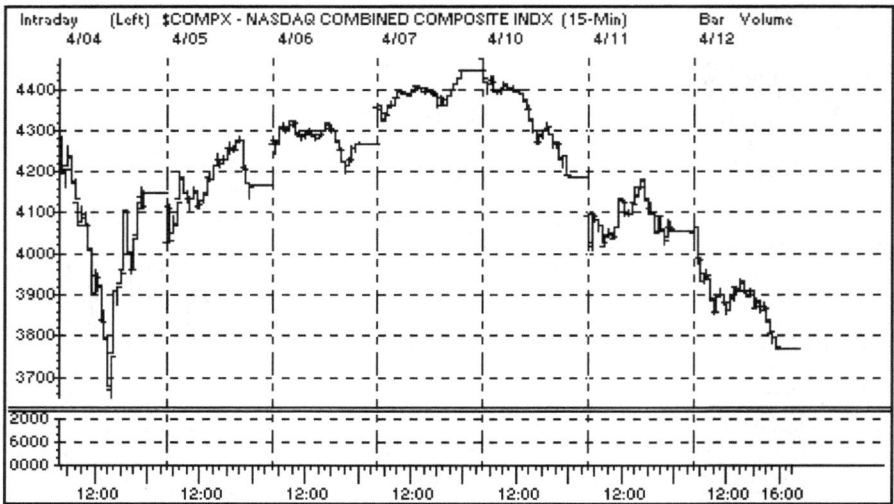

Intraday (Left) $COMPX - NASDAQ COMBINED COMPOSITE INDX (15-Min) Bar Volume

Reprinted with permission of Townsend Analytics, Ltd.

Here is another look at what the Nasdaq has done over the last seven trading days. We are about 100 points higher than the low we made last week. Volatility is the highest I have ever seen. I thought that the downside risk at this point was limited. I felt that 3650 would hold if it gets tested again, and the Nasdaq would go back to 4200 in a heart beat, so I was willing to carry my two positions in PMCS and JDSU overnight.

PMCS was trading higher after-hours. I offered out 100 shares at 152 on ISLD ECN. I got hit for 89 shares. I sold 89 shares at 152. I was following the activity on the ISLD book very closely because I had an open order to sell the remaining 11 shares at 152. It was almost 8:00 PM EST, and there were two traders who desperately wanted to sell their shares of PMCS. The best bid on ISLD was 148.25 for 300 shares. I joined the bid at 148.25 for 89 shares. I felt that the trader with the 1000 shares was going to sell at that price. He was competing with another trader who wanted to sell 400 shares. As one will offer his shares on ISLD at a certain price, the other will jump in front offering his shares at a 0.06 lower. The best offer was at 149.50. With three minutes left, I finally got my fill. Someone sold me 89 shares at 148.25. My position was 200 shares again, so I cancelled my order to sell 11 shares at 152.

Source	Investment	Proceeds	COM	P&L	Return
Constant List	13,083	13,528	8.03	436.97	3.33%

212

Today was an incredible busy day. I started the day on the wrong foot, and I was never able to recover. I felt that I was trading very poorly as I was trying to play catch-up. Only God knows how the day would have ended if I was to sell INTC in the morning for profit, or sell PMCS when I was up well over $1,000 on that position and green for the day, or sell AAPL for a minimal profit or loss. These were the pivot points of the day. I was trying to fight the tape on many occasions, yet I felt that the reward was worth the risk. The Nasdaq was down 285 points today, yet I only lost $1,109.50 after starting the day down $585 on INTC. The market is looking very ugly, yet I am holding long positions overnight. I guess we will find out tomorrow if I was right or wrong.

Open positions: 200 JDSU, 200 PMCS
Total profit for 4/12/00: $-1,109.50

Day Eighteen Lessons

Set two alarm clocks or even three.

If you did a big booboo in the morning quit trading.

CHAPTER 22

Traffic Jam

DAY NINETEEN

Thursday, April 13, 2000

I had two alarm clocks set to go off at 4:30 AM, and they didn't fail me. When the annoying beeping sound broke the silence, I quickly jumped out of bed. It was still dark out. Thank God I didn't sleep in.

I didn't do any overnight analysis, and I had no trades planned out. My main concern was to manage my overnight positions properly. I went upstairs, turned on the computer and logged in to my RealTick Trading Account. My P&L total was showing +$800. This means that my positions were trading higher in pre-market action. Since I felt the market was over-sold, I was going to wait for the opening bell and see if my stocks could run higher. I was hoping for a short squeeze this morning.

Ding! Ding! The market was now open. Both PMCS and JDSU were holding their gains. It was 5 minutes into the action when my cable modem service came to a halt. I was now completely blind. I couldn't see where anything was. I immediately picked up the phone and called my broker's trading desk. My call was answered immediately. The broker on the other side asked me what I wished to do, and I told him to sell both PMCS and JDSU at the market. This was as painless as painless can be for this kind of experience. I was very impressed. The broker executed my orders very quickly.

Since I have been in these scenarios many times in the past with different brokers, I have a note posted to my monitor with directions of how to speed up the process of placing trades over the phone.

Hi, this is Tony Oz. I'd like to place a trade. My four letter ID is XXXX. Sell to close 200 shares of PMCS at the market. Sell to close 200 shares of JDSU at the market.

If you care about speed, always place market orders. Avoid small talk. Let the broker know you want to place a trade immediately. Have all your info ready. Make sure to use the words to open or to close. This will save the time of him asking you if you own the stock or not.

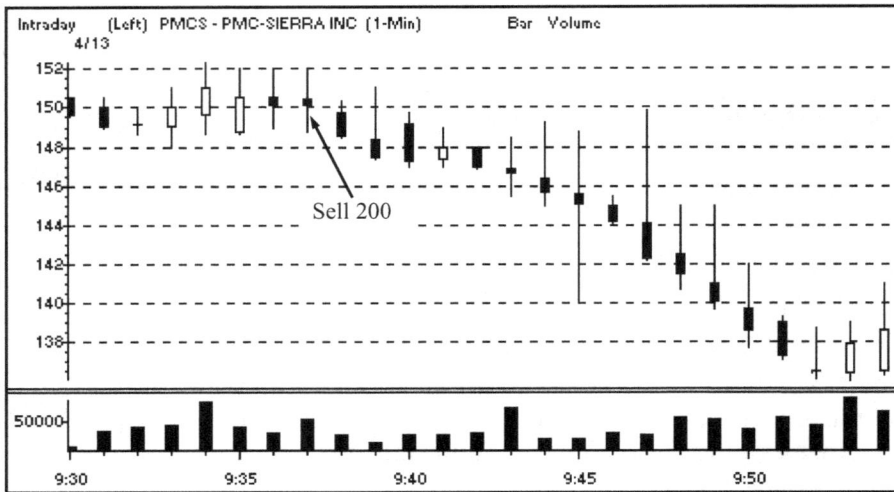

Reprinted with permission of Townsend Analytics, Ltd.

I sold 200 PMCS at 149.31.

Source	Investment	Proceeds	COM	P&L	Return
Constant List	29,503.89	29,862.5	21.57	337.04	1.14%

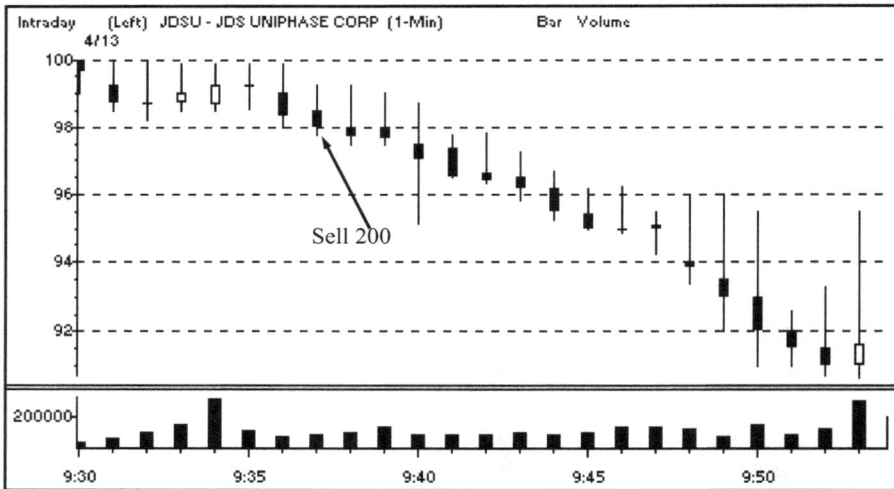

Reprinted with permission of Townsend Analytics, Ltd.

I sold 200 JDSU at 97.69.

Source	Investment	Proceeds	COM	P&L	Return
Constant List	19,612.5	19,537.5	10.66	-85.66	-0.44%

216

It was about 9:50 AM, and it seemed that my ISP was back in business. My quotes seemed to be working now.

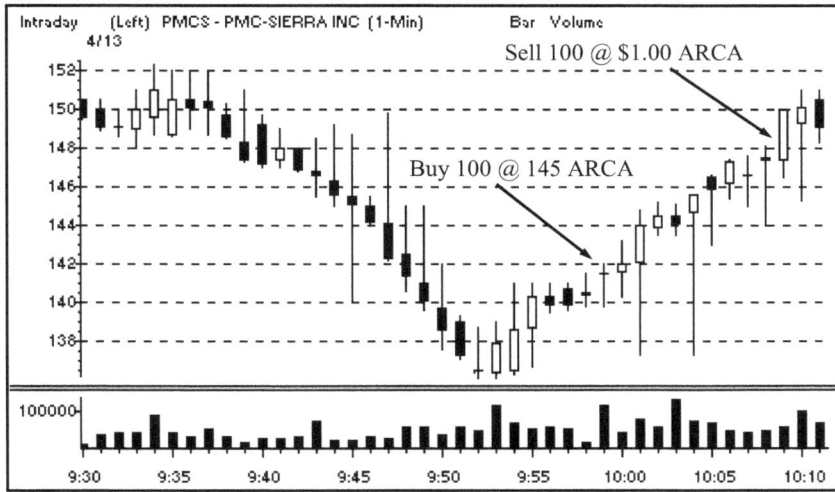

Reprinted with permission of Townsend Analytics, Ltd.

PMCS sold off hard but had bounced from a low of 138.25. It was racing up. I entered an order to buy 100 shares at 145 on ARCA. The best offer was at 142 at the time. It took a long minute, and I got a confirmation that I bought 100 shares at 144.50. PMCS was still running. I was getting spurts of data that were inconsistent. I entered a sell order on ARCA for 100 shares at $1.00. I was basically telling ARCA to get me out at the best possible price. PMCS was at the high of the run at the time, trading at 148.50. I got my confirmation. I sold 100 shares at 148.37.

Source	Investment	Proceeds	COM	P&L	Return
Constant List	14,450	14,837.5	10.50	377.00	2.61%

I felt very fortunate to get out of the trade without any harm as my cable connection was now completely lost. I didn't want to trade on my backup machine which is connected via DSL, because it seemed to be slow as well. I later found out that the problems I was having with my @home service was widely spread. In fact, users from California all the way to Florida had trouble connecting to the net.

I didn't make a lot of money, but I was very happy to have a profitable day. My cable connection came back on around 1:00 PM, and I watched the market carefully for a high percentage trade. The market was tanking hard again.

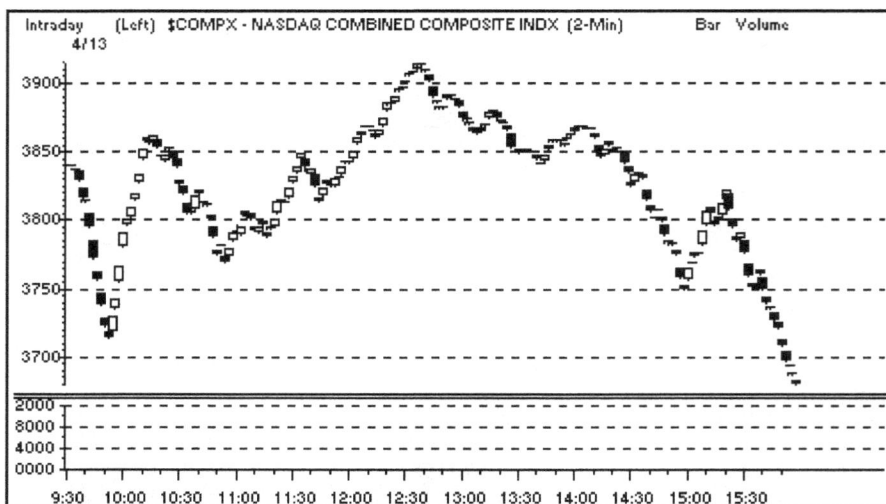

When the final bell rang, the bears won another battle. The Nasdaq, which was up as much as 145 points for the day, managed to reverse direction and close down 93 points. It wasn't looking good for the bulls.

Open positions: None
Total profit for 4/13/00: $628.38

Day Nineteen Lesson

Be prepared should you have to call the trading desk.

23

Cash is a Position

DAY TWENTY

Friday, April 14, 2000

In preparation for the last day of the challenge, I spent a lot of time researching the highest probability long setups. I wrote down price levels of support and resistance for the indexes and all stocks on my Constant watch list. I then started a word processing program, I selected 72 point bold fonts, and I typed "**TRADE SMART**." Next, I printed out four copies. I stapled each one of the copies to the wall, so I could see it no matter what monitor I was sitting behind.

I had no problem getting out of bed this morning. I was ready for the last day of the challenge, and I wanted to make this one count. I felt that the Nasdaq was approaching support levels again, and I was looking to buy my favorite stocks at bargain prices. I went upstairs and sat at my computer. As I was logging into my MB Trading software, I glanced over the monitor and saw the mini-posters I made last night. I chuckled in amusement, and promised myself that I will obey the command. I was ready to trade.

The futures were down sharply, and pre-market trading showed great weakness. I was licking my chops. This is the day I have been waiting for.

The Nasdaq gapped down big this morning, and it took out the previous low made last week, at the open.

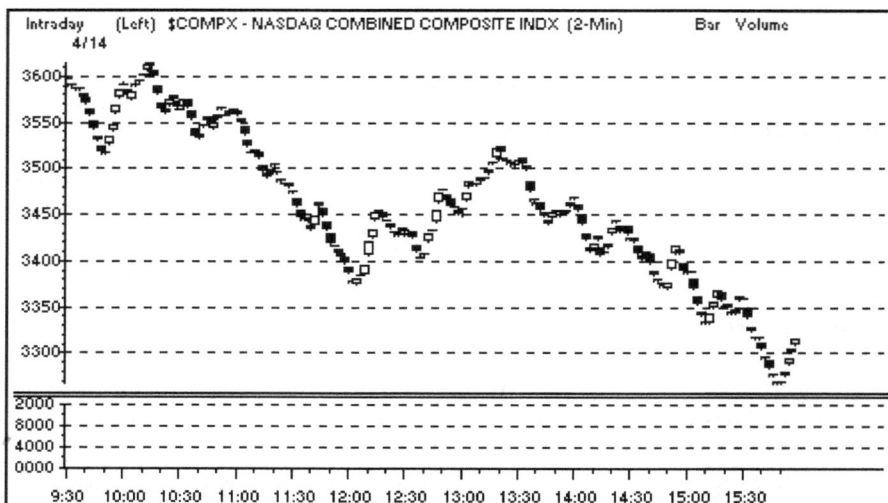

I almost got suckered into the first bounce, which took out the morning highs at 10:15. I decided that the smart thing to do will be to wait for a pullback, because the index raced about 100 points in 18 minutes. My strategy was to wait for a pullback, then look to see if the next rally can take out the intraday high. This will be the sign of a trend reversal.

The index failed to do so, and at 11:00, it broke down hard and took out the low of the day. The index broke through 3500. The lunchtime rally was not convincing for the simple reason that margin selling was not over yet. At 1:30, things turned around again. It was the worst blood bath I have ever seen, and there was no way I was going to contribute any of my own blood to the brutal bear assault.

It was the last day of the challenge, and I was going to play it as a golfer who has a 15 shot lead going into Sunday in Augusta. I just want to shoot par today. I was watching this painful display, and at 2:00 PM we blew the whistle. The challenge was now officially over, and I ordered a check.

However, once I saw all the blood in the street, I just could not hold myself back, and I bought $100,000 worth of QQQ for a swing trade. I knew this trade would not count as a part of the statistics for the challenge, but I just *had* to make that trade. I felt that at 3300, my risk/reward ratio was high.

Total profit for 4/13/00: $0.00

The forth and final week of the challenge was now over. It was a major down week for the market. The Nasdaq Composite lost 1125 points, a 25.3% decline in five days. The Dow Jones Industrial Average lost 7.9% for the week, and the S&P 500 Index lost 10.6%. It was a broad market sell off.

I started the week trading very well. I felt that my trading on Monday and Tuesday was in top form. I struggled on Wednesday from the minute I woke up. On Thursday, I had connectivity problems, but I still managed to have a profitable day. On Friday, I sat on the sidelines and watched the sharpest single-day point drop on the Nasdaq as it lost 355 points

I was amazed that I actually turned a profit this week. My total profits for week four were $3,046.23. I faxed my broker a request for a check in the amount of $3,000.00. After all, Friday is payday!

Southwest Securities 1201 Elm St. Suite 3500. Dallas, TX 75270	SIPC	88-88 1113 216507
	DATE	AMOUNT
PAY ********3,000DOLLARS 00CENTS Pay To	4/17/00	$*****3,000.00
TONY OZ LAGUNA HILLS, CA 92654		

Day Twenty Lesson

Cash is a position.

The market can decline sharply, you must manage risk properly, especially if you trade on margin.

Make yourself a mini-poster saying "TRADE SMART" in big bold letters.

221

CHAPTER 24

Thank You, But No Champagne for Me

My wife and I had plans for a celebration dinner following the last trading day of the challenge. But I was very depressed. I had just witnessed a brutal bear market in which trillions of dollars were lost. You would think that I would be glowing with my success in making decent returns in such a down market, but the truth is that I have experienced the worst weekend of my life as a professional trader.

I am very close to the trading community and correspond with many day traders who vary in their level of expertise. Some are professionals, some are amateurs, and some are just starting out. The stories were very similar. Many traders lost a lot of money over the last few weeks. There were a few success stories as well, which were uplifting, but many of the stories were horrifying.

I had a very long talk with my dad on Friday night. He was very concerned that the crash of the market would reduce consumer spending and result in a recession. I didn't know what to tell him, but his concern was not very comforting.

My uncle, who lives across the Atlantic Ocean, called me early Saturday morning. He was concerned about my financial situation as he heard on the news that the stock market crashed. He was happy to hear that I survived. I later learned that he lost a big chunk of his own trading account. "The market gives it, and the market takes it away," said his wife.

These were the types of conversations I had with many individuals over the weekend. The devastation and turmoil so many of my friends and family were experiencing took all the air out of the satisfaction I would have otherwise been feeling about my own accomplishments. I was definitely in no mood to celebrate. "It will have to wait," I told my wife, who was very understanding.

CHAPTER 25

The Secret to Success

I think I have learned many great things from this four-week challenge. For the first time in my life, I really understand the meaning of the phrase, "Bulls make money, bears make money, and pigs get slaughtered." I have proven to myself that my simple trading system can be traded successfully, on the long side, in a bear market. This was a question I was asked many times by my students, and at the time, I couldn't answer it, because I never traded in a bear market before. I think this diary answers that question very well.

The most important lesson, however, is found in each and every case study I have featured. It has to do with religiously adhering to the rules and guidelines of a trading system. I know for a fact that my discipline in executing each and every trade according to my trading system is the secret to my success. This is why I had the courage to accept this challenge.

When I started teaching seminars about high probability short-term trading, my performance chart was improving on a consistent basis. The reason was that every time I was tempted to break a rule, I would ask myself, "How are you going to explain this one to your students?" This question has taken my trading to the next level.

If you want to improve your trading, what you need to do is very simple. Before you enter any trade, think that you will have to explain this trade to the world in a case study format. You have to explain the reason for entry, your risk management guidelines, and why you exited the trade. If you can truly do this, I strongly believe that you can enjoy the same type of success I have enjoyed in this challenge. And that, my friend, is the greatest lesson of this book. Trade as if the world was standing behind you watching each and every trade.

As you should all know by now, my trading system is very simple. It is made of two words: Support and Resistance. I don't use sophisticated technical indicators. I keep things very simple, and as far as I am concerned, simple strategies make an advanced trading system. I have featured the technical setups and Level II order execution methods in my online trading course which you can get at SFO Academy, *sfoacademy.com*. I hope that you were able to follow, throughout this book, how I actually trade these setups in real life.

Day Trading has been greatly disparaged by the media, with reporters focusing on those who have lost all their money, while ignoring those who are successful. Many of the subjects of these reports were inexperienced and untrained, and hadn't yet learned the fundamentals of the business they had chosen. They risked all they had without a plan, without rules, and without any tested, systematic methodology whatsoever. No business can survive without a solid business plan rigorously followed, yet we see no sensationalized media stories about all the small businesses that fail each year in other industries as the result of the same lack of planning.

In this book, I have provided you with a simple system of trading that I believe most anyone can follow. I have proven my system in combat, in the midst of a 30% market crash, where I netted a 32.5% Return. I have given numerous examples and details regarding the various circumstances of each trade, allowing you to get the "feel" of trading my system, that goes beyond mere theory. I have been very honest in showing you the consequences I suffered as a result of not practicing my own rules, and I have shown you those times when I did everything right, yet I still lost money just the same. But, through it all, I made a comfortable living every week for the duration of the challenge, in the midst of some very rough times in the market. And the only reason is, because I stuck as closely as I could to the rules of my system. That is the secret to my success. And that is how I make a living trading stocks.

CHAPTER 26

Challenge Summary

For the four weeks of the challenge, I made a total profit of $16,277.25. This was a 32.55% return on the $50,000.00 I opened the account with. There was no compounding of profits, since I ordered a check at the end of each week. My overnight risk management kept me in small positions or no positions overnight due to bearish market conditions. The longest I held any open position was two days.

Since all the stocks I traded were in the tech sector, the performance of the Nasdaq stock market will be the most realistic measure for any kind of performance comparison. The following chart covers the Nasdaq performance for the same period of time as the challenge.

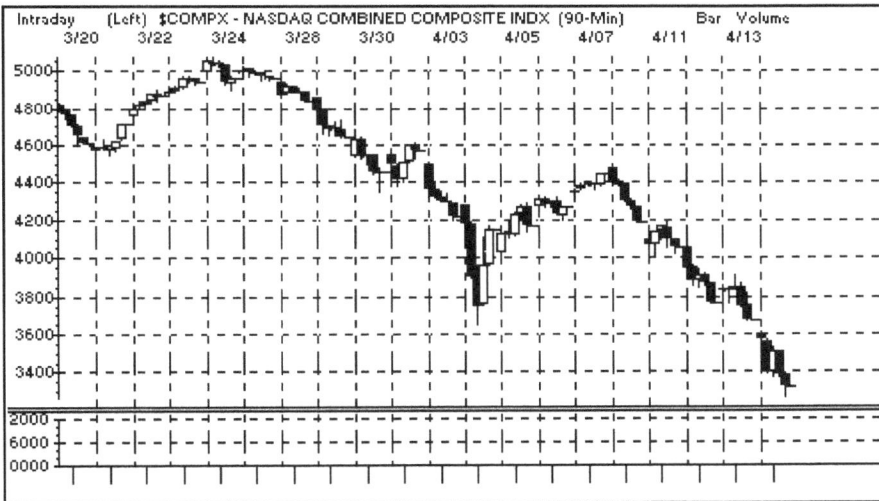

Reprinted with permission of Townsend Analytics, Ltd.

The Nasdaq lost 1476 points, or 30.78% in the time frame of the challenge. A bear market by definition is a price retracement that is greater than 20% from the highs, so my trading took place in a bear market for technology stocks.

Only time will tell what these four weeks will be called by the experts, or if this was just the beginning of a much steeper decline. Was this the buying opportunity of the new millennium? The bulls and bears can argue about this one for as long as they wish. I will still trade the market the very same way I did in this book - Support and Resistance.

There are some very important numbers that you can study from your trading records that can help make you a better trader.

The first number is Win/Loss Ratio.

There are 116 trades illustrated in this challenge of which 75 are winners and 41 are losers. So I have executed a winning trade 64.6% of the time, and I have executed a losing trade 35.4% of the time. This stat may seem impressive, but it doesn't mean much, because you can have this win to loss ratio every month and still lose money consistently. I have mentioned that my only goal is to trade well, so I study my numbers a little bit differently than you might expect. I have designed a performance chart to give me a clearer picture of my trading.

At the end of every month, I create a performance table which covers all my trades. This table tells me if I am trading well or not. In this table, I will include the dollar amount I have made or lost on each trade I executed over the last month. The table on the next page is broken into four weeks, and a range of dollar amount made or lost on each trade I have executed. Most of the battle takes place at the gray shaded area where I expect the number of winners and losers to be very close. As I move from the gray shaded area to the extremes on both the left and right side, it tells me how many BIG winners I have had versus how many BIG losers. This is where the difference between good trading and bad trading lies. I want the numbers on the extreme right to be bigger than the numbers on the extreme left. If there is one secret to being successful in this business, it is simply to have more trades executed on the extreme right than on the extreme left.

Using the *Areas* on the table and the *Total*, we can learn much more about our trading. First I want to answer the questions of which area is bigger:

B1>B2 - Yes.
C1>C2 - Yes.
D1>D2 - Yes.
E1>E2 - Yes.
F1>F2 - Yes.

Next, I can calculate the ratio of winners to losers within a certain area.

B1/B2 = 2.11
C1/C2 = 7
D1/D2 = 2

I'd like to see a number greater than 1.75 as a ratio of area 1 divided by area 2, (excluding area A where I expect the numbers to be closer).

228

Performance Table 3/20/2000 - 4/14/2000

Winning Trades

Area	1-200	201-400	401-500	501-600	601-700	701-800	801-900	901-1000	1001-1500	1500+
	A1	B1	C1	D1	E1	F1	G1	H1	J1	K1
Week 1	3	5	2	2	1	1	1			
Week 2	8	5				1	1			
Week 3	14	3	3	1		1	1	1	1	1
Week 4	8	6	2	1			2			
Total	33	19	7	4	1	3	5	1	1	1

Losing Trades

Area	1-200	201-400	401-500	501-600	601-700	701-800
	A2	B2	C2	D2	E2	F2
Week 1	4	1				
Week 2	7	2	1			
Week 3	11	3		1		1*
Week 4	5	3		1		1
Total	27	9	1	2		2

I suggest that you use a similar table to tabulate your own performance based on the dollar range of your winners versus your losers. This table should answer the question, am I trading well?

*A basket trade of five stocks

EPILOGUE

I am sure many of you are wondering what happened after the last day of the challenge. On Friday, which was the last day of the challenge, I bought 1,200 shares of QQQ. I held this position for three days, and I sold it on Tuesday, April 18, 2000 for a profit of $8,806.30. I also bought and sold 300 shares of KLAC, twice, for a total profit of $1,970.93. Next, I bought and sold 300 shares of BVSN for a profit of $280.43. Finally, I bought and sold 300 shares of INKT, twice, for a profit of $798.78. My total profit for the two days following the challenge was $11,856.50. I have not executed one trade in this account since then.

It is a shame that my best week of trading the account did not make it into the book, but the guidelines which I followed were to include only realized profits from the four-week period of time, so although I bought the 1,200 QQQ shares on the last day of the challenge, the profits were not realized until two days after.

For those of you who keep score, the total amount I have made in this account is $28,133.75. That is a 56.26% return in one month.

Once I closed my positions, I devoted all my time to the writing of this book. One of my goals in writing this book is to show everyone, and I mean everyone, that trading stocks for a living is a legitimate business, and I hope that the media will finally see it this way, as well.

Once this book is finished, I will be doing what you have just witnessed in this book, day in and day out – I will be taking money out of the market.

TRADE SMART!

To learn more about smart stock trading, please visit *sfoacademy.com*.

Don't forget to follow Tony Oz on social media and subscribe to his YouTube Channel.

Please visit SFO Academy, *SFOACADEMY.COM*, and register for Tony Oz's Premier Stock Trading Course and learn more about his money management system, position sizing, price target forecasting, stop loss placement levels, and stock picking techniques.

231

Training, Coaching, & Consulting

SFO Academy offers a **Premier Stock Trading Course** by Tony Oz
which compliments this book perfectly. Get 50% off the Premier
Stock Trading Course at www.sfoacademy.com when
you use the exclusive coupon code: **TradeSmart**
The course contains five modules, 32 video lessons,
session notes, Stock Market Calculator software,
and Tony Oz's proprietary scan formulas.

www.sfoacademy.com

****

For all inquiries please email:
info@tonyoz.com

****

TonyOz.com

www.ingramcontent.com/pod-product-compliance
Lightning Source LLC
Chambersburg PA
CBHW080529220326
41599CB00032B/6249